SOUTHEAST ASIA

By the Editors
of Sunset Books
and
Sunset Magazine

LANE PUBLISHING CO.   Menlo Park, California

With striped umbrellas held high, *red-sashed members of Malay wedding party sashay toward celebration.*

Edited by Joan Erickson

Special Consultant:
**Frederic M. Rea,
Publisher, Pacific Travel News**

Photo Editor: **Barbara J. Braasch**

Design: **Joe di Chiarro**

Illustrations: **H. Tom Kamifuji**

Maps: **Jim Norris**

Cover: Flaming sunset silhouettes ship anchored in Manila Bay. To view such spectacles, Philippine residents gather nightly along sea wall. Photographed by Dick Rowan.

Acknowledgments

We are grateful to the many individuals and organizations that helped in the preparation of this travel guide. We wish to acknowledge the assistance and cooperation of the editorial staff of *Pacific Travel News,* particularly Phyllis Elving and James Gebbie. And a very special thank you goes to Jane Keator, who produced the manuscript for the Philippines chapter.

For assistance in information gathering and manuscript checking we extend special thanks to the following: Virginia Brunner; Lorraine Reno; Joan Storey, Mediapacific; the Indonesian Tourist Promotion Board in San Francisco and Jakarta; the Tourist Development Corporation of Malaysia in San Francisco and Kuala Lumpur; the Philippine Ministry of Tourism in Los Angeles and Manila; the Singapore Tourist Promotion Board in San Francisco and Singapore; and the Tourism Authority of Thailand in Los Angeles and Bangkok.

Editor, Sunset Books: David E. Clark

First printing February 1982

Hours, costs, telephone numbers, and highway designations in this book are accurate as of press time.

CONTENTS

SPECIAL FEATURES

SOUTHEAST ASIA

A well-packed travel treasure chest — lush tropical greenery, ancient architectural wonders, timeless traditions, exquisite art forms, thriving urban centers, quiet hamlets, and a multicultured population

Southeast Asia—the mere mention of it conjures up images of things exotic. For centuries this intriguing region has lured travelers. Drawn by tales of the rich spice islands and the romance of Singapore and the fabled isle of Bali, adventurers journeyed here to discover other riches—the jeweled spires of Bangkok, the archeological splendor of ancient Borobudur, and the incomparable Philippine rice terraces.

A treasure chest resplendent with tropical greenery, beautiful beaches, delicate art forms, and varied ethnic groups and cultures, Southeast Asia is one of the world's most diverse regions. For the visitor, it offers a multitude of fascinating travel experiences.

NATURE'S INFLUENCES

Southeast Asia stretches more than 4,828 km/3,000 miles—from the southeast corner of the Asian mainland out over the island-studded Indian Ocean and South China Sea. Contained within the mainland portion of this tropical wonderland are Thailand, Burma, Cambodia (Kampuchea), Laos, and Vietnam. Extending southward from the mainland is the Malay Peninsula, occupied primarily by Malaysia, with Singapore forming an exclamation point at its southern tip. The rest of the area is fragmented into thousands of islands comprising Indonesia and the Philippines.

Violent earth forces

Until some 300 million years ago, most of Southeast Asia was beneath the sea. Then the mainland rose out of the water, part of a colossal continent that included today's Europe and Africa. During the next 200 million years, this huge land mass underwent constant changes. Violent upheavals occurred in the earth's crust. Volcanoes erupted, and mountains reared up. Then the wind and rain went to work, grinding down the mountains until the land surface became a vast, featureless plain, cut by broad, shallow rivers.

About 25 million years ago, the earth's crust once more began to churn and heave, thrusting up gigantic mountain ranges. The Alps rose in Europe, and the Himalayas appeared between India and China. Hundreds of volcanoes, forming a giant arc from Burma south through the Indonesian archipelago and then north through the Philippines, began spewing forth molten black lava. Their eruptions brought destruction, but they also deposited mineral-rich ashes over territory destined to become some of the richest agricultural land in the world.

The melting of the polar ice cap, some 10,000 to 20,000 years ago, caused the oceans to rise, covering vast areas of coastal lowlands. Parts of Southeast Asia disappeared underwater, forming the Sunda Shelf—the largest continental shelf in the world. The warm waters atop this shelf make up large portions of the South China, Java, Celebes, and Sulu seas, and the Gulf of Thailand. The higher land in this area remained above sea level, forming the thousands of islands of Indonesia and the Philippines. The area is still a center of much volcanic activity, with 10 active volcanoes in the Philippines and 77 in Indonesia.

Tropical plants and animals

Over the millenniums, Southeast Asia has been graced by warm sunshine, plentiful rain, and gentle winds. Its lands and waters teem with a seemingly endless array of plant and animal life. Naturalists estimate that the area contains more than 1,500 vertebrates. The varieties of plant life are too staggering in number to record.

Tropical forests cover much of the land. A small area may provide growing space for a number of different types of trees, ranging from teak forests to stands of ironwood, mahogany, and mangrove. Rubber trees—introduced from Brazil—grow on vast forest plantations, making Southeast Asia the greatest rubber-producing area in the world. The bamboo tree, common throughout the area, supplies Southeast Asia with its most important building material; bamboo is also used for furniture and utensils. Hillsides support highly cultivated plantations of tea plants, pepper bushes, and tapioca plants.

Since rice is the basic food of Southeast Asia, rice fields are a dominant feature of the landscape. On the plains, the geometric patterns of the rice fields stretch for miles, separated by earthen dikes and connected by an ingenious network of irrigation waterways. In mountain areas, rice is cultivated in terraces that climb the mountains almost to their crests in a series of giant, contour-hugging steps. Masterpieces of engineering, they are among the wonders of the world.

Still other Southeast Asian plants add notes of color to the landscape. Included among the area's flora are frangipani, bougainvillea, roses, flame of the forest trees, morning glories, rafflesia, and thousands of varieties of orchids.

Southeast Asia is the natural habitat of orangutans, huge lizards, one-horned rhinoceroses, "banteng" oxen, long-nosed tapirs, wild boars, monkey-eating eagles, and deer. Here, too, are tigers, leopards, elephants, panthers, monkeys, and pythons. The waters of the Sunda Shelf provide a plentiful food supply for seemingly endless varieties of fish and coral. Rivers, deltas, and coastal mud flats support millions of crabs, as well as crocodiles.

A CULTURAL CROSSROADS

The dawn of Southeast Asia's human history begins with that of mankind. In Java, anthropologists discovered the fossilized remains of *Pithecanthropus erectus* — Java man. Carbon dating indicates that this early inhabitant lived on Java some 500,000 years ago. He was succeeded by later races of primitive man in various stages of human and cultural development.

Restricted by oceans and rugged mountain terrain, these early Southeast Asian inhabitants existed for thousands of years in splendid isolation. But as waves of migration surged from the north and west and as man became more mobile and more acquisitive, most of that isolation disappeared.

Mingling of ethnic groups

Tribes of Negritos found in the Philippines and Malaysia are considered representative of some of Southeast Asia's earliest inhabitants. But most of the people of Southeast Asia are Mongoloids of various types who migrated south from mainland Asia before the Caucasoids arrived from India. Because of this, you'll find remarkable similarities in appearance among the native people of the different coun-

tries. For example, it's not uncommon to find Malaysians who look very much like their neighbors in Thailand, Burma, or the Philippines.

Each successive wave of people added to the existing cultures; yet each group retained its own identity. You'll recognize Indians by the men's turbans and the women's saris. The Chinese, numbering in the millions, live in city Chinatowns, belong to a clan house, and worship at neighborhood Chinese temples. In Malaysia and Indonesia, you'll find Arabs living in their own ethnic communities and retaining their culture. Each country also has small concentrations — principally in the cities — of British, Europeans, and Americans. You'll find a British-style cricket club in many of Southeast Asia's major cities.

The multiplicity of racial groups in the area has encouraged a multitude of languages. Though English is commonly spoken in the cities, each country has its own national language, and often a second language, as well as numerous local dialects.

Historical notes

By the 2nd century, traders and adventurers from India, Arabia, and China were paying visits to Southeast Asia. Geographically, Southeast Asia was on the east-west trade route between India, Arabia, and China. These early traders soon discovered that Southeast Asia had riches of its own—gold, tin, sandalwood, teak, ivory, and most importantly spices like nutmeg and cloves. These flavorful items were riches found only in Southeast Asia.

A legacy of ancient empires. Archeological discoveries in Southeast Asia have revealed the existence of ancient cultures and great empires. These empires experienced their greatest growth and development from A.D. 600 to A.D. 1200.

The 8th century saw the rise of the Sri Vijaya empire in Sumatra. Its authority and influence swept through islands of Indonesia and the Malay Peninsula. It was a Sri Vijaya prince who discovered and named Singapore. In the 13th century, the Majapahit empire grew powerful, and the Sri Vijaya empire gradually disappeared. The Majapahits, based in Java, gained control of Indonesia, destroyed the Sri Vijaya settlement on Singapore Island, and extended their influence into Malaysia.

To the north lay the Khmer empire. Controlling much of the Southeast Asian peninsula between China and the Gulf of Thailand, the Khmers' reign lasted from the 9th through the 15th centuries. In 1238, the Thais, emigrants from China, founded the Sukhothai kingdom on the Southeast Asian peninsula. This was followed by the kingdom of Ayutthaya in 1350. During Ayutthaya's 417 year history, there was much warring between the Thais and their neighbors, the Khmers and Burmese. Burma finally invaded and destroyed Ayutthaya in the mid-18th century.

Ruins of these early empires' monuments provide an intriguing glimpse into the highly advanced civilization of each empire. The matchless wonders of the Khmer rulers at Angkor in Cambodia and at Pimai in Thailand and the great Hindu and Buddhist temples in central Java and at Pagan in Burma rank among the finest architectural achievements of man.

The colonialists arrive. In the 16th century, the western powers began to arrive in Southeast Asia, lured by the area's riches. For the next 400 years, European powers — Portuguese, Spanish, British, Dutch, and French — dominated various parts of the region.

Western influence, characterized by commercial and trading enterprises, began with the arrival of the Portuguese in Malacca in 1511. This important rendezvous port, at the junction of the maritime routes linking the Indian Ocean and South China Sea, was wrested from the Malacca Sultanate.

During the 16th century, the Portuguese set up trading posts in Thailand, gained control of the spice trade in Indonesia, and built a fortress in the Moluccas (now known as the Maluku Islands) to protect their interests. In the late 1500s, the Spanish, desiring control of the Moluccas' toothsome riches, took possession of the Philippines — a harborage from which to engage in sea battles with the Portuguese. The Spanish efforts to gain control of the Moluccas failed, however.

It was the Dutch who were to be the rulers of Indonesia and the Molucca spice trade. In 1596 they defeated their rivals and took over the government of Indonesia to rule the country for more than 300 years. The Dutch East India Company dominated the Molucca spice trade. In 1641, the Dutch captured Malacca from the Portuguese. Here, they ruled for more than 180 years. During the 17th century, the Dutch and the British established trading posts in Thailand.

The 19th century saw the British make inroads into Southeast Asia. The British East India Company incorporated Penang, Malacca, and Singapore as the Straits Settlement, later making it a British Crown Colony. Finally a series of treaties induced all the Malay states to accept British advisers. The British annexed Burma in 1885.

During this century, the French gained control of Vietnam, Cambodia, and Laos and administered the three countries as French Indochina.

Independence. Today, Southeast Asian countries once controlled by European colonists are now independent nations, in some cases undergoing economic, social, and political upheaval.

Influences from outsiders

The shores of Southeast Asia's mainland peninsula and innumerable islands served as harbors for many waterborne traders and missionaries. Each new wave of visitors brought fresh concepts that aided and modified the area's development.

Indian culture. The region's most important cultural influences came from India. Merchants and priests introduced Buddhism, Hinduism, and Islam — Southeast Asia's major religions — statesmanship, and the Indian concept of kinship. Indians also brought their literature and arts, classical dance, and language.

The town of Pagan in central Burma became a great center of Buddhism from 1084 to 1113. From Pagan, the religion expanded eastward to other Southeast Asian countries.

Though Islam was first introduced in northern Sumatra in the late 13th century, its major growth came two centuries later. When Malacca became a trading center, Islam spread throughout the Malay Peninsula. Today you can find Muslims and their mosques in Sumatra and Java in Indonesia, and in Malaysia, Singapore, and the southern Philippines.

China's contribution. Southeast Asia is geographically situated midway between India and China, yet China's influence seems slight compared to that of India. The Chinese influence was most important in Vietnam, where many elements of China's culture were adopted — including Chinese Buddhism, Confucianism, and Taoism.

Elsewhere, China's most important contribution was its people. Chinese business practices and commercial activities strongly influenced the development of trade in Southeast Asia. Even today, the Chinese of Southeast Asia play an important economic role. Chinese influences also appear in the region's decorative arts, especially the ceramics of Thailand in the 13th and 14th centuries. Chinese temples and Chinatowns are found in most of the area's major cities.

European influences. It is in the region's cities that the European influence is most prevalent.

The ancient empires of Southeast Asia considered cities merely ceremonial or symbolic centers. The strength of the empire remained in the countryside with the scattered villages of rice farmers, who fed the ruler's slaves and soldiers. When these empires fell, the ruling cities disappeared.

In Europe, though, cities provided the focal point for survival and for the development of culture. Consequently, when the colonial powers constructed cities in Southeast Asia, they built them to endure as power centers. Tacked onto the rural landscape, these river-mouth settlements or harbor-hugging towns along the major shipping routes prospered.

Today, wherever you travel in Southeast Asia, you'll

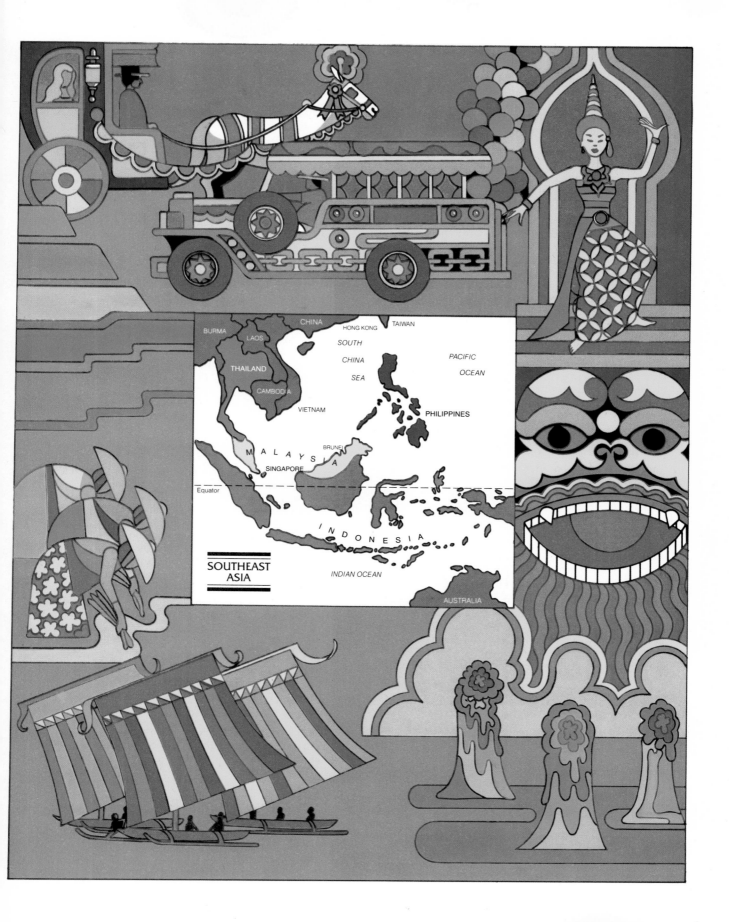

SOUTHEAST
ASIA

BURMA
CHINA
HONG KONG
TAIWAN
LAOS
SOUTH
THAILAND
CHINA
PACIFIC
CAMBODIA
SEA
OCEAN
VIETNAM
PHILIPPINES
MALAYSIA
BRUNEI
SINGAPORE
Equator
INDONESIA
INDIAN OCEAN
AUSTRALIA

see this legacy. Singapore's city center, with its colonial buildings, resembles a British township; Rangoon and Penang are well-provided with British-inspired buildings. In Indonesia's capital of Jakarta, you'll see the buildings and canals reminiscent of those in the Netherlands. Filipino architecture reminds many travelers of the gracious architecture of Spain.

DIVERGENT LIFE STYLES

Of the 250 million people who live in Southeast Asia's Philippines, Thailand, Malaysia, Singapore, and Indonesia, only about 25 million cluster in the capital cities. Most of the inhabitants live outside the cities — in small rural towns, on the lush farmlands cut by winding rivers, along the sparsely settled fringes of tropical rain forests, in tiny settlements in the cool mountainous highlands, or in coastal stilt villages built above shallow, muddy waters.

Rural living

Rice is the food staple of Southeast Asia. Since antiquity, it has been the people's major sustenance. The face of the land is an endless geometric pattern of *padis* (rice fields), broken only by occasional villages or meandering streams. Many of Southeast Asia's rural people are involved in the growing of rice.

The planting, cultivating, and harvesting of rice is a backbreaking task that is repeated several times yearly. First the fields are tilled by heavily yoked water buffalo. Then the seeds are scattered into muddy planting beds. When the tiny green seedlings emerge, they are set out in the shallow waters of growing beds. Ripened grain, shimmering golden brown in the tropical sun, must then be harvested.

Shrines are built in the fields to protect growing grain against the displeasure of spirit gods; religious rites are celebrated in the villages to insure a good crop; and festivals thank the gods for the bounty. This agricultural cycle has changed little in the last thousand years.

Over the centuries, the countryside's small, isolated villages, their houses of bamboo topped by palm leaf roofs, have become the region's most important social and economic units. Villagers join together not only to grow and harvest the rice but also to raise animals, grow vegetables, create handicrafts, and celebrate secular and religious events.

City life

City dwellers live a far different life than their country relatives. No longer physically and culturally isolated, people from different races have had to learn to live and work together. The result is a mingling of customs and ways.

Many cities are experiencing growing pains. Providing adequate and affordable housing for their rapidly increasing populations is the biggest problem facing these metropolises. Tucked between blocks of high-rise luxury apartments are paint-worn shophouses, sometimes housing several families under one small roof. At the edge of the cities are villages of squatters, their wooden houses and yards inhabited by chickens, goats, and pigs. A plethora of humanity is very much in evidence.

The scene is changing, though. More and more, governments are seeking to provide low-cost, high-rise housing for working class people.

A DOMINANT THEME

Throughout Southeast Asia religion is pervasive. Striking temples, mosques, and churches tower above city streets. In the countryside, most villages surround a temple or local shrine; in the fields, shrines are erected to the gods of fertility. Religion often dominates the social life as well. Many of Southeast Asia's colorful festivals are primarily religious celebrations.

The area's religions

Though each Southeast Asian country has a dominant religion, you'll find that many other religions are practiced as well. Buddhism and Islam are the area's preeminent religions; Hinduism and Christianity rank second in importance.

Ninety percent of Thailand's people follow Buddhism. However, there are also Muslims, Taoists, and Christians. Thailand's hill tribes still practice ancestor worship and animism. Predominantly Chinese, Singapore's major religion is Buddhism, frequently combined with elements of Taoism and Confucianism. Christianity is also practiced here. The island's Malays are Muslim; its Indians, Hindu or Muslim.

Islam is the state religion of Malaysia as well as the major religion of Indonesia. However, in both countries you'll find Buddhists, Christians, and Hindus. The Balinese of Indonesia practice Balinese-Hinduism, a form of Hinduism that has been highly modified by ancient Balinese beliefs drawn from animism and ancestor worship. Indonesia's Christian converts include certain tribal groups — the Torajas, Minahasans, and Bataks. Their Christian beliefs have also been tempered with animistic practices.

Ninety percent of the Filipinos are Roman Catholic, a religious heritage from early Spanish conquerors. This makes the Philippines the only predominantly Christian nation in Southeast Asia. You'll find Muslims in the southern Philippines, the legacy of 14th century Arab traders. Scattered throughout the Philippines are Protestants, Buddhists, and Taoists.

A brief understanding

Because many of Southeast Asia's attractions (wats, ancient temples, and festivals) reflect the area's religions, it is helpful for visitors from the West to know a little about Eastern religions.

Islam. Islam is monotheistic. Its followers — Muslims — believe in one supreme deity, Allah. Their holy scripture is the Koran, a collection of words of Allah as revealed to his prophet Mohammed. Devout Muslims spend much time reading and studying the Koran. Children memorize verses from it and recite them in annual Koran reading competitions.

(Continued on page 11)

HANDICRAFT TREASURES

Southeast Asia is truly a shopper's paradise. There are so many beautiful, locally made craft items, you'll have a difficult time choosing what to buy. In many cases you can watch workers using century-old, traditional skills.

Craftspeople at work

Many of the local handicrafts are produced by tiny cottage industries. Sometimes a whole village specializes in the making of one type of product. Visitors are welcome to tour many of Southeast Asia's cottage industries. Products made on the premises can be purchased.

Cottage industries along Peninsular Malaysia's east coast specialize in the making of *kain songket* (a hand-loomed fabric interwoven with gold or silver thread), pewter, and delicate, silver filigree jewelry. In cottage industries near Chiang Mai—Thailand's center of traditional handicrafts—you can see silversmiths, silk weavers, and umbrella makers at work. Whole villages on Bali specialize in a particular craft skill such as stone or wood carving or painting. The craftspeople in and around Yogyakarta are known for their talents in batik making and silver crafting. In the Philippines, an entire village might be involved in the abaca industry. Tasks—from the stripping of the fibers and the spinning of the twine to the final braiding of mats and bags—are divided by households.

In each of Southeast Asia's major cities, you'll find handicraft centers where you can view craftspeople at work as well as buy some of the country's native craft items. Many of these handicraft centers are part of cultural complexes that also feature local architecture, dance, and music.

Things to buy

Each of Southeast Asia's countries is noted for particular craft items. The following are a few things you'll want to look for in each country.

Philippines. Here you'll find abaca hats, mats, and baskets; brightly colored, handwoven place mats and table runners; and delicately embroidered dresses and shirts.

Thailand. Thailand's most famous product is Thai silk, which comes in a variety of colors, patterns, and weights. However, you shouldn't overlook colorful Thai cotton. Other specialties include *nielloware* (silver inlaid with a black alloy), Thai celadon (high-fired stoneware), hand-painted silk or paper umbrellas, bronze tableware, and Thai dolls in elaborate dance costumes.

Malaysia. This country's fine craft items include kain songket, batik, pewter, web-fine silver filigree jewelry, and woven-leaf products.

Singapore. You'll find handicrafts from throughout Southeast Asia sold in Singapore's shops and markets. Locally made products include pewter and carpets. Singapore's tailors can fashion suits in just a few days.

Indonesia. Batik is one of this country's famous products. Other local handicrafts include wood and stone carvings, paintings, silver bowls, flatware, and tea sets, silver filigree jewelry, and leather products like wayang kulit puppets.

Things not to buy

The United States restricts the import of products made from animals and plants it has officially listed as endangered or threatened. This includes tortoise-shell jewelry; items made from the skins or fur of certain animals like the cheetah, jaguar, ocelot, leopard, and tiger; products carved from elephant ivory or whale's teeth; and items made from crocodile and sea turtle skin, including shoes, handbags, belts, wallets, and luggage.

Even though you can buy these items abroad, you will not be allowed to bring them into the United States. If you are in doubt about a purchase, check with the local United States embassy or consular office. The vendors' assurances may not always be correct. There is no refund for purchases confiscated by the United States customs or wildlife inspector. There may even be a fine.

Only a few of the restricted items have been listed here. For a more complete listing, write the Fish and Wildlife Service District Law Enforcement Office in your area.

EASTERN REFLECTIONS

Nowhere else on earth is there more diversity of races and cultures than in Southeast Asia. Over the centuries, the area has served as a crossroads for the world's people. Today, you'll find a multiplicity of inhabitants—Chinese, Arab, Thai, Indonesian, Indian, Malay, European, American, Burmese, Filipino, and tribal people such as Dayaks, Bataks, Torajas, Bajaus, Meos, and Lahus. Each group has added a special flavor to the fascinating cultural blend that is Southeast Asia.

The colorfully garbed child (top right) belongs to a Thai hill tribe whose language, culture, dress, and traditions differ from those of other Thais. Lines of time edge the face of a Singaporean Chinese man (bottom left). A beautiful Thai dancer (bottom right) pensively awaits her turn on stage. Her delicate hands with their long brass fingernails will help tell the dance's tale.

... *Continued from page 8*

The Muslims' house of worship is the mosque, which contains a tall tower called a minaret. From this tower the muezzin calls Muslims to prayer five times daily — at dawn, noon, midafternoon, sunset, and midevening. All the Muslim faithful, wherever they may be, turn to face in the direction of Mecca and fall to their knees in prayer.

Hinduism. In the Hindu religion there is a holy trinity of gods — Brahma, the creator; Vishnu, the preserver; and Siva, the destroyer. Brahma, with its four heads, represents creativity and intellect. Vishnu has four arms and exemplifies versatility and strength. Siva, the most popular god, not only stands for destruction but also regeneration; he is believed to be the most sympathetic of the gods. Each of these major gods has a consort and many minor deities. When you visit a Hindu temple, you'll see statues and carvings of these gods and deities.

Buddhism. Buddhism was founded in India in the 6th century B.C. by Gautama Siddhartha, who later became known as Buddha. Buddhists follow the teachings of Buddha, and their temples and *wats* (Thai Buddhist monasteries) contain many statues of Buddha.

Like the Hindus, Buddhists believe in reincarnation. The goal of all devout Buddhists is nirvana—a total release from earthly pain, sorrow, and desire. Though nirvana is seldom reached in just one life, Buddhists believe that it can eventually be gained by right living, believing, and peace of mind through meditation. When attained, nirvana releases man from the trial of repeated earthly existences.

Others. Confucianism follows the teachings of Confucious, who emphasized devotion to parents, family, and friends. Taoism, based on the doctrine of Lao-tse, advocates simplicity and selflessness. Often practicing Buddhists adhere to the tenets of Confucianism and Taoism as well.

Animism (the belief that inanimate objects and natural phenomena contain spirits) and ancestor worship are still practiced by some of Southeast Asia's primitive, isolated tribes. In numerous areas of Southeast Asia, animistic observances color the rituals of Buddhists, Muslims, Hindus, and Christians.

FESTIVALS AND EVENTS

Festivals are an important part of every Southeast Asian's life. These local celebrations also add color to any vacationer's Southeast Asian trip. Visitors are welcome at most events.

Below are some of the festivals and events celebrated in a similar manner in several Southeast Asian countries. Check the "Festival Time" special feature in each chapter in this book to learn about each country's particular festivals.

The same festival may fall on different dates in different countries. Since some events are based on the lunar calendar, dates change from year to year in concurrence with a full moon. In planning your trip, check with the appropriate government tourist office for a current calendar of events.

Rhythm of the seasons

In Asia, agricultural festivals have been celebrated for generations; most of them follow the cycle of the rice harvest. Though modern high-yield rice strains and other agricultural advances have made traditional communications with the gods less significant, rice festivals are still observed.

Rice planting. In late April or early May, village and regional festivals celebrate the new rice season and invoke the patronage of the spirits. Ploughing and rice planting ceremonies include prayers for a good crop, music, dancing, and other fair activities.

Life-giving rains. Since the success of the rice crop is largely dependent on the annual rains, special festivals are held to encourage the rain and to give thanks for it.

Folk dancing accompanies celebrations in Malaysia. At festivals in Thailand and Singapore, enthusiastic participants douse everyone with water.

Buddhist festivals

Because millions of Southeast Asia's inhabitants follow the precepts of Gautama Buddha, many celebrations revolve around Buddhism's ancient ceremonies.

Ordination of monks. When rice seedlings are transplanted in July, young boys are ordained as Buddhist monks in Thailand. Young monks serve in this capacity for three months, until the rice harvest begins in October. This initiation to manhood — reenacting Buddha's great departure — is similar to the Christian confirmation or Jewish bar mitzvah.

Buddhist Lent. The Buddhist Lenten period begins in April or May, with the onset of the rains and continues through the rainy season. During this period those who are followers of Buddha are expected to be devout, and Buddhist monks spend much of their time meditating in the wats.

In September or October, the end of the Lenten period is celebrated with the Festival of Lights in Thailand, Singapore, and Indonesia. For three nights, all lights—candles, oil lamps, and electric bulbs — burn. The celebration also includes dancing.

Celebration of Lord Buddha. After the rains begin in May, Buddhist celebrations commemorate the birth, enlightenment, and death of Lord Buddha. Lantern processions and religious rites are celebrated at major temples in Indonesia, Malaysia, Thailand, and Singapore.

Muslim festivals

In those parts of Southeast Asia where Islam is practiced, Mohammed's birthday and Muslim holy days mark the calendar.

The fasting period. The Muslim fasting month, Ramadan, occurs during the ninth month of the Muslim year. Malaysia, Indonesia, and the southern Philippines celebrate the end of fasting with a day of mass prayers in the mosques followed by feasting and giving of gifts.

Mohammed's birthday. The birthday of Prophet Mohammed is usually celebrated in April. Each country has its own name for this celebration. It is called Maolod en Nabi in the Philippines and Mauloddan Nabi in Malaysia, where it's a national holiday. All of Indonesia's Muslims honor Mohammed's birth as Grebeg Maulud.

Pilgrimage to Mecca. Every follower of Islam wants to make a *haji* (pilgrimage to Mecca) at least once in his lifetime. In Malaysia, Singapore, the Philippines, and Indonesia, followers who have made the pilgrimage gather at the principal mosques to rejoice. Here, they celebrate their haji with the Hari Raya Haji.

Hindu festivals

The origins of Hinduism go back more than 4,000 years and embrace dozens of sects. So pervasive is this religion that, in regions where Hinduism is practiced, its rituals become part of everyday life for its followers. Many daily activities — prayers, food offerings, bathing — are part of a year-round religious observance.

Two of the great Hindu epic dramas — the Ramayana and the Mahabharata — are performed in whole or in part in Indonesia, Singapore, and parts of Malaysia. Many Balinese dances and celebrations are based on the colorful, emotional Hindu epics.

Birthday of Lord Subramaniam. Hindu devotees in Bali, Malaysia, and Singapore honor the birthday of Lord Subramaniam in late January or early February with the festival of Thaipusam, which features an elaborate procession. Many penitents carry ornately decorated *kavadis*, wooden frames pinned to the back and chest by long metal skewers. Worshippers line the procession's route, chanting and wailing prayers. Thousands of other devotees, some carrying religious images, join the procession as it passes through the streets.

Festival of Lights. Usually held in early November, Deepavali, the Hindu Festival of Lights, marks the victory of Lord Krishna over a mythical king. On the night of the festival, all Hindu homes in Singapore, Penang, and Bali are lighted with oil lamps or candles.

Chinese celebrations

Wherever you go in Southeast Asia, you find enclaves of Chinese who continue to celebrate their traditional holidays. Among the major events are Chinese New Year (in January or February), Cheng Beng, similar to All Soul's Day (in early April), the Birthday of the Goddess of Mercy and the Festival of Seven Sisters (each in August), the Moon Cake Festival (usually about mid-September), and the Festival of the Nine Emperor Gods (late October). Of these, Chinese New Year and the Moon Cake Festival are the most interesting to the visitor.

Chinese New Year. The New Year bursts into being with popping firecrackers, exploding fireworks, colorful dragon parades, feasting, and visits to Chinese temples. During this 3-day period of festivities and great good will, Chinese decorate their homes, and worshippers wear their most colorful clothing when visiting temples.

Moon Cake Festival. Legends relate that Mongol overlords were overthrown by Chinese who hid messages in moon cakes (pastries filled with sweet bean paste and lotus seeds). During the Moon Cake Festival (also called the Mid-Autumn Festival), Chinatown shops are filled with boxes of moon cakes, and the shop fronts are decorated with colorful, whimsical paper lanterns of every size and description.

SOMETHING FOR EVERYONE

Whether lured by tales of once-great civilizations, now lying forgotten amid lush, rice fields or images of wild orchids growing profusely in dense jungles where monkeys chatter unceasingly, the Southeast Asia traveler will be captivated by the region's myriad sights and activities. You can climb the time-worn steps of an 8th century stone temple; travel by horseback to the top of an active volcano; para-sail high above a beach resort; join the locals for an all-night outdoor puppet show; or dine on Peking duck in an elegant restaurant. The choice is yours.

Nearby, isolated beaches, caressed by warm waters, beckon seekers of solitude.

Architectural treasures

With a history that dates back to the dawn of mankind, it's not surprising that some of Southeast Asia's important sights would have historic significance. Long before many of Europe's important buildings were even designed, Southeast Asian craftsmen had put the finishing touches on Indonesia's Borobudur (a Buddhist sanctuary) and Prambanan (a Hindu temple complex). Completed in the 8th and 9th centuries, respectively, the two stone complexes feature intricately carved bas-reliefs — a tribute to the artisans of that period.

Crumbling walls, gateways, temples, and towers attest to the magnificence of Southeast Asia's ancient civilizations. Thailand is replete with vestiges of past empires. Pimai, east of Bangkok, was built by the Khmers in the 1000s. Sukhothai, south of Chiang Mai, was the center of the Siamese civilization in the 1200s and 1300s. Ayutthaya, north of Bangkok, was the Thai capital for 417 years before the Burmese destroyed it in 1767. In Indonesia, remnants of the once great Majapahit empire, an advanced and powerful 13th century Hindu civilization, lie scattered across a plain south of Surabaya.

Not all of Southeast Asia's architectural attractions are crumbling reminders of yesteryears. Spectacular palaces remain. Bangkok's Grand Palace, its shimmering spires of gold and distinctive tiled roofs with eaves dramatically upturned, is the ceremonial center of Bangkok. The Sultan's Palace in Yogyakarta features gracious open-air pavilions with gleaming marble floors and intricately carved teak pillars.

Intriguing, too, are the wats, mosques, and temples of Southeast Asia. The spires of Bangkok's wats soar toward the sky, their golden surfaces gleaming in the tropical sun. In Malaysia, onion-shaped mosque domes bring back childhood memories of tales from the *Arabian Nights*. Singapore's Sri Mariamman Temple is delightfully decorated with brightly painted stucco sculptures of deities, animals, and humans.

A breath of fresh air

Outdoor enthusiasts will find a wealth of fresh-air sights and activities. Southeast Asia is endowed with dense rain forests, lava-spewing volcanoes, cool mountain retreats, and pristine beaches.

National parks and wildlife reserves abound. Indonesia's many nature reserves provide a protective home for native animals like the banteng, one-horned rhinoceros, black monkey, barking deer, orangutan, or komodo dragon. Visitors to Malaysia's Taman Negara (National Park) can spend the evening in a treetop blind positioned above a salt lick in the hope of viewing jungle animals that come to feed.

Even crowded Singapore Island has a nature reserve —Bukit Timah. Here, city dwellers have an opportunity to escape the people-clogged streets to stroll quiet footpaths that meander through tropical jungle. Across the South China Sea in Sabah, climbers can challenge the heights of Mount Kinabalu in Malaysia's Kinabalu National Park. The hike to the top is an arduous one, but the view makes it all worthwhile.

Southeast Asia is the center of much volcanic activity. For a glimpse into the bubbling depths of an active volcano, you can take an overnight horseback trip to Indonesia's Mount Bromo. A boat excursion to Indonesia's newest volcano, Krakatoa, gives you an opportunity to learn about the development of a volcanic island. The original Krakatoa erupted with such force in 1883 that it blew itself apart.

For a gentler view of nature, visit one of Southeast Asia's resort areas. The highland resorts of Malaysia and Baguio in the Philippines offer cool mountain climates, quiet paths for strolling, and spectacular views. Beach resorts such as Singapore's Sentosa Island, Malaysia's Penang, Indonesia's Bali, and Thailand's Pattaya are famous for sun and sand. The Philippines, 7,107 islands washed by clear, warm waters, offers divers countless possibilities for underwater exploration. Coral reefs and colorful marine life thrive offshore. Throughout Southeast Asia, sun seekers and water lovers will find deserted beaches, protected bays, and inviting seas with clear, warm water.

The entertainment scene

Like cosmopolitan communities everywhere, Southeast Asian cities have their fair share of nightclubs, discotheques, and cocktail lounges featuring the latest in popular entertainment. However, the cultural heart of Southeast Asia's entertainment scene is its traditional dance and drama accompanied by native music. Visitors can experience these local performing arts at special restaurant and hotel shows or during colorful, local festival celebrations.

Southeast Asia's dances require skill and agility. The classical dance-dramas of Thailand demonstrate a controlled grace. Beautiful girls, adorned in richly embroidered costumes, jeweled headpieces, and long brass fingernails convey the emotions of a story through the careful movements of their hands and feet. Equally graceful and controlled are the female *legong* dancers of Indonesia. The men of Malaysia have turned the traditional art of self defense, *bersilat*, into a dancelike repertoire of slow, graceful movements; its flow is broken by the staccatos of lightening fast punches and swift kicks. It's all done in time with accompanying music. In Philippine villages, the people entertain themselves by dancing the *tinikling*. Bamboo poles are placed parallel on the ground and clacked together in time with music. Agile dancers must hop in and out between the poles.

Wayang kulit (shadow plays with leather puppets) are a popular form of entertainment in Indonesia as well as in parts of Malaysia and Thailand. The audience sees only the shadows of the puppets, which are manipulated behind an illuminated screen. Performances, consisting of tales from the Ramayana, can last all night.

Time-honored legends of ancient China are portrayed by brilliantly costumed and elaborately painted Chinese opera performers. These shows are usually held on temporary outdoor stages. Opera troupes lead a nomadic life, wandering from place to place to perform for festivals or other special occasions.

Culinary pleasures

A feast of culinary delights awaits the visitor to Southeast Asia. Palate pleasers can vary from innocently sweet to daringly spicy hot. Each country has its own taste-tempting surprises.

Regional dishes of China can be sampled in Singapore. Dine on Peking duck, Hokkien *mee* (noodles), Shanghai bird's nest soup, or Hainanese chicken rice. One of Indonesia's most famous dishes — *sate* — can also be enjoyed in Malaysia, where it's called *satay*. In both countries, the dish consists of pieces of marinated meat skewered, barbecued, and served with a peanut dipping-sauce. Peanut sauce also flavors Indonesian *gado gado* (a vegetable salad).

The cuisine of Thailand is never bland. Instead, it's usually spicy, very spicy! The favorite ingredient—used in large quantities—is chile peppers. A popular dish is *tom yam gung* (a hot and spicy soup). Filipino favorites include *lechon* (roast pig) and *lumpia* (flour wrappings called spring rolls filled with chopped vegetables).

Types of dining spots are almost as plentiful as cuisine choices. You can dine in elegant surroundings at a posh restaurant, join the locals at a small neighborhood cafe, eat a quick bite at a fast-food establishment, or take to the streets for a little food stall sampling.

TRAVEL TIPS

Modern transportation has made Southeast Asia easily accessible to the traveler. International airlines and cruise ships transport visitors to the major cities; guided tours, traveling by air-conditioned buses, follow established sightseeing routes to popular destinations in the various countries. Hotels, restaurants, and other tourist facilities in the big cities and resorts rank with the world's best. You can visit Southeast Asian attractions in comfort and get around with ease; yet the travel experience remains unique.

Since Southeast Asia offers such an array of choices— a seemingly endless variety of destinations, accommodations, and transportation — prospective travelers should seek the advice of a knowledgeable travel agent when planning a trip. A mere capsule of travel information appears below, your travel agent can fill you in on the important details.

By air or sea

Travelers can reach Southeast Asia from virtually any direction: from the United States, Europe, India, the Orient, and the South Pacific. More than 50 international air carriers touch down at the international airports of Southeast Asia. Every country in the area has at least one international airport, and some have several.

An increasing number of airlines are offering discount fares (APEX, excursion, budget) to Southeast Asia. Some airlines offer special packages that include air transportation, accommodations, and some meals.

Sightseeing by cruise ship in the island-studded waterways of Southeast Asia is still another possibility. Some cruise itineraries feature only the Orient and Southeast Asia. Average length for one of these cruises is a month. Other cruise itineraries include Southeast Asian ports as part of an extensive round-the-world cruise, lasting several months. Popular Southeast Asia ports of call include Bali, Jakarta, Singapore, Manila, and Penang. Lesser known ports in Indonesia, the Philippines, and Malaysia can also be reached by sea.

If you want to escape the tourist scene, take a cruise that eschews the popular ports for remote islands that are accessible only by sea. From your offshore anchorage, you visit villages and see cultures that have existed in near isolation for centuries.

A number of cargo/passenger liners also sail the busy seaways of Southeast Asia. Travel on one of these is usually less expensive than on a cruise ship. Since the number of cabins available is limited, you'll need to book your trip well in advance. You'll also need a somewhat flexible schedule. The main purpose of the ship is to carry cargo from port to port, and the dockside unloading/loading process can cause delays.

A word about tours

Group tours are a popular way to see Southeast Asia. They can be less expensive than solo travel since tour operators can take advantage of package prices on accommodations and transportation. The tour price usually includes air fare, accommodations at first-class hotels, local sightseeing, and one or two meals per day. Knowledgeable guides show you the sights and provide information in your own language. The tour escort worries about settling the hotel bill, taking care of the luggage, and getting you to the airport on time.

Generally tours to Southeast Asian countries also include countries in the Orient on their itinerary. Along with your Southeast Asia destinations, you might stop in Japan, Taiwan, Hong Kong, or, in some cases, Korea or China. One or more of these Orient destinations is usually included with several Southeast Asian stops. Longer tours might even include India or, in the case of a circle-Pacific tour, Tahiti, New Zealand, Australia, and Fiji.

Length of tours featuring Southeast Asian destinations can vary from 15 to 36 days. Length of stay at each place is usually no more than 2 to 3 days. Little or no exploration is done beyond the major destination points such as Kuala Lumpur, Singapore, Bangkok, Bali, and Manila.

Once you get there

For the traveler not on a group tour, there are a variety of ways to traverse Southeast Asia once you've arrived. Traveling by air is the fastest; however, it can be expensive. Trains can be a less costly alternative, and they're also a good way to meet local people as you journey through the countryside. Thailand, the Philippines, Malaysia, and Indonesia have train service. Express trains link Singapore, Malaysia, and Thailand. You'll also find air-conditioned express buses throughout Southeast Asia. If you plan to travel by car (rental cars are readily available in major Southeast Asian cities), be sure to hire a driver too. Road signs are not always in English, and local driving habits can be disconcerting to the uninitiated.

Colorful transport. Cities and towns offer a colorful variety of local transportation. Besides the usual buses and taxis, you might find *tuk-tuks* or *helicaks* (motorized trishaws); *pedicabs* or *becaks* (bicycle-powered trishaws); *jeepneys* (jeeplike vehicles with bench seating); or even horse-drawn *calesas* (two-wheeled buggies).

Local tours. Southeast Asia's major cities and tourist areas offer a variety of local tours. These include short city-sights tours as well as longer full-day tours to nearby countryside attractions. Available also are several-day trips that explore the major sights of the country.

A place to stay. In Southeast Asia's major cities you can stay in first-class, high-rise hotels. Amenities include swimming pools, shopping arcades, numerous restaurants and cocktail lounges, and air conditioning. Fashionable beach resorts offer first-class bungalow accommodations and seaside amenities such as water-skiing, boating, and snorkeling.

Beyond the major tourist destinations, accommodations may be limited. However, even in some of the more out-of-the-way places, you may discover comfortable accommodations, good food and drink, and companionship of congenial people. Off the principal routes, you'll find Southeast Asia to be an almost virgin travel land. Elephant roundups, bull races, colorful markets, island hideaways, spectacular river trips, festive celebrations — an almost endless list of discoveries awaits the curious traveler.

Weather wise

The countries of Southeast Asia lie near or on the equator. The climates, therefore, are tropically hot and humid the year around. Temperatures in the lowland areas average between 27°C/80°F and 32°C/90°F. The highland areas can be up to 10 degrees cooler.

Expect some rain the year around. However, during the rainy season be prepared for very heavy rains — monsoonal, in fact. At this time temperatures rise even higher, and it becomes very sultry. Torrential downpours cause roads to flood, making them impassable.

The best (coolest and driest) time to visit varies from country to country. The Philippines and Thailand are at their best from November through February; March through September is a good time to visit Malaysia. You'll find good weather in Singapore from June through September and in Indonesia from April through September.

Wide woven hat *protects rice field worker from tropical sun in timeless Southeast Asian landscape.*

A GLIMPSE OF BURMA AND INDOCHINA

Burma and Indochina (Vietnam, Laos, and Cambodia) are also part of Southeast Asia. However, because of limited tourism possibilities they have not been featured elsewhere in this book. A glimpse of these areas follows.

BURMA

The second largest country in Southeast Asia (Indonesia is the largest), Burma covers an area of about 678,580 square km/262,000 square miles. Bordered by China on the north, India and Bangladesh on the northwest, and Thailand on the southeast, Burma occupies a strategic location in Southeast Asia.

Traditionally Burma has been one of the most isolated areas in Southeast Asia. Now, following a decade of particularly tight military control, Burma is taking its first tentative steps to reestablish relations with the world. This has resulted in increasingly relaxed restrictions for travelers to Burma. In the 1960s visitors could only stay 24 hours in the country. At present you can obtain a 7-day, nonrenewable visa.

You'll find tourist facilities limited, however. Because of a shortage of both accommodations and transportation, it's best to take a group tour into Burma. There are 4 and 6-day Burma tours out of Bangkok, and some U.S. tour operators occasionally include several days in Burma on a Southeast Asia/Orient excursion. Sights you might see on a tour include Rangoon, Pagan, and Mandalay. Because of tight security, travel is restricted in the north.

For the visitor

Burma offers the visitor a culture relatively untouched by the Western world. The Burmese people—kind, gentle, and friendly—still adhere to traditional ways. You will rarely see Western dress. Both men and women wear the Burmese *longyi* (sarong) tied at the waist.

Burma is known as the "Land of the Golden Pagodas." Throughout the country are beautiful temples. Nearly all Burmese are Buddhists, and most of their cultural activities are related to Buddhism. The country's main pagodas are not only places of worship, but often also commercial and social centers. The Burmese express a deep respect for their religion by removing footwear in pagodas and other religious places; visitors should do the same, removing both shoes and stockings.

Rangoon, city of golden pagodas

The old colonial city of Rangoon—on the Hlaing (or Rangoon) River 34 km/21 miles inland from the Gulf of Martaban—is Burma's main port and business center and capital. The present city was originally laid out by the British at the turn of the century. (The British occupied Burma from 1852 to 1948.)

Rangoon's major sights include several pagodas.

Shwe Dagon Pagoda. Towering above Rangoon, the bell-shaped Shwe Dagon Pagoda—Rudyard Kipling's "golden wonder"—forms a landmark that has dominated the city since the first shrine was built almost 2,600 years ago. Of the thousands of Buddhist temples in Burma, it is probably the most revered by Buddhist pilgrims because of the eight sacred hairs of Gautama Buddha enshrined here.

You may be unprepared for the size and brilliance of the pagoda. Its spire soars 99 meters/326 feet, the entire surface shimmering with gold plate. Atop the spire is the *hti* (umbrella), encrusted with more than 5,000 rubies, diamonds, and other precious stones. Numerous ornate smaller pagodas cluster around the base of the spire.

Other pagodas. Situated in the heart of the city, the octagonal Sule Pagoda equals the Shwe Dagon in beauty but not in size. Built about 2,250 years ago, this pagoda contains relics of Buddha brought from India.

The gilded Botataung Pagoda, near Strand Road, has six interior chambers whose walls and ceilings are covered with semiprecious stones.

The lost world of Pagan

Nestled in a broad curve along the east bank of the Irrawaddy River 563 km/350 miles north of Rangoon, the ancient ruins of Pagan seem to meditate beneath the tropical sun. Slowly crumbling walls, rain-eroded shrines, and an occasional broken stupa mark the passage of time in this former center of Buddhist learning. The size of the complex is startling—roughly 41 square km/16 square miles, containing the remains of almost 5,000 temples. Stretched along a 13-km/8-mile bend of the Irrawaddy on a parched plain, the ruins are the survivors of an estimated 30,000 pagodas and temples that once blanketed the Pagan landscape. Centuries ago, 3 million people lived on this plain; now the small village of Nyaung-U stands alone among Pagan's ruins.

Although many of Pagan's temples and pagodas suffered damage in July 1975 when the area was hit by a severe earthquake, the character and general view of Pagan and its attractions have not changed. You can still wander among thousands of temples and pagodas. Some are small and have exquisitely carved designs; others are great hulking masses of stone.

Three temple ruins you'll most assuredly want to visit are Shwezigon Pagoda with its massive golden dome; Ananda Temple, one of Pagan's most impressive monuments; and Thatbyinnyu Temple with its wonderful panoramic view.

Historic Mandalay

Mandalay sprawls over a 65-square-km/25-square-mile area on the east bank of the Irrawaddy River, 692 km/430 miles north of Rangoon. For hundreds of years a large village stood on the site; then, in 1857, King Mindon built the royal capital city of Mandalay. It was the heart of Burma until 1885, when the British annexed the country and deposed Burma's last king. During World War II more than a third of the city was destroyed by Japanese and Allied bombing. Though only a fragment of its once grand past remains, enough older monuments have survived to provide a vivid contrast to the modern era.

Among Mandalay attractions are sacred Mandalay Hill; traces of the Royal Palace; the ancient Shwekyimyint Pagoda; and the venerated Mahamuni (Arakan) Pagoda.

INDOCHINA

The countries of Indochina—Vietnam, Laos, and Cambodia (Kampuchea)—were closed to normal tourism following their takeover by Communist forces. The doors remain closed and the future of tourism in this area is uncertain. The following is a brief sketch of the geography and people of each country.

Vietnam

Vietnam stretches along the eastern coast of the Indochina peninsula, from the border of China south to the Gulf of Thailand. Laos and Cambodia border the country on the west, while Vietnam's east coast faces the Gulf of Tonkin and the South China Sea.

Vietnam's 328,930 square km/127,000 square miles encompass forested hill country and the fertile Red River Valley and delta in the north. To the south are the lush rice lands of the Mekong River delta. The two areas are joined by the Truong-Son mountain chain in central Vietnam.

The great majority of the people in Vietnam are ethnic Vietnamese. Racial minorities account for about 15 percent of the population. These minorities include Chinese and Khmers. The highlands are inhabited by some tribespeople of non-Vietnamese racial background known as Montagnards (highland peoples).

Laos

Laos is a landlocked kingdom in the heart of Southeast Asia. Burma and China border it on the north, Vietnam on the east, Cambodia on the south, and Thailand on the west.

The country covers an area of 236,799 square km/ 91,428 square miles, with a shape similar to Italy minus the toe. The landscape is dominated by jungle-covered mountains and deep river valleys. Many of the country's inhabitants live in the fertile valley of the Mekong River, a waterway that functions as a main transportation route.

Laos has a fascinating cultural mixture influenced by the Indo-Khmer, French, Burmese, and Khmer people. The dominant ethnic group, the Lao, is of Thai stock. Other segments of the population include the Black, Red, and White Thai; the Meo; the Yao; and a variety of tribal groups. The country also has large groups of Chinese, Pakistani, Indian, and Vietnamese inhabitants.

Cambodia

Part of a once-powerful empire, Cambodia (currently called Kampuchea) occupies a southeastern portion of the Indochina peninsula. Generally characterized as a flat plain ringed by low, densely forested mountains, it is bordered by Thailand on the west and north, Laos on the northeast, Vietnam on the east and south, and the Gulf of Thailand on the southwest.

Covering 181,036 square km/69,898 square miles, Cambodia is roughly the size of Washington state. The people live along the Mekong River and in the tributary lake basin of the Tonle Sap, or Great Lake which drains the alluvial central plain.

In Cambodia, the Khmer people dominate the ethnic groups by comprising more than 85 percent of the country's population. Minority groups include Chinese, Vietnamese, and smaller groups of Cham-Malays (a Muslim group) and scattered hill tribes.

One of Southeast Asia's most important ancient temple complexes—Angkor Wat—lies within the well-guarded borders of Cambodia. Angkor was the capital of the Khmer empire which flourished in this part of Southeast Asia between the 9th and 15th centuries. Angkor Wat, the largest and most magnificent of the Khmer's monuments, was built in the 12th century.

For a frozen moment, colorfully clad Filipino performers hold pose during evening show at Manila's Folk Arts Theater, center for preservation of provincial music and dance.

PHILIPPINES

An island world of steeply tiered rice terraces,
prosperous cities, reef-protected lagoons, time-worn
cathedrals and forts, lively festivals, skilled artisans,
and a unique Spanish heritage

Though the Philippines is part of Southeast Asia, in many ways it differs from the rest of the region. Almost everyone in the Philippines speaks English in addition to the dialect indigenous to his province. Filipinos have Malay features, but many people speak Spanish and Spanish names prevail. Most of the population is Christian, though the major religions of Asia are also evident.

With its rice fields and cloud-capped volcanoes, the countryside resembles other parts of Southeast Asia. In addition the landscape includes sugar cane fields and pine-forested highlands. You'll see the well-ordered urban complex of Makati, Manila's commercial center, as well as fishing villages of stilt houses built over the water; old baroque cathedrals dominating town squares and red-domed mosques set in palm groves; islets and atolls that disappear when the tide is high and mountain peaks rising to the clouds; *carabaos* (water buffalos) pulling plows across farmland and entire mountainsides terraced in rice.

Filipinos possess an uncommon warmth and courtesy derived from their Asian and Spanish heritages. Women enjoy an independence and hold a respected place in the community. Upon arriving in the Philippines, you will hear a word that will be with you throughout your stay. It is "Mabuhay," pronounced ma-BOO-hai. Strictly translated it means "long live," but it has also come to mean "welcome," "farewell," "good luck," and "Godspeed."

SOME GEOGRAPHIC FACTS

Lying some 965 km/600 miles off Asia's southeastern coast, the 7,107 islands of the Philippine archipelago stretch 1,770 km/1,100 miles from north to south. The northernmost part

of the chain, the rocky Batanes Islands, lies 161 km/100 miles south of Taiwan, and the southernmost part, the islands of the Sulu archipelago, lies only 23 km/14 miles east of Borneo. The entire chain is bounded by the Pacific Ocean on the east, the South China Sea on the west and north, and the Celebes Sea on the south.

The archipelago falls into three groups—the island of Luzon in the north, the Visayas in a central cluster, and Mindanao, with its own archipelago, the Sulu chain, trailing off to the south. Only about 10 percent of the islands are inhabited, and more than half unnamed.

Geologic characteristics

Geologic features of the Philippine archipelago include mountainous islands marked by a multitude of natural harbors, active volcanoes, and hot springs.

Volcanic origins. Most of the islands are the exposed tips of extinct volcanoes or the ridges of an underwater mountain range that once joined the Asian mainland. Coral overlays some of the low mounds, and many of these tiny atolls disappear when the tide is high. The larger islands, particularly Luzon and Mindanao, have coastal plains, edged by rolling hills and high mountains and narrow central valleys.

Natural formations. Natural phenomena include hot springs and volcanoes, of which 10 are still active (Taal Volcano and Mayon Volcano on Luzon are popular visitor spots). The highest point in the archipelago is 2,954-meter/9,690-foot Mount Apo on Mindanao, and the lowest is the Philippine Deep, east of Mindanao, where the ocean sinks to a depth of 10,802 meters/35,440 feet. The irregular Philippine coastline has many natural harbors. Manila Bay, with its 193-km/120-mile shore, is one of the finest natural harbors in Southeast Asia.

Flora and fauna

Centuries of volcanic activity have given the Philippines rich soil yielding varied plant life. Tropical evergreen rain forests cover much of the land; pine forests grow in the mountains, and bamboo, coconut palm, and banyan trees cover the lower slopes.

Lush growth. According to botanists, there are 10,000 species of flowering plants and ferns; orchid species alone number 1,000. You'll see fragrant, white *sampaguita* blossoms, the national flower, made into garlands. The national tree is the *narra* (a type of mahogany). Chief agricultural products are rice, sugar, abaca, coconuts, tobacco, corn, vegetables, and a variety of fruit — some that you'll never find at home. Look for pineapples, mangoes, bananas, citrus, as well as the succulent chicos, rambutans, and lanzones, and the infamous durians, foul smelling and sweet tasting.

Abundant wildlife. Among the hundreds of varieties of birds and animals inhabiting the islands are the rare monkey-eating eagle of Mindanao and the short-horned *tamaraw* (half boar and half water buffalo) of Mindoro Island. Omnipresent is the gentle, hard working *carabao* (water buffalo). The waters yield pearls, corals, sponges, and an abundance of fish and mollusks.

THE HISTORIC PERSPECTIVE

Archeologists have found evidence that prehistoric tribes occupied the Philippines long ago, when its land mass was still attached to the Asian mainland. However, the first inhabitants generally are considered to be the primitive Negritos (small Negroes), descendants of whom still live in the forests of the major islands. These pygmylike people trace their origins back some 25,000 years to the great migration of Stone Age people from Asia.

Centuries of settlement

Next came Indonesians ("island Indians") from Sumatra and Java, who eventually became the hill people of the Mountain Province in northern Luzon and of central and eastern Mindanao. Soon the seafaring Malays began to cross the South China Sea in large canoes, first reaching the islands by 300 B.C. and continuing to arrive until A.D. 1500. As the Malays settled along the coastal plains and in the valleys, the earlier arrivals were displaced and permanently driven into the high mountain ranges. Chinese and Arab traders were early visitors to the island ports, but it was not until about A.D. 700 that the Chinese began to settle in the islands.

Western explorers. In 1521, Ferdinand Magellan, the Portuguese navigator sailing under the flag of Spain, landed at a tiny, uninhabited island in the Leyte Gulf off the coast of Samar. He claimed the islands for Spain and celebrated the first Roman Catholic mass. After planting the Christian cross at the already thriving port of Cebu, Magellan and several of his men were killed by native chief Lapu-Lapu on nearby Mactan Island in a conflict over Christianization of local tribespeople.

Bringing the cross and the sword, Miguel Lopez de Legazpi and his band of conquistadores arrived in 1565 to establish the islands as a Spanish colony. They named the islands Las Felipinas after Philip II of Spain. These first colonizers found people living in tribal units, with laws, their own culture, and a thriving trade with neighboring countries. Establishing the first capital of Las Felipinas at Cebu City, the conquistadores spent the next seven years conquering the islands. They reached Manila in 1571, overpowered the Muslim tribes living there, and established it as the capital. The port of Manila flourished, for the Spanish galleon trade with Mexico brought Mexican silver from Acapulco to be traded for Chinese silks and jade.

Towards independence

During the 333 years of Spanish rule, more than a hundred revolts were organized by the Filipinos. In 1896 the colony was rocked by widespread insurrection following the execution of Dr. Jose Rizal, a Filipino author, sculptor, and physician who sought reform in government and religion.

Spanish-American War. After unsuccessful efforts to establish a republic, insurgents led by General Emilio Aguinaldo joined American forces in the Spanish-American war. Commodore George Dewey defeated the Spanish navy in Manila Bay on May 1, 1898, and Filipino and American ground forces captured the city of Manila. The Treaty of Paris awarded the United States control of the Philippines—a disappointment to the Filipinos, who expected complete independence.

First Philippine Republic. Immediately, hostilities broke out between the Americans and Filipinos. On January 23, 1899, the First Philippine Republic was inaugurated with General Aguinaldo as its president. A year later Aguinaldo was captured; in trying to avoid further strife, he swore allegiance to the United States, officially ending the armed resistance. Peace did not come, however, until 1902, when the United States began laying the foundations for Philippine independence and self-government.

President Woodrow Wilson was prepared to end the U.S. administration of the Philippines but was prevented by the onset of World War I. Succeeding presidents did not favor ending the relationship.

GOVERNMENT IN TRANSITION

Finally, in 1935 the Commonwealth of the Philippines was formed, with Manuel L. Quezon as president, and the country looked forward to independence within the decade. Before this goal was reached, the Japanese invaded the islands.

World War II

Japanese troops occupied the country until it was liberated by U.S. forces under General Douglas MacArthur in 1945. During those years, Filipino and American forces fought side by side during some of the heaviest battles in the Pacific. Devastated by war, the country began to rebuild after liberation.

Complete independence, as promised in an earlier U.S. plan, came on July 4, 1946. Manuel A. Roxas, the last president of the Commonwealth, assumed office as first president of the Republic of the Philippines.

The government today

The Philippines has a parliamentary form of government with the president also acting as the prime minister. A pool of nationally elected cabinet members is responsible to the Interim National Assembly, which runs day-to-day matters.

In 1969, Ferdinand E. Marcos, sixth president of the Philippines, won an unprecedented second term. Three years later, in response to security disturbances and separatist movements in Mindanao and the Sulu Archipelago, he declared martial law. Martial law was lifted January 17, 1981, and legislative powers were transferred to the Interim National Assembly.

THE FILIPINO PEOPLE

The people of the Philippines reflect the blending of Asian and Western influences. Most of the 40 million island inhabitants are Asians, predominantly of Malay origin. Yet they are the most westernized people of all Southeast Asia. Most of them speak English, wear western clothes, play western music, drive western and Japanese cars, and have the manners and friendly hospitality of old Spain.

Many old-time Filipino families trace their ancestry back to Spain; others to Europe, America, Indonesia, India, China, Mexico, and Japan.

Ethnic diversity

Despite general similarity in appearance, the Filipinos belong to some 43 distinct ethnic groups, many retaining particular dress, religions, customs, and dialects.

Largest of these minority ethnic groups are the Filipino Muslims from Mindanao and the Sulu Archipelago. Spanish colonizers called all Muslims "Moros" (for Moors); however, the name is not commonly used today. Other groups include the Ifugao tribespeople, whose ancestors built the rice terraces in northern Luzon; the Badjaos or sea gypsies, who spend most of their lives afloat on the Sulu Sea; and the Negritos, a dark race of pygmies from central Luzon.

Language

From among 87 different Filipino languages and dialects, the government chose the Tagalog dialect as the basis for the national tongue—which they call Pilipino. For more information on the language, see "Speaking Pilipino," page 24.

In the schools, English is the medium of instruction. Spanish is a social language, spoken mainly by the older generation.

Religion

Roman Catholicism, a heritage from the Spanish conquerors, is the religion of 90 percent of the Filipinos, making the Philippines the only Christian nation in Southeast Asia or the Orient. Islam, introduced during the 14th century by Arab traders, is limited mainly to the Muslim population of Mindanao. Also found in the Philippines are Protestants, Buddhists, and Taoists.

PLANNING YOUR TRIP

Situated some 7,000 air miles west of the United States, the Philippine islands lie 17 hours flying time from California. Twenty-two international airlines, including Philippine Airlines (PAL), serve the country. Steamship companies maintain regular service—both cruise ships and cargo/passenger ships—from the United States' west coast to Philippine ports. Manila is the country's capital and gateway city.

The hotel scene

Greater Manila has many luxury and first-class international hotels where hospitality—for which the Filipinos are famous—is evident. At Baguio, Cebu, Davao, Zamboanga, and other major visitor destinations, you'll find hotels with restaurants, nightclubs, shops, and tour services; some have swimming pools and health clubs. Rates are subject to a 10 percent service charge and a 10 percent government tax.

New on the hotel scene, particularly near Manila, are luxurious beach resorts. Emulating native architecture, the resorts' bungalows have thatched roofs.

Local transportation

Philippine Airlines provides regular service to major cities throughout the country. Available for charter from several Manila-based companies are small planes and helicopters.

By train and bus on Luzon. The Philippine National Railways operates first-class, air-conditioned cars as far north as San Fernando and south to Camalig (for Legazpi). Railway and bus connections made in San Fernando proceed farther north to Vigan, Bangued, and Laoag.

Interisland boat trips. Several Manila-based companies offer regular passenger service from Manila to ports in the Visayas and Mindanao. Air-conditioned cabins with private facilities are available on all lines.

Car and driver touring. For navigating Manila traffic and the highways that ribbon the country, a chauffeur-driven car is advisable. Luzon has the best highway system, but all islands have paved roads. Avis, Hertz, and National rental car companies have offices in Manila. Avis is also represented in major tourist destinations. Traffic keeps to the right.

By jeepney and taxi. Found careening through Manila and other cities are jeepneys, jeeplike vehicles that accommodate up to 12 passengers, hunched together on bench seats (see "Filipino Jeepneys — Folk Baroque on Wheels," page 32). At rates lower than those charged by taxis (determined by zones), the jeepney will stop to load or unload anywhere along its route. Jeepneys are plentiful, as are metered taxis. In provincial towns, you'll also find the tricycle (a motorcycle fitted with a side car). It's comfortable for two average-size people for short rides. The two-wheeled horse-drawn *calesa* (buggy) still rolls through the older sections of Manila and some provincial towns. Calesas can be hired for leisurely sightseeing.

Tours. Philippine tour operators run trips throughout the country. They have air-conditioned buses and provide guides. You can arrange a tour to satisfy almost any special interest whether it's diving or deep-sea fishing, playing golf or studying archeology, hunting for shells or arts and crafts, watching birds or wildlife, or exploring caves or World War II battle sites.

Food and drink

A variety of taste sensations await when you dine in the Philippines. The country's hotels and restaurants offer Filipino, Chinese, Japanese, Thai, Korean, Indonesian, Spanish, Scandinavian, French, Italian, and American dishes. Dining styles range from elegant to fast-food-casual. Allow for regional differences when it comes to seasonings. Food may be merely broiled or steamed in some places, embellished with garlic, onions, and chile peppers in others.

Edible delights. In a nation of islands with a coastline measuring twice that of the United States, expect a great deal of seafood. Try *lapu-lapu* (a white meat fish native to Phillipines) served boned and stuffed as *relleno*, wrapped in banana leaves and broiled as *inihaw*, marinated with onions and peppers and eaten raw as *kinilaw*, or stewed with vegetables in a garlic sauce as *paksiw*. The national favorite is *adobo* (a pork dish that has chicken and beef variations). It is cooked with garlic and peppercorns in one version, coconut milk in another, or merely fried crisp and dry.

If you are fortunate enough to be invited to a Filipino family celebration, you will be offered *lechon* (whole roast pig)—the country's feast dish. Stuffed with tamarind leaves, which preserve its shape and impart a slightly tart flavor to its meat, the suckling pig is turned on a spit over hot coals for several hours. When done, the skin is so crisp it stands out taut from the body. Restaurants serve lechon if you order it in advance. Crisply browned, the whole roast pig is brought to the table on a platter and served with a spicy sauce.

Staples at a Filipino meal include rice—a reminder of Spanish cuisine—and two Chinese derived foods: *pancit* (a noodle) and *lumpia* (a noodlelike spring roll filled with chopped vegetables). Fresh vegetables and tropical fruits are plentiful. A whimsical dessert for hot weather is *halo-halo* (layers of sweet fruit topped with shaved ice and sugared milk). Literally translated, it means "mix-mix," and that's exactly what you do to the layers of jackfruit, garbanzo beans, coconut meat, cubes of a glutinous purple jam, and chunks of sweet potato. Served in a tall glass, everything is stirred together with a long-handled spoon and enjoyed.

Thirst quenchers. For a hot weather cooler nothing satisfies as much as soda water mixed with *calamansi* (a round, marble-size green citrus) juice. The locally brewed San Miguel beer is also popular. Sip native drinks such as *basi* (wine made from fermented sugar cane) and *tuba* (a coconut sap wine) with care—they're strong.

The entertainment picture

Filipinos are the musicians and entertainers of Asia. Their bands, singers, and specialty acts are popular in the entertainment capitals of Southeast Asia. Hotels offer floor shows with local and imported talent and dance music —from gentle strains to fiery disco beats. You'll find nightclubs in Makati and along "the strip" at the south end of Roxas Boulevard in Manila.

An interest in folk entertainment is keeping alive the music, dances, and costumes of the provinces. You can see performances in some hotels and in Manila's Folk Arts Theater. The best known Filipino dance is the *tinikling*: men hold bamboo poles parallel and click-clack them in time to the music, while dancers hop between the poles and away again at an ever faster pace. The movements of the dancers represent the movement of long-legged herons.

If you itch to cast the dice, head for one of the casinos along the tourist route. Located in Manila, Baguio, Iloilo, Cebu, and Davao, they offer craps or dice, roulette, black jack, and slot machines.

In search of good buys

Cottage industries operating in small towns throughout the provinces keep shelves in Manila shops and local markets filled with handicrafts. Prices are set in large stores, but bargaining is permissible in small shops and expected in the markets.

Here are some of the handicrafts you can find at very reasonable prices: mats and baskets of abaca; textiles of *jusi* (raw silk fiber), *pina* (pineapple fiber), and *ramie* (linenlike fiber); wooden chests, trays, and boxes; wooden tables often inlaid with carabao bone; capiz shell lampshades and Christmas tree ornaments; bamboo and rattan furniture; brassware and silver pieces; and bright-colored place mats and table runners woven on ancient looms.

Other good buys are shoes, increasingly available ready-to-wear fashions, and custom-made shirts and dresses, sewn up overnight by local tailors. At a reasonable price, men can order a *barong tagalog* (the loose-fitting embroidered shirt worn by Filipinos). Long-sleeved for formal occasions and short-sleeved otherwise, the diaphanous garment is a cool, comfortable substitute for a coat and tie.

The sports scene

Sports are a year-round passion for Filipinos. When they can't be players or spectators outside (usually only during a period of heavy rain), they move inside to sports arenas. Visitors have ample opportunity to watch or participate in the Filipino sports life.

From the sidelines. Called the "game of a thousand thrills," the Basque-derived game of jai alai is similar to handball but played with a hook-shaped wicker basket strapped to each player's arm. On a court half the length of a football field, two players alternately catch the small ball in the basket before it bounces twice and then hurl it back against the court's wall for the other player to catch on the

"Most is best" *might be motto for flamboyant Filipino jeepneys, local form of transportation. Romantico's owner makes a statement about his vehicle's horsepower.*

Venerable Manila Hotel, *only one of city's many tourist hostelries, offers deluxe service amid elegant surroundings.*

rebound. In Manila, you can watch and place bets on jai alai matches nightly except Sunday at the *fronton* (stadium) on Taft Avenue.

Staged on weekends and holidays in cockpits near cities and towns throughout the country, cockfights are a popular spectator sport. Passions run deep. Though spectators are to sit in galleries, they frequently surge against the pit as they root for their favorite, yelling out bets to the *kristo* (bookie). The kristo never writes down a bet, yet remembers who bets what and pays up exactly.

A fight is a brief and bloody affair. The birds have sharp metal spurs strapped to their left feet, and blood spurts as they slash each other. The winner of the match either kills or sets to flight the other bird. Cocks that survive several matches are allowed to retire. Losers usually end up in the stew pot.

You can also watch *pelota* (a cross between tennis and jai alai) matches at hotel and resort courts and horseracing at Manila's San Lazaro Hippodrome or Philippine Racing Club. Basketball, volleyball, and baseball are played in various sports arenas in Manila, among them the Araneta Coliseum (the largest dome in Asia) and Rizal Memorial Stadium.

Sports to play. Golf courses dot the country. You'll find beautifully manicured greens and astonishingly low greens fees. In Manila, the municipal links spread out alongside the old walled city of Intramuros. The Manila Golf and Country Club in Forbes Park has a championship course, as does the suburban Wack Wack Golf and Country Club, traditionally the site of the Philippine Open. Visitors can usually arrange to play at private clubs on weekdays.

SPEAKING PILIPINO

Your chances of encountering a language barrier in the Philippines are minimal, since English is widely spoken. If there's a breakdown in communication, or you have an urge to test your linguistic ability, here are some phrases in Pilipino, the national language. The words are pronounced just as they are spelled.

Good morning— *"Magandang umaga"*
Good afternoon— *"Magandang hapon"*
Good evening— *"Magandang gabi"*
Thank you— *"Salamat"*
You are welcome— *"Walang anuman"*
How much is this?— *"Magkano ito?"*
Expensive— *"Mahal"*　Cheap— *"Mura"*
Where is the hotel?— *"Saan naroon ang otel?"*
Where is the restaurant?— *"Saan naroon ang restoran?"*
Is it far?— *"Malayo ba?"*
Help me— *"Tulungan mo ako"*
Yes— *"Oo"*　No— *"Hindi"*

Tennis courts of shell, clay, and synthetic substances are part of the facilities at hotels in Manila and other tourist destinations and beach resorts near the capital. Permission is needed to play at such private clubs as the Manila Polo Club and the Army and Navy Club.

If you like to hike, head for Mount Apo on Mindanao, Taal Volcano, 64 km/40 miles south of Manila, or Mayon Volcano near Legazpi, 330 km/205 miles southeast of Manila. Popular water sports are swimming and snorkeling at any one of numerous beaches, sailing, scuba diving (see page 41), and white-water boating (see page 33).

MANILA

Located in the southwestern part of Luzon, Manila dates back to 1571, when Spanish conquistadores chose the site — then a tiny Muslim kingdom called May-nilad — for a settlement. The Spaniards built their walled city of Intramuros on the delta where the river emptied into the large protected bay.

Getting your bearings

Today Manila spreads out over the broad plain that borders Manila Bay. The Pasig River separates Intramuros, the oldest section of the city, lying on the south bank of the river, from Manila's historic sections on the north bank. Modern Manila lies to the south of Intramuros.

The cosmopolitan capital, a city of 8 million, is a mix of modern hotels and office buildings, ancient ruins, flower-filled plazas, and spreading suburbs. The main waterfront thoroughfare, parklike Roxas Boulevard, follows the bay's curving shoreline. Visitors travel this route to reach hotels that border it and cluster near Rizal Park, at its north end. On Sunday morning, most of Manila's residents seem to be on an outing along the boulevard—swimming in the bay, buying fish from a stall on the beach, and settling along the seawall for family picnics. The bay has an irresistible attraction for the locals. They walk along the waterfront at sunrise and again in the evening, as the fiery orb sinks below the watery horizon.

Metropolitan Manila consists of four cities — Manila, Pasay, Quezon City, and Caloocan—and 13 towns. Arterial highways lead north to Quezon City and southwest to modern Pasay and Manila International Airport. Still experiencing growing pains, Manila is expanding onto land west of Roxas Boulevard that is being reclaimed from Manila Bay. Zoned for business and residential use, the so-called New City now holds the Philippine Cultural Center complex.

Downtown walking tour

Manila is a cluster of districts — Ermita, Santa Cruz, Quiapo, Escolta, and Binondo — all fanning out from the city center. None of the districts is far from the heart of the city, yet each has a distinct character and interesting landmarks. You can cover many of Manila's sights during a 2-hour walking tour starting from Rizal Park.

Rizal Park. A swath of green, this memorial park extends eastward from the bay into the city. It has gardens and expanses of lawn, fountains, monuments, playgrounds, a

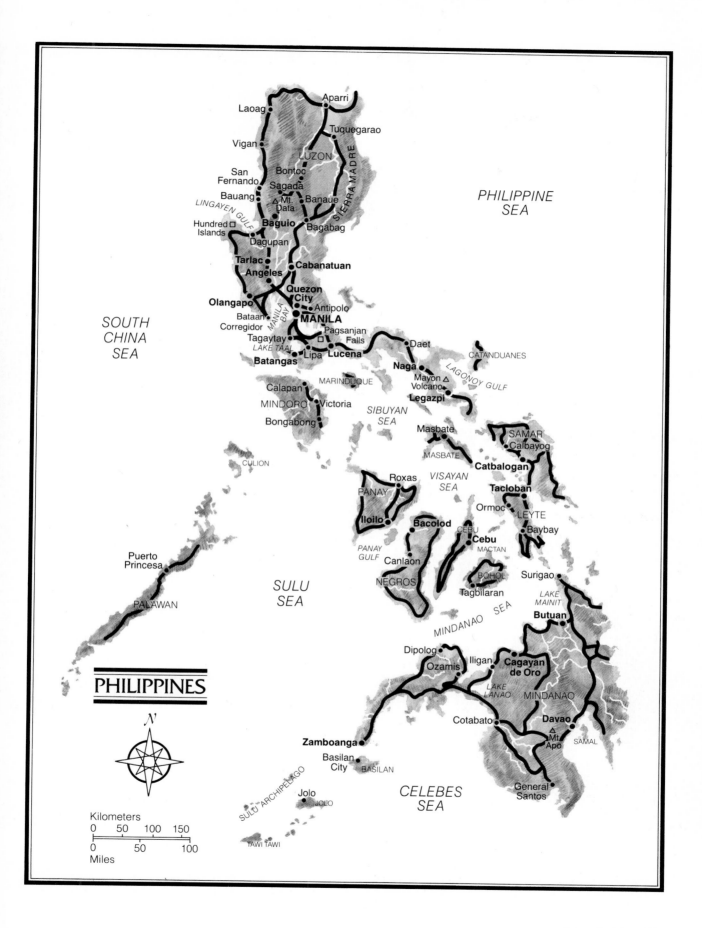

PHILIPPINES

N

Kilometers
0   50   100   150

0   50   100
Miles

Explore Corregidor's reminders *of grim World War II battles; tours visit Pacific War Memorial, artillery sites, and jungle-covered barracks.*

Brooms from Baguio *make interesting, if large, souvenirs; smaller handicrafts from northern Luzon's summer capital include silver filigree, bamboo wares, handwoven items.*

circular roller skating rink, and promenades. At the park's west end, a monument marks the spot where Dr. Jose Rizal, the Philippines' national hero, was executed by the Spaniards in 1896. His remains are buried here, and members of the Armed Forces of the Philippines keep vigil.

Rizal Park is probably the best place in Manila to go people-watching by day or night (it's well lighted and patrolled). At the first light of dawn, young and old walk through the park on their way to work; others take their morning exercise roller skating on the circular concrete rink. Hundreds of people visit the park during their lunch hour, and on Sunday families come to promenade or picnic. You can go strolling in the park's Chinese and Japanese gardens or enjoy open-air concerts held regularly on Sundays and holidays at the grandstand by the breakwater. A sidewalk cafe, found at the western end of the park, is open for lunch.

Facing upon the east end of the park are several government buildings, including the Ministry of Tourism building.

Intramuros. A five-minute walk from the park, north across P. Burgos Drive, is Manila's old walled city, reminiscent of a tiny medieval enclave. Built in the 16th century by the Spaniards (aided by some 3,000 Filipinos), it was badly damaged during World War II.

Though it's partly in ruins, you can inspect crumbling walls, cobblestone streets, the ancient church of San Augustin (dating from 1599 — the oldest stone church in the Philippines), Manila Cathedral, and the former palace of the Spanish governors general. The city's original seven gates have been partially restored.

Fort Santiago. One of Spain's oldest garrisons stands at the northwest corner of Intramuros, between Aduana Street and the Pasig River. Built nearly 400 years ago near the river's mouth, the restored fort is a national shrine. It was once the seat of Spanish colonial powers; its dungeons and inner chambers served as a prison during the Spanish regime and the Japanese occupation. The fort was almost completely destroyed during the battle for the liberation of Manila in 1945.

In one of the dungeons, Dr. Jose Rizal spent his last hours before his execution in 1896. Inside the fortress is the Rizal Museum, housing memorabilia of the man who, to the Filipinos, is a martyr and a revolutionary symbol.

The fort attracts visitors not only for its historical significance but also as a pleasant place for evening strolls. Like Rizal Park, it is well lighted and patrolled at night. Seasonal open-air drama is presented in the Rajah Sulayman Theater, occupying the area where barracks once stood. The fort is open daily from 7 A.M. to 9 P.M.

A walk or taxi ride south on Roxas Boulevard will return you to Rizal Park.

North of the river

Half-day trips by taxi, jeepney, or a guided coach tour take you north of the Pasig River to the older sections of Manila.

Escolta district. The heart of the city's old commercial section lies across Jones Bridge. It is a small area of stores and coffee houses.

The name *escolta* (meaning "escort") comes from the days when the Spanish viceroy and his mounted escort would clatter down the cobblestone streets. Shopkeepers would dash out at the "escolta" sound, hoping to make a sale. A reminder of Manila's early days is the baroque structure of Santa Cruz Church. Nearby, the Plaza Cervantes (named after the creator of the fictional Don Quixote) still retains its old Spanish atmosphere.

Chinatown. A few blocks north of the Escolta district lies the home of many of the city's Philippine-born Chinese. Ongpin Street, the center of Chinatown, is lined with dozens of noodle shops and family-run Chinese restaurants. Narrow streets branching off Ongpin contain hundreds of shophouses. The district's architecture is more Filipino than Chinese, and most of the signs are in English. Though many Chinese families practice their ancestral ways, their children have names like Carlos, Manuel, Rosann, and Maria.

Quiapo district. Located just north of the Quezon Bridge, this district is one of Manila's oldest. Plaza Miranda, at the head of Quezon Boulevard, is Manila's Hyde Park and the people's political forum. Beneath the plaza is a pedestrian underpass with several shops, a bank, and young people selling lottery tickets.

Facing the plaza is Quiapo Church, home of the Black Nazarene shrine. On Friday, great crowds gather here to venerate the ebony-carved image. Twice a year, at the saint's feast day in January and on Good Friday, a milling crowd gathers to watch the male penitents carry the Black Nazarene through the district's streets. Women devotees dress in the garb of the Nazarene — maroon robes or dresses, with crowns of green branches around their heads.

Under Quezon Bridge you'll find the Quiapo Market, resembling an underground department store. Hundreds of stalls sell fresh produce, fruits, fish, and meats brought in from the provinces at dawn. By midmorning, late-arriving housewives are haggling with vendors over the price of picked-over vegetables and fruit. Some stalls sell handicrafts—hats, handbags, place mats—at lower prices (if you bargain) than in the city.

Central Market. North on Quezon Boulevard is one of the city's largest markets. Here under one large roof are all the items a family will need in its lifetime. You'll see electronic items from Japan and expensive brocades from Paris, handembroidered *jusi* (silk) from Iloilo, and handloomed cottons of the mountain tribespeople near Baguio. In the food section, you'll discover that the Filipino gourmet has a multitude of choices, among them snails, frogs, beetles, and New Zealand steaks.

University of Santo Tomas. A few minutes' walk east of the Central Market, the university occupies a 60-acre site fronting on Espana Street. Santo Tomas is an old university; it was founded in 1611—25 years before Harvard—by Spanish Dominicans. For 300 years the university was located inside the old walled city of Intramuros; the present buildings were dedicated in 1927.

Santo Tomas is noted for its medical school, museum of biological and zoological rarities, and tower, a historical landmark. A colorful student quarter surrounds the university. During the Japanese occupation, some 3,000

American and Allied men, women, and children were confined here for more than 3 years.

Malacanang Palace. The imposing official residence of the president of the Philippines stands on the bank of the Pasig River, east of the Quiapo district. Originally built as a country residence by a 19th century Spanish aristocrat, the palace has also housed the Spanish and American governors general.

The main building is closed to visitors, but by prior arrangement you can stroll through the gardens and visit the Executive Building. Just inside the main gate stands a *nipa* (bamboo) hut, shaded by banyan and acacia trees; the structure is made entirely of handrubbed bamboo, with furnishings of bamboo and rattan.

South of Rizal Park

Heading south from Rizal Park, the "tourist belt" of the Ermita district extends 2 km/1 mile along Roxas Boulevard and its tree-shaded promenade bordering Manila Bay. Some of the area's attractions are within walking distance of hotels; others are only a short taxi or jeepney ride away.

Many of the city's leading hotels, shops, art galleries, restaurants, and night clubs line the thoroughfare and streets running parallel to it. Before the war, Roxas Boulevard (formerly Dewey Boulevard) was considered Manila's "millionaires' row," and several stone-walled mansions still remain. On the bayside, the U.S. Embassy occupies spacious grounds. Further down the avenue is the headquarters of the Philippine Navy and the Manila Yacht Club.

Cultural Center complex. Set on land reclaimed from Manila Bay, the Philippine Cultural Center is a showcase for the Filipino performing arts. Its architecture combines modern sculptured forms with native Philippine materials.

The building contains a concert hall and theater, music and art library, historic art gallery, and a museum with archeological finds and Muslim artifacts. Also part of the complex is the Philippine International Convention Center, with facilities for up to 5,000 people. A major conference center for Southeast Asia, it has exhibits of Philippine natural resources and an audio-visual program highlighting the country's history.

Behind the Cultural Center is the Folk Arts Theater,

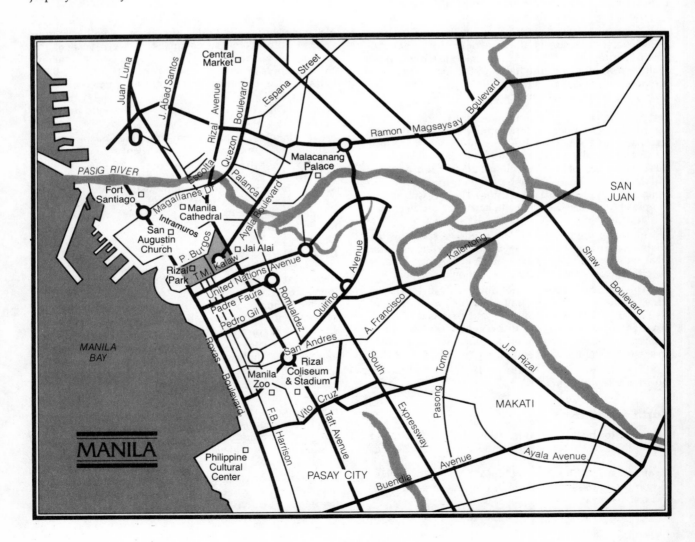

Here are some basics to help you in planning a Manila visit.

Getting there

Manila is served by air, sea, bus, and train transportation.

By air. Serving Manila's airport are twenty-two international airlines from major cities in the United States, Europe, Australia, and Asia. Philippine Airlines (PAL) is the country's international and domestic carrier.

The airport is located 7 km/4 miles south of downtown Manila.

Taxis and limousines of specific hotels are available to transport visitors from the airport into the city.

By sea. International cruise and cargo/passenger ships call regularly at Manila Bay. Several Philippine lines sail from Manila to ports throughout the islands.

By bus. Philippine National Railways operates bus service from Manila to major tourist destinations on Luzon.

By rail. Philippine National Railways operates air-conditioned trains from Manila, with routes extending north to San Fernando, and south to Camalig (for Legazpi). Local lines traveling north to Laoag make connections with the express train in San Fernando.

Where to stay

Major hotels are concentrated along Roxas Boulevard and amid the office buildings and shops of Makati. All are air-conditioned and have nightclubs, discos, and swimming pools; in addition, some have tennis courts, saunas, and massage services. Most hotels add a 10 percent service charge and 10 percent government tax to room rates.

Roxas area hotels include the Manila Hotel, Manila Hilton International, Manila Midtown Ramada, Silahis International, Century Park Sheraton Manila, Holiday Inn Manila, Philippine Plaza, Hyatt Regency Manila, and Regent of Manila. The Philippine Village is south of these, next to the airport.

In Makati you'll find the Inter-Continental Manila, Manila Garden, Manila Peninsula, and Manila Mandarin hotels.

Within a few hours' drive south of the city are two luxurious beach resorts, the Puerto Azul resort on the southern coast of Manila Bay and Punta Baluarte in Batangas Province. An air-conditioned bus makes daily trips between the Philippine Village Hotel and Puerto Azul. Punta Baluarte can be reached by bus or helicopter from the Inter-Continental Manila.

Getting around Manila

Traffic presents the greatest problem in traveling about the city. The drive between the Ermita tourist belt and Makati can take from 20 to 45 minutes. Be sure to allow time when going from one part of the city to another.

Taxis are plentiful and inexpensive, but even cheaper are jeepneys and buses. If the jeepney and bus crowds bother you, try the Love Bus, a blue bus with a large red heart painted on its sides. It follows established routes in Ermita, Makati, and Quezon City. Though it costs a bit more than a jeepney or a regular bus, it is air-conditioned and takes on no more passengers than can be seated.

Tours

Half and full-day tours take in city sights and go farther afield to Corregidor (see page 32), Tagaytay and Lake Taal (see page 33), and Pagsanjan Falls (see page 33). Night tours include a jai alai game, the casino, and nightspots.

Dining variety

Manila offers the venturesome diner an array of cuisines—Filipino, Oriental, French, Spanish, and other European menus.

Chinatown is the best place for Chinese dishes. Restaurants along Ongpin, Chinatown's main street, serve full banquets.

For a casual Filipino-style meal try Nayong Pilipino's Turo-Turo sa Nayong, loosely translated as "Point-Point." It features regional specialties eaten with the fingers—hot, spicy items from Bicol, such traditional dishes as adobo and seafood. For a meal on the run, try the fast-food outlets called "Eat and Split" and "Big-20 Hamburgers."

Lively night life

Look to the hotels for piano bars, floor shows with local and imported talent, and dancing to easy rhythms and disco beats. Makati and a neon-lighted section on south Roxas Boulevard have nightclubs with live bands. The Manila Bay Casino is located in the Philippine Village Hotel near the airport.

Traditional music. Several dance troupes specialize in Filipino folk music and dances. Notable among them is the Bayanihan Dance Company, which performs during the week at the Folk Arts Theater in the Cultural Center complex. The evening program includes a buffet of Filipino specialties, table-to-table serenading by madrigal singers, and costumed dancers performing Spanish, Muslim, and Malay routines to native rhythms. This group and other colorful cultural troupes perform at various Manila restaurants also.

where dinner shows of provincial music and dance are given several evenings during the week (see page 29). The Design Center, a showplace for industrial designs, and Trade Center are also in the complex.

Nayong Pilipino. Within earshot of jets warming up at Manila International Airport, you can explore the architecture, crafts, and culture of the Philippines' far-flung regions. *Nayong Pilipino* (The Filipino Village) is a Philippines-in-miniature compound of regional villages that covers some 36 hectares/90 acres.

Focal point is the administration center, patterned after a typical town plaza during the Spanish era, with a *residencia* (town hall), chapel, and small shops. Eight miniature villages, a Filipino restaurant, and the Museum of Traditional Philippine Cultures surround a manmade lagoon.

Filipino guides and a fleet of jeepneys are available to take you from village to village. Each of the settlements depicts a region of the Philippines — Mindanao, with a Muslim mosque, stilt houses in the lake, and some *vintas* (outriggers with bright sails) anchored offshore; northwest Luzon with a Spanish colonial-style house; the Mountain Province (encompassing northern Luzon's Cordillera Range) with an Igorot village; the Bicol region of southern Luzon with a replica of Mayon Volcano; the Visayas with women weaving *pina* (pineapple fiber) cloth; and central Luzon with a Tagalog village. Nayong Pilipino is open daily from 9 A.M. to 6 P.M., and guides are available until 5:30 P.M.

Suburb sightseeing

Some of Manila's sights overlap into the suburbs. Many tours include the spacious campus of the University of the Philippines near Quezon City, the nearby suburbs of Makati and Forbes Park, and the Manila American Cemetery and Memorial.

Makati. Approximately 10 km/6 miles southeast of the downtown district, this planned community of stores, supermarkets, homes, and office buildings is one of the most modern suburbs in Asia. Trees shade the broad main street, Ayala Avenue — Manila's Wall Street. Modern glass buildings facing the boulevard house the stock exchange, banks, apartments and condominiums, the offices of some of the country's largest companies, and the Philippine branches of many foreign firms.

At the far end of Ayala Avenue is the Makati Commercial Center, a complex of stores, boutiques, restaurants, and dozens of small shops. Several hotels are within walking distance. Spreading out from the commercial area are residential areas.

Forbes Park. Just east of the Makati Commercial Center is Manila's wealthiest residential area; its contemporary mansions are protected by an encircling wall with guarded gates and patrolled streets. Some tour buses drive past this area.

Fort Bonifacio. Just a few minutes beyond Forbes Park is the site of the Manila American Cemetery and Memorial. Encircling the marble memorial are some 17,000 white crosses, marking graves of American World War II dead.

Missing servicemen, grouped according to their branch of service, are listed on a series of semicircular walls. On several other walls of the memorial, mosaic maps record major battles and theaters of operation in the Pacific campaign.

Museums and galleries

Throughout the city, you'll find dozens of art galleries, some private and others public. Check with the local tourist office or call ahead to find out if a particular gallery is open to the public.

Museums are usually open daily from 9 A.M. to 5 or 6 P.M. Some are closed Sunday or Monday. Here are four to include in a museum tour — two within Manila's city limits and two just a short drive away.

National Museum of the Philippines. Located in the former Congress Building on Padre Burgos opposite Rizal Park, this national museum has a collection of ancient Chinese porcelains, many dating from the 14th and 15th centuries. The west wing, dedicated to Philippine art and history, displays the Ifugao culture of northern Luzon. Ethnology Hall houses cultural artifacts of Mindanao's Muslims. The museum is open from 9 A.M. to 5 P.M. daily.

The Museum of Philippine Costumes. Occupying a seven-story building near Rizal Park, the museum has one floor devoted to thousands of dolls dressed in regional costumes. Other exhibits show tribal dress of the country's ethnic minorities, tribal dress of pre-Spanish days, and contemporary Filipino designer styles. Museum hours are 9 A.M. to 6 P.M. daily.

The Museum of Traditional Philippine Cultures. Part of Nayong Pilipino, this museum has four galleries, showing the life and arts of 60 ethnic minorities. Included are the Tasaday cave people, discovered on Mindanao in the early 1970s.

Ayala Museum. Located in the Makati area, this museum emphasizes the history of the Philippines. Sixty dioramas show episodes from pre-Spanish times to the present. Other exhibits feature the work of early Filipino artists, musical artifacts such as old instruments, and Filipino publications, including the first book ever printed in the country. The museum is open daily except Monday from 9 A.M. to 5 P.M.

Shopping around

Manila offers an array of shopping experiences. Within walking distance or a short taxi ride from Manila's major hotels are the prime shopping areas of the Ermita district's tourist belt. South of United Nations Avenue, A. Mabini Street and adjoining streets are crammed with shops and galleries. The belt includes Pistang Pilipino, a square block of handicraft stalls. Just south, showrooms of Filipino couturiers front on Remedios Circle, and west on Vito Cruz is Harrison Plaza, with restaurants, galleries, and stores. Most shops are open Monday through Saturday from 9 A.M. to 8 P.M.

In Makati. Across town, the Makati Commercial Center on Ayala Avenue takes up several blocks with department

Tiny village near Banaue huddles among flooded rice terraces carved 20 to 30 centuries ago from precipitous mountain ridges

FILIPINO JEEPNEYS — FOLK BAROQUE ON WHEELS

That flamboyant, chrome-plated, gold-tasseled, vehicle that careens past you on Manila's Roxas Boulevard is called a jeepney. If the vehicle's shape is reminiscent of something and the word "jeepney" rings a faint bell, it's because you have seen this wonder machine before, when it was going through its drab phase as a World War II U.S. jeep. You're now seeing it with its Filipino facelift. An abstract painting on wheels, the jeepney has created an art style unique to the Philippines—"folk baroque."

The Filipinos' natural competitiveness and love of flamboyance have developed the jeepney into a riotous blend of colors—crimson red on canary yellow, peacock blue on electric pink, or kelly green on adobe white. The long bodies, capable of carrying 10 to 12 passengers, are further adorned with gargoyles and handpainted with Filipino designs. Standard accessories might include white sidewall tires, chrome bumpers, shiny hubcaps, an eye-catching hood ornament, tassels dangling from the windshield, and fringe draped from the roof along the open sides.

A short, fast, bumpy jeepney ride costs 50 centavos and follows a regular route in the cities and barrios. The jeepney picks up and lets off passengers anywhere along its route. Wherever you travel in the Philippines, you'll find the jeepneys. In many rural villages, they are often the only form of motorized transport.

Colorful history. The jeepney has an interesting history. After World War II, the Philippines had a taxi shortage and some form of transport was vitally needed. A group of enterprising Filipinos secured surplus U.S. Army and Navy jeeps and, by cannibalizing several of the jeeps, managed to get a few running. These were outfitted with temporary tops against the sun and weather, fitted with extra seats, and used to haul passengers. The fancy decorations came later.

Visiting a jeepney factory. Located some 16 km/10 miles from Manila are jeepney factories where this process continues today.

In the assembly yard, you can follow the entire reconstruction process of the surplus jeeps. Amid tumultuous hammering on sheet metal and sparking welder's torches, new and longer bodies are added to the jeep chassis. The engines (gasoline or diesel) are all reconditioned—good for another 10 to 12 years.

In the paint shop, jeepney bodies are primed gray, sprayed with rainbow colors, and decorated by freehand artists with fantastic, fanciful, and sometimes meaningful designs.

---

stores, specialty shops, restaurants, and markets. Rustans and the Shoemart are department stores with ready-to-wear clothing, household goods, and handicraft sections. In the basement of the Shoemart, fast-food stalls do a brisk business in Chinese sweet and sour dishes, Korean *kimchi* (spicy pickled cabbage), pizza, and barbecued meat.

Farther afield. If you're searching for handicrafts, spend a few hours at Nayong Pilipino, a large complex located next to the airport that features a collection of traditional houses. Each house features crafts from a particular region: woven goods from the Mountain Province, abaca goods from the Legazpi region, and brassware and shell work from the island of Mindanao.

You'll find other shopping opportunities north of the Pasig River in Chinatown and in the Cubao district of Quezon City.

TRIPS OUT OF MANILA

Popular excursions out of Manila include a 1-hour trip by hydrofoil to Corregidor Island with its impressive wartime reminders and a leisurely drive to Tagaytay to view its beautiful lake and volcano. The latter excursion provides glimpses of rural life en route.

Hydrofoil to Corregidor

Infamous as a World War II battleground, the island today is a green and pleasant spot, tranquil and even a bit cooler than the city. Shaped like a giant tadpole, its head facing westward toward the South China Sea, the 8-square-km/3-square-mile rock is one of five guarding the entrance to Manila Bay, some 45 km/28 miles west of Manila.

Waterless Corregidor served as a pirate hideout during

pre-Spanish times. By the early 18th century, it had become the site of a Spanish dockyard and navy hospital. In 1902 the island became a U.S. military reservation and six years later an Army post—Fort Mills. Its strategic site made it an important World War II stronghold; after the Japanese invasion of the Philippines in December 1941, the island became headquarters for Allied resistance under generals Douglas MacArthur and Jonathan Wainwright. Today, Corregidor is a national shrine.

Passengers are transported from Manila to Corregidor by hovercraft, departing in the morning and afternoon from a pier near the Cultural Center. You can book the trip through any Manila travel agent or buy tickets at the dock.

After skimming across Manila Bay past a host of anchored freighters and small outrigger fishing boats, you transfer to an air-conditioned bus for a ride to the various sights. You'll see the 274-meter-long/900-foot-long Malinta tunnel (which sheltered the military command post) and its numerous side tunnels, the barracks where 8,000 soldiers once lived, skeletons of various military structures,

giant rusting guns, and pockmarked walls amid the jungle growth.

Corregidor's Pacific War Memorial of white concrete and marble tablets is located on the island's western side at Topside, the highest point of the island. A sculptured steel "Eternal Flame" juts skyward from a setting of landscaped gardens and reflecting pools. The memorial has a map mural showing campaigns that led to liberation. A documentary film on General MacArthur is shown in the memorial's theater.

Nearly devoid of vegetation following World War II bombing, the rocky island is once again covered with dense jungle, mostly *ipil ipil* trees. At various spots on the island, you'll see wooden crosses inscribed in Japanese, erected by widows and family of Japanese soldiers.

A country drive to Tagaytay and Taal

You see a condensed version of rural Philippine life during an hour-long drive to Tagaytay, a hillside resort area 64

WHITE-WATER BOATING

One of the most spectacular day trips out of Manila is the dugout canoe ride on the Pagsanjan River to roaring Pagsanjan Falls. The 2-hour drive southeast from Manila to the river goes through rural towns and villages of palm-thatched stilt houses, rich green coconut plantation, and fields of rice and sugar cane. Often you'll see small boys riding a *carabao* (water buffalo), roadside stands laden with fruit, or bright laundry spread on buses to dry.

At the town of Pagsanjan, you stop at the Pagsanjan Rapids Hotel on the riverbank to change into a bathing suit or waterproof attire. The boat ride is neither dangerous nor strenuous, but you'd better plan on getting wet.

Two or three passengers and two oarsmen sit or kneel in the *bancas* (canoes) for the upriver ride to the main waterfall. Using short, snubnosed paddles, the boatmen push, pull, and shove the craft over 14 rapids. When the water is low or when the boatmen come to a tight squeeze between rock and boulders everyone jumps out and the sinewy boatmen actually lift the small boat over the rapids.

You pass between 90-meter/300-foot-high gorge walls, hung with curtains of orchids and begonias. Dozens of small waterfalls cascade down the cliffs. Cries of monkeys and tropical birds break the stillness; palms and dense vines crowd the river's edge.

You disembark near the thundering, main waterfall, taking in the vista of falling water crashing into the lagoon below. A small, makeshift refreshment stand sells cold

drinks and snacks (prices are high, since supplies must be hauled upriver).

If you feel adventurous, ride a bamboo raft across the lagoon and go behind the falls (a drenching experience) to explore a cave, or you can swim in the deep pool at the base of the waterfall.

Your return trip downstream is fast, through turbulent white water. You'll find yourself hanging onto the sides of the small but sturdy craft as the oarsmen maneuver around the rocks.

Wherever rice grows *in the Philippines, you'll see picturesque thatch-roofed huts, raised high on stilts to provide dry homes for field workers.*

Coconut palms *shade cove on Luzon's west coast. Calm waters of Lingayen Gulf offer excellent opportunities for swimming, fishing, skin diving, water-skiing, boating.*

km/40 miles south of Manila. The half-day excursion provides an interesting contrast with the busy city. The road winds through fishing villages and farming barrios, past rice fields, neat *nipa* huts, coconut plantations, orchards, and a succession of *sari-sari* stores, the Philippines' version of the variety store.

As the road ascends, you have an exhilarating view of the lush, green countryside. From Tagaytay Ridge, 685 meters/2,250 feet above sea level, you see Taal Lake and Taal Volcano, spewing steam from an island in the middle of the lake. The volcano erupted in 1971 without much damage, but earlier eruptions in 1965 and 1911 killed hundreds of people in the fishing villages on the island. (Volcano-watchers scrutinize the volcano the year around.) Taal Lake itself is in the crater of a once mighty volcano.

Standing on cool and quiet Tagaytay Ridge, you view a far-reaching mix of blues and greens—lake and convoluted shoreline and even the South China Sea beyond. Weather can be unpredictable, with fog sometimes sweeping in to hide the volcano in a matter of minutes; be sure to bring along a sweater.

At the rustic Taal Vista Lodge, perched on the edge of the ridge across from the volcano, you can enjoy the scenery from outdoor tables during a snack or lunch.

About a half hour outside Manila (on your return trip from the volcano) is the Las Pinas Church, renowned for its bamboo organ. Constructed by a Catholic priest in 1794, the organ (containing 950 bamboo tubes) is still in working order.

NORTH TO BAGUIO

Noted for its cool, pine-scented air, Baguio lies at an altitude of 1,524 meters/5,000 feet in the Cordillera Range of northern Luzon. The American architect Daniel Hudson Burnham laid out this pleasant city—originally envisioned as a rest haven for the American administrators in Manila — in the early 1900s. Basing his overall plan on that of Washington, D.C., Burnham designed this city of parks and gardens and pine-shaded residential areas around a well-ordered street scheme.

In past years, the entire government moved each summer from Manila to Baguio, but now only the courts hold summer sessions here. Still known as the summer capital of the Philippines, Baguio sees its winter population of 100,000 nearly triple as lowlanders take up temporary residence during the summer months to escape the hot, muggy weather below. Mansion House, the president's summer residence, is located in Baguio, as are summer residences of cabinet officers and the justices of the Supreme Court. The natives of the area are the Igorots, a mountain tribes people. You see their handwoven fabrics, baskets, and other handicrafts at the city's central market.

Since Baguio can be a cool 17.8°C/64°F and evenings are even cooler, you'll need a sweater or light jacket. Baguio has most of its rain from May through October; January and February are the driest months. Humidity averages 86 percent the year around.

Baguio is within a day's drive of the Banaue rice terraces (see page 36), Bauang beach resorts (see page 37), and, off the coast the Hundred Islands National Park (see page 37).

Some basic facts

The most traveled route from Manila to Baguio follows the MacArthur Highway northward across the plains of central Luzon to the Cordillera Range. There, the scenic Kennon Road winds upward to the mountain resort. It takes 4 hours to drive the 250 km/155 miles from Manila. You can hire a car and driver in Manila for the trip or take the air-conditioned bus operated by Resort Hotels Corporation. The latter comes complete with a folk singer and on-board refreshment service. You can also reach Baguio from west coast beach resorts at Bauang via the Naguilian Mountain Road, a drive of approximately one hour.

Twice every morning, a plane from Manila lands at Baguio's Loakan Airport, usually swathed in fog by early afternoon. It's a 50-minute flight. The northern line of the Philippines National Railway goes to Damortis, and from there you drive to Baguio.

Places to stay. The city has numerous inns and hotels. Among the choices are the Hyatt Terraces Baguio and the Pines Hotel, both centrally located. The Hotel Milton International lies a half mile from the business center; the Diplomat Hotel is on Diplomat Hill, one of the city's highest points. The Ruff Inn is 6 km/4 miles out of town in the mountains.

Dining and entertainment. The hotel restaurants offer a variety of cuisines, including Filipino, Spanish, Chinese, and American. Look for other restaurants along Session Road, Baguio's main street. Most of the hotels have dancing, and some feature floor shows. The Pines Hotel has a casino.

City sights

Major attractions are the extensive parks and the native handicrafts. You can see the highlights during a leisurely day of touring. Start with a view over the city from Baguio Cathedral. Situated on a hill at the top of Session Road, the twin-spired structure dominates the heart of town.

Burnham Park. Named after the architect who designed Baguio, the city's major park resembles an American village green. It has playing fields, a skating rink, parade ground, children's playground, and a lagoon, where rowboats and sailboats can be rented.

Imelda Park. Located south of Leonard Wood Road, this park was formerly called the Baguio Botanical Gardens. It features a scale model of an Igorot village, with houses representing architecture of various Mountain Province tribes. There is also a zoo and a children's playground.

William Wright Park. Horseback riding is a favorite pastime in this park north of Leonard Wood Road. Opposite a reflecting pool bordered by tall pines is Mansion House, originally built for the American governor general and now serving as the summer residence of the Philippine president.

Mines View Park. As the name suggests, this park, perched on a cliff, overlooks the Benguet gold mining district. The partially denuded hills you see in the distance cover miles of tunnels leading to gold-bearing rock.

Camp John Hay. This U.S. military rest and recreation area, southeast of Baguio, is the site of the summer residence of the U.S. ambassador, Italian landscaped gardens, and the Bell Amphitheater, with terraced-lawn seating. A pass from the base commander grants golf privileges for the 18-hole course. World War II in the Philippines began and ended at this base, target of the first Japanese bombs to hit the country and site for the signing of the Japanese surrender papers.

City market. The cleanest and best organized in the country, Baguio's market on Magsaysay Road has clearly marked sections for fish, meat, fruits, vegetables, and dry goods. In the latter section, look for woodcarvings, bamboo trays and mats, abaca products, silver jewelry, and Igorot handwoven mats.

Easter School of Weaving. Tattooed Igorot tribeswomen weave vivid strips of fabric on upright and back looms at this center northwest of the city. You can buy fringed belts, placemats, tobacco pouches, and bolts of material.

Nearby attractions

South of the city limits, 2,286-meter / 7,500-foot Mount Santo Tomas offers a splendid view on a clear day. From the resthouse near the mountain top, you have a broad panorama stretching from Luzon's central plains west to the South China Sea. An altar atop the mountain commemorates the establishment of Christianity in the Philippines.

North of the city is the Trinidad Valley, known as the Salad Bowl of the Philippines. An area of vegetable and strawberry cultivation, Trinidad Valley nightly trucks its produce to Manila's hotels and restaurants.

Roads southwest lead to an Igorot woodcarving village, Asin Hot Springs, and views over city and country from Mirador Hill, Dominican Hill, and Lourdes Grotto. You climb 225 steps to reach the grotto, a shrine housing an image of the Lady of Lourdes.

THE RICE TERRACES

Sometime between 2,000 and 3,000 years ago, the Ifugao tribespeople drifted into the mountainous interior of northern Luzon and began the task of carving the precipitous land from valley floor to ridge top into neatly terraced rice fields. Working with bare hands, primitive wooden and stone tools, and empirical engineering skill, they created a system of terraces that would extend around the world if laid end to end.

Ranked among the marvels of the world (Filipinos consider them the eighth wonder of the world), the terraces are also difficult to travel to, but the long, tiring drive over mountain roads to reach them is a discovery trip in itself.

Banaue, the terrace gateway

Center of the rice terrace country is Banaue, home of the Ifugao tribespeople. From Manila, you have a choice of two routes to the terraces. One goes through Baguio to Bontoc, dropping south to Banaue; the other approach is from the

east, through Bagabag. From Baguio, it's an 8-hour drive along the Halsema Mountain Highway; from Bagabag, it's a 3-hour drive. The shorter route is less interesting but serves to create a loop trip.

If you want to break up the longer trip, spend the night at Mount Data Lodge, about halfway between Manila and the terraces. Otherwise, stay at the Banaue Hotel, set on a plateau overlooking the terraces.

Journey to the terraces

Driving north from Baguio, you take a road through Mount Data that is a scenically exciting engineering marvel.

A rugged trip. A sign outside Baguio reads "Drive with Care, Courtesy & Discipline"—and you soon see why you are so advised. The drive is an 8-hour bone-jogging and nerve-shattering trip. There are many obstacles along the curving highway—jeeps, cars, trucks, open-sided buses, and road crews repairing landslide damage. Vehicles use their horns constantly to warn others of their approach.

Near Mount Data Lodge, the road reaches 2,286 meters/7,500 feet. The lodge is a convenient lunch stop if you are headed to Banaue for the night. After Mount Data, the road winds deeper into terraced country, often cutting across planted slopes and becoming another lateral shelf itself, with rice fields stepped into the slope above and below.

Scenic compensations. There are visual rewards for those enduring the rugged drive—roadside sunflowers, terraced vegetable gardens, pine forests, wild orchids, even a stretch of rain forest. Dusty buses, which started down from the north before dawn, bounce past, piled high with baskets of chickens and sacks of rice. Trucks pass, loaded with bamboo baskets of cabbages. Occasionally you see tattooed women, dressed in wraparound *tapis* (skirts with distinctive stripes) topped with faded shirts, balancing straw mats or baskets on their heads, which are encircled by snake spines. In some places, men are clad only in G-strings.

At the terraces

For years Filipinos have urged visitors to see the rice terraces, and those visitors who have viewed this monument to man's ingenuity and fortitude find it difficult to comprehend what they see.

The visual impact. Imagine yourself looking across a river canyon at a sharply sloping mountain. Visualize the entire mountainside, from river bed to ridge top — reaching as high as 1,524 meters/5,000 feet — cut into hundreds of curving steps, each stone staircase a product of laborious hand cutting and digging. Picture these terraces with rice plants forming patterns of green — from delicate seedlings to strips of mature plant — with water trickling gently from one level to the next.

The builders tapped springs and constructed channels, often stone-lined, to transport the water along the breadth of the slopes and down from plot to plot so that it moistened the soil, rather than washed it away. Rims along the outside edge of each terrace form little dams and also serve as walkways.

Exploring terrace country. A day at Banaue allows time to hike the slippery pathways—walking sticks are available at the Banaue Hotel — up and down the shelves. Sights include Ifugao weavers working in a native hut, a forge where blacksmiths use crude tools to make jewelry from old metal, and a picnic spot beside a pool and waterfall. A full-day trip goes to the remote village of Batad, where you see tattooed men and women cultivating the terraces. This trip entails an 11-km/7-mile drive to the end of the road and a 3 km/2 mile (2-hour) hike to the village.

NORTHWEST LUZON

Luzon's northwest coast, a 241-km/150-mile stretch extending from the colonial city of Vigan south along the beaches of Bauang to the Hundred Islands National Park on the Lingayen Gulf, offers towns with baroque churches built by the Spaniards, crumbling watchtowers, sandy beaches, and deserted islands.

Though not easy to reach, this scenic coastline is well worth your effort. You can drive to the various destinations from Manila, swing west from Baguio by car, or fly to Laoag, north of Vigan, and then drive down the coast. Flights from Manila go to Laoag three times weekly—Tuesday, Thursday, and Sunday. The northern line of the Philippine National Railways goes to San Fernando (for Bauang), and a spur line continues to Vigan.

Colonial Vigan

A 2½-hour drive from Laoag, Vigan lies on a river near the coast of the South China Sea. The town has two hotels and several privately owned homes that welcome guests.

A sense of history. Vigan was founded in 1595, after Cebu and Manila. Stepping back in time, you can tour the narrow streets bordered by stately old Spanish houses in a horse-drawn calesa. Stop at the town square to see the Cathedral of San Pablo and Burgos House, the restored home of priest-patriot Jose Burgos, who was martyred in 1872 for advocating equal status among native and Spanish clergy. Now a branch of Manila's Ayala Museum, the house features rooms furnished as they were for the Burgos family, paintings recording the *basi* (sugar cane wine) revolt of 1807, and dioramas with authentically costumed scale-model figures portraying historic scenes.

Cottage industries. Vigan also supports some cottage industries. You are welcome at a pottery works where potters turn local clay into jars that are exported throughout the country. In small homes along the road, family members take turns at hand looms, weaving brightly colored mats and napkins, which are for sale.

Bauang attractions

The resort area of Bauang is a 13-km/8-mile drive south of San Fernando, a stop on the northern train line. The drive from Baguio takes approximately 1 hour via the Naguilian Mountain Road. You'll find plain but comfortable accommodations at several beachfront hotels.

Beach scenes. Lapped by gentle surf, the white sandy beach stretches for miles north and south of Bauang. At dawn, fishermen coming in from the sea take their catch to a stand under the coconut palms to sell to the villagers. They leave their orange, red, and green boats on the beach during the day, then launch them in the evening for another night's work. Wandering along the sand are shell venders who are willing to bargain over the price of a coral necklace or shells.

Inland attractions. A short drive inland, a sugar cane wine operation is run by carabao power. Hooked up to the cane crusher, the animal activates the machinery by walking around and around in a circle. North of San Fernando, you can watch weavers working at the Bangar Weavers Cooperative.

Hundred Islands National Park

Lying off the northwest coast of Luzon in the Lingayen Gulf, Hundred Islands National Park is one of the world's largest marine reserves. The drive to the town of Alaminos, departure point for the islets, takes 6 hours from Manila, 3 from Baguio, and 2 from Bauang. Motorboats transport visitors to the islands.

The park is habitat for some 2,000 species of marine life. The tiny islands also offer sandy beaches, coral gardens, and underwater caves.

SOUTH TO LEGAZPI

The gateway to attractions in southern Luzon is Legazpi, a port city on the Albay Gulf 330 km/205 miles southeast of Manila. Named for the explorer who claimed the Philippines for Spain, Legazpi is the home of the symmetrical, "perfectly shaped," Mayon Volcano. If you fly into the city on a clear day, the pilot is likely to take the plane alongside the cone to give you a close look. The area also offers boiling pools and other thermal attractions, abaca-craft cottage industries, and some lively markets. Don't miss the area's Bicol cuisine, one of the country's spiciest. Giant prawns and other seafood turn up in hearty chowders, and the locally grown, almondlike pilinut is ubiquitous in plain and sugared form.

Even rainfall the year around keeps the countryside a vibrant green, a striking counterpart to the deep blue waters of the Albay Gulf. Days can be hot—to such a degree that carabaos pulling carts along the city streets wear rubber "shoes" for comfort. Nights are cool.

A word about spelling: you'll see Legazpi spelled with both a "z" and an "s." The former reflects Spanish spelling and the latter Tagalog, one of the Filipino dialects.

Some helpful facts

A 1-hour morning flight leaves Manila daily for Legazpi; Philippine Airlines (PAL) also runs a 1-hour morning flight from Cebu to the city. If you take the train, plan on a full-day or overnight trip. The bus is a 15-hour drive. Negros Navigation's 7-day cruises out of Manila dock at Legazpi.

Set on a hillside at the edge of town is the Mayon Imperial. From its bougainvillea-festooned terrace, you can view the Mayon Volcano. Downtown, the tallest building in town is the six-story Hotel La Trinidad, with marble lobby abutting on the marble-columned foyer of the local movie theater.

Mayon, the perfect volcano

Its name derived from the word *magayon*, meaning beautiful, Mayon Volcano soars 2,438 meters/8,000 feet above the rice fields in triangular perfection. If clouds don't obscure the cone's tip, you can see a plume of smoke drifting skyward. Very much alive, the Mayon Volcano appears to follow a 10-year eruption cycle, venting its fury most recently in 1978. Photos of molten lava streaming down the volcano's flanks are the proud possession of the locals, who can be persuaded to sell one for a few pesos.

Adventurous hikers can arrange with local tour operators to take on the Mayon. The 1½-day trek to the top is best attempted from March through May. For a panoramic view of the southern Luzon countryside, drive part way up the volcano to the Mayon Vista Lodge, situated at 762 meters/2,500 feet.

In Mayon's shadow

You'll see evidence of Mayon's past fury at Cagsawa, a 6 km/4 mile drive west of Legazpi. En route to or from Cagsawa stop in Daraga and Camalig to stroll through a church and busy marketplace, and to tour a museum and a thatched-roof shade factory.

Destruction of Cagsawa. The blackened stump of a church belfry rising above ground is all that remains of this village, buried during the Mayon's eruption of 1814. Cagsawa, located at the foot of Mayon Volcano, is now a study in tranquility: cosmos flutter in the breeze, and farmers till the rich soil at the base of the cone.

Daraga's church and market. From the breezy hillside vantage point of the 18th century church at Daraga, 5 km/3 miles west of Legazpi, you discern the awesome volcano on the horizon. The weather-worn carvings on the exterior of the church give no inkling of the surprise within—a bright, like-new interior. Take time to wander down the hill into town. A covered market, alive with locals who shop for fruits, vegetables, and household items at the many stalls (several crammed with abaca products from local cottage industries) sprawls over two blocks. Small businesses line the main street.

Camalig's artifacts. located 10 km/6 miles west of Daraga, Camalig is the site of funnel-like caves in which ceramic items showing Malayan and Chinese influence have been found recently. Beads and bowls believed to be from ancient burial sites are on view in a small museum in the Camalig church. The nearby caves are open to visitors who wish to walk a short way into the caves' damp interiors.

Also at Camalig is Simor Abacacraft, a complex of thatched-roof cottages where abaca window shades are made for export. Each cottage represents a step in the production line. As you walk through the cottages, you'll see the abaca fiber evolve into shades.

North for cottage industries

Cottage industries and thermal attractions lie along the scenic coast road north of Legazpi.

Malilipot for twine. This small town located 23 km/14 miles from the city is dedicated to the abaca industry. Skeins of bright orange hemp lie bundled beside the road, ready to be distributed among the various houses. Every house has someone working with abaca, stripping away the fibers, spinning it into twine, and braiding it into slippers, mats, and bags.

Tabaco for shears. Scissors-making is the main concern in a group of roadside cottages 5 km/3 miles beyond Malilipot. Since 1912, the same family has been melting, bending, and filing pieces of old railroad track and other scrap metal into shears and cleavers. Filipino barbers are their best customers. You can wander from house to house to observe the heating and chiseling process. Scissors and other implements are for sale, at startlingly reasonable prices. Don't miss the Tabaco market. On the street level of the two-story building are countless booths crammed with abaca hats, bags, mats, slippers, and hammocks.

Tiwi's thermal action. At Tiwi, 11 km/7 miles beyond Tabaco, geothermal energy is harnessed to provide power for a salt-making plant. The plant also utilizes hot springs to generate electricity for the Legazpi region. Tours of the plant can be arranged, often upon your arrival. Small bags of salt, converted from salt water, are for sale. Boys anxious to show how quickly thermal activity can hard boil an egg stand around a nearby pool of steaming green water and wait for sightseers to appear.

A 5-minute drive from the plant is the Putsan pottery works. In this one-street town every house has a pile of clay in the front yard and, by the road, a stack of finished jars, which are ready to be carted to market. Hidden from view at least one family member works at a wheel. You can buy pottery here if you wish.

THE VISAYAS

The cluster of islands called the Visayas lies midway in the Philippine archipelago. The group comprises seven of the chain's largest islands—Bohol, Cebu, Leyte, Masbate, Panay, Negros, and Samar. Key tourist destinations are Iloilo on the southeast coast of Panay and Cebu City on the eastern shore of Cebu.

Getting there

You can fly to Iloilo and Cebu from Manila. Flights are scheduled three times daily for Iloilo, a trip of 1 hour, and five times daily for Cebu, a trip of approximately 1½ hours. If you have more time, you can arrive aboard one of the ships plying the waters weekly between Manila and the islands, reaching Iloilo in 19 hours and Cebu in 24.

The Visayas are the home of a relaxed and casual people known for their charm and beautiful women. Sandy beaches, marked by palms and fishing boats, line the coast; coconut and sugar plantations predominate inland. You'll sense the area's Spanish heritage as you tour old churches.

Iloilo on Panay

Viewed from the air, the port of Iloilo appears to be a huge nose (the city's original name Irong-Irong meant

Cebu women kneel *in kiosk that shelters Cross of Magellan, planted here by famous navigator in 1521; ceiling mural depicts event.*

Happy smiles *on faces of guitar makers reflect pride of workmanship. Visitors are welcome at ukulele and guitar factories on Mactan Island.*

"noselike") outlined by two rivers—the Iloilo and the Batiano. The greater city is composed of a central downtown area and the two districts of Molo and La Paz. Outrigger fishing boats grace the waterfront of the busy harbor. Driving along the coastal road and through bougainvillea-splashed villages you see carabao, long-skirted women carrying water jars on their heads, and farmers threshing rice on a bamboo platform by stamping their feet so that the grain cascades into a golden pile below. The Ilonggo people, who live in this part of Panay, speak in a soft cadence that makes even a heated remark sound like a caress. It's said that only the natives can tell when someone is angry.

You can stay in any of several hotels located downtown or near the beach. Among these are Hotel Del Rio, River Queen Hotel, Sarabia Manor, and the Anhawan Beach Resort a short drive west of town. In the evening, you'll find music and dancing featured at most hotels; Sarabia Manor has a casino.

Churches and watchtowers. The area's Spanish heritage is most evident in the Iloilo countryside, where a succession of Spanish-Filipino churches and watchtowers is strung along the coast. A massive fortresslike church in Miagao, 40 km/25 miles west of Iloilo, is typical of colonial church architecture. On the facade, European and Filipino influences blend in a relief sculpture: against a backdrop of papayas, coconuts, and other tropical plants, St. Christopher holds the Holy Child. Sturdy sandstone towers flank the facade. Each tower has four tiers; the two uppermost tiers on each are of different design. When built in 1787 by an Augustinian friar, the church served as a refuge

FESTIVAL TIME

What are your chances of encountering a festival when you're in the Philippines? Very, very good in this fiesta-loving land. There are springtime revels, summer fluvials focusing on waterways, harvest rites, historic celebrations, tribal festivals, and Muslim ceremonies. You're bound to come across something. Some celebrations are local—nearly every village has its own saint's day—and some are nation-wide. The Christmas season, the most joyous time of year, is celebrated for 22 days. Holy week in this primarily Catholic Asian country is the most sacred. Festival time is your chance to see pageantry at its most colorful, to get caught up in drumbeat and song, and to taste some of the country's most lavish cookery. Here are some of the events that are celebrated about the same time each year. Check with the Ministry of Tourism for exact dates.

Feast of the Black Nazarene. Manila's most fervent religious event takes place in Quiapo from New Year's Day to January 9. At the climax, men walk through the streets barefoot, pulling a carriage bearing a 200-year-old image of the saint.

Ati-atihan. People in Kalibo, Panay, blacken their faces and dance in the streets for three days in January to honor the Holy Child and to commemorate the barter of Panay between aboriginal *atis* (a Panay people) and Borneo chiefs.

Moriones. During Holy Week on Marinduque, participants don masks and costumes of Roman soldiers to reenact the story of the centurion Longinus, whose sight was miraculously cured with a drop of Christ's blood. The climax is the beheading of Longinus on Easter Sunday.

Santacruzan. During May, young women throughout the country don Biblical or mythical costumes and walk in candlelight processions to commemorate the search of Empress Helena and Prince Constantine for the Holy Cross.

Carabao festival. During May, farmers in provinces near Manila honor the farmer's patron saint with a carabao parade. The animals are scrubbed clean and decorated with flowers.

Bocaue fluvial. In July, Bocaue, Bulacan, located north of Manila, celebrates the rescue of the Holy Cross of Wawa from the river. The cross found in the river by a fisherman during the days of Spanish rule, is borne through the streets and put aboard a decorated barge for a trip down the river.

Hari-raya Poasa. This Muslim event, held around November, marks the end of Ramadan, the 30-day fasting period. The day is filled with horse racing, boat races, and games.

Lantern festival. On Christmas Eve in Pampanga, north of Manila, people stage a parade with enormous lanterns called *parols*. Some measure more than 6 meters/20 feet in width and height and are intricately wired to give a kaleidoscopic lighting effect. The most impressive lantern wins a prize.

Rizal Day. This national holiday, observed December 30, honors Jose P. Rizal, the country's greatest hero, who was executed by the Spanish in 1896.

PHILIPPINE DIVING — AN UNEXPLORED WORLD

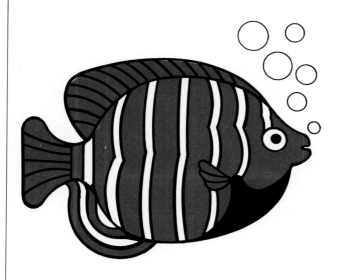

Its expansive coastline—one of the world's longest—and more than 7,000 islands, warmed by a tropical sun and washed by warm waters, make the Philippines a diver's paradise. The islands have everything a diver dreams of—coral reefs with abundant marine life, steep drop-offs, year-round sites and, most significantly, pristine water, much of it yet uncharted, yet unexplored. Where do you start?

If Manila is your base of operations, you'll find several diving resorts in the Batangas area, a 2-hour drive south of the capital. Conditions are good all year. North of the capital, off the eastern shore, are the less visited Polillo Islands. It's a 3½-hour drive and 1½-hour ferry ride from Manila to these waters—a treasure house of coral and reef fish. Best diving is from April to October.

In the Visayas, Cebu is considered the diving center of the Philippines. Cliff and coral divers will be happy here the year around. On Mindanao, areas off Davao and Zamboanga have good diving all year.

You enter the realm of manta rays, sharks, and pilot fish in dive areas off the islands of Mindoro and Marinduque, southeast of Luzon. Apo Reef, off the west coast of Mindoro, is accessible from March to June. Nearby, the reef of Apo Island, dropping to 45 meters/150 feet, has even more marine life than the big reef.

Palawan—and the hundreds of tiny islands adjacent to it—is the center of a marine area with an underwater shelf that harbors 60 percent of the country's corals. Only small outriggers can navigate the uncharted coral reefs and mounds in these waters. Here the Sulu Sea offers the serious diver one of the best diving experiences in the world. But come prepared to ration drinking water and camp on the beach or in a small *banca* (dugout canoe). The diving season varies with location.

North of Palawan in the Calamianes Islands, you'll find virgin coral reefs accessible the year around. Also in this area are the remains of Japanese World War II ships, sunk to depths of 27 meters/90 feet. To the east of Palawan, the waters of the Cagayan Islands, teeming with fish, are ideal for underwater photography from March to June.

Boats, equipped for 4 to 34 passengers, are available for Philippine diving excursions. Accommodations are in bunk cabins. Dive shops in Manila, Cebu, and Davao have rental equipment and can arrange trips. The Philippine Ministry of Tourism publishes a guidebook for divers that lists diving sites, charter boat outfits, tour agencies, and dive shops.

from Muslim pirates as well as a place of worship. Today the church fronts on a busy street lined with small shops selling rice and other daily necessities. Fish merchants, baskets of fish balanced on poles across their shoulders, walk past the church's doors and sputtering tricycles rush by.

The white coral San Joaquin church, located on the coast road approximately 13 km/8 miles west of Miagao, was built in 1869 as a sign of local loyalty to Spain—notable because rebellions were disrupting other parts of the country at the time. On the facade, a bas-relief depicts a scene from the Battle of Tetuan in Morocco in 1859, when invading Spanish troops conquered the Moroccans.

You'll find another 18th century church in the Molo district just west of downtown Iloilo. The Gothic-Renaissance structure has a tall, spired belfry and classic columns. Inside, woodcarvings of women saints line the aisle to the wooden altar, carved from a single tree trunk. The Molo district with its many fine homes was once known as the "Athens of the Philippines."

Restoration of old churches is a continuing project of Iloilo. In recent decades, well-meaning priests attempted to repair old structures by plastering over walls. Restoration efforts are removing these layers to reveal structural brick and coral. Also being preserved are watchtowers, built when Muslim pirates terrorized coastal villages. Guards manning the towers used smoke signals to warn the townspeople to flee to the hills.

Museo Iloilo. The only government-built museum outside Manila, this one-story building is easy to cover in one visit. There are displays of Ilonggo culture, pottery from

Bright *geometric designs swell with tropical breezes as Muslim vintas glide across lagoon near Zamboanga.*

Mindanao men *prepare fish for drying; most of island's food still comes from fish-rich seas.*

the 13th century China trade, gold eye and nose masks from pre-Spanish burial coffins, wine bottes from 19th century shipwrecks, and World War II relics. The museum is open daily.

Handicrafts. The Iloilo region is known for its hand-woven cloth, available for purchase in lengths or made up into ready-to-wear garments. Though especially known for their *pina* cloth (fabric woven on old wooden looms from pineapple fibers), weavers also turn out lengths of *jusi* cloth (cloth made from raw silk fibers). Both are used for the barong tagalog and other fine clothes. You can see demonstrations at the weaving center of Arevalo, known also for its flowers. For pina and jusi cloth, stop by the orphanage at Jaro, where girls embroider church vestments, barongs, tablecloths, and dresses.

Several shellcraft stores have the *capiz* (round, paper-thin .shells) made into boxes, trays, lampshades, and numerous other items. The local market has an assortment of fabrics and shell items in addition to baskets, mats, and woodcarvings. If your interest is antiques, seek out the city's various collectors. They have pottery, strings of lapis lazuli (a bluish violet gemstone) beads, and *santos* (the worn wooden figures of saints) that once graced the interior of country churches.

Ilonggo food. Take a break from sightseeing to sample some Ilonggo cooking, a more mildly seasoned cuisine than found in other parts of the country. Start your meal with a bowl of soup. In La Paz try *batchoy*, (a noodle soup with pork, liver, and chicken); in Molo sample *pancit Molo* (a noodle soup with meatballs). The Molo bakery supplies Manila and Mindanao towns with distinctively flavored breads and biscuits. After sampling, you can buy a tin to take home. For other treats, try rice cakes from Arevalo and, by all means, the catch of the day from local waters.

Festive occasions. Cockfighting has gone big time in Iloilo. Bets can reach thousands of pesos at the January Derby, a showcase for fighting cocks from throughout the country. Throughout the year, cockfights are scheduled on Sundays and holidays at the city's three cockpits. One of the country's most raucous festivals, the Dinagyan, is held in Iloilo in January, and its counterpart, the Ati-atihan, is celebrated the same month in Kalibo on northwest Panay (see "Festival Time," page 40.)

Cebu, oldest Philippine city

On the east coast of Cebu Island is Cebu City, the cradle of Christianity in the Philippines. It was here that the Portuguese explorer Ferdinand Magellan, sailing under the flag of Spain, landed in 1521, planted the Christian cross, and baptized the reigning king and queen and their subjects. Since Magellan was killed shortly after his arrival by the native chief Lapu-Lapu, it was the Spanish explorer Legazpi, who arrived in 1565, that moved northward through the islands to claim the land for Spain and Christianity. Relics of that era remain today.

The largest commercial center outside Manila, Cebu has the country's main brewery, grows acres of flowers for daily export to Manila, harvests grapes for wine, and supports several cottage industries. The area's mangoes are considered the best in the country.

You'll find comfortable accommodations in the city at the Cebu Plaza and Magellan International hotels, and in the suburbs at the Montebello Village Hotel. Beach resorts include Santa Rosa by the Sea and Tambuli Beach Resort, both near Cebu, and Argao Beach Club, 86 km/53 miles south of the city. For night life, there's a casino, located aboard the *Philippine Tourist I,* which is docked at Pier 1 in Cebu City.

In Magellan's memory. Fragments of the cross this explorer planted in Cebu ground when he landed are contained in a hollow cross that stands in an old kiosk across from City Hall. A mural on the ceiling depicts the event. On nearby Mactan Island, monuments honor Magellan and Lapu-Lapu—the first Filipino to resist foreign aggression.

The image of the Holy Child Jesus that Magellan presented to the newly baptized native queen is kept in Basilica Minore del Santo Nino, formerly San Augustin Church. The oldest religious relic in the Philippines, the red velvet and-jewel clothed image is removed from its vault only on special feast days. The January Fiesta of the Santo Nino is one of these occasions. At other times, a stunning replica of the image stands on an altar in the basilica.

Fort San Pedro. A wooden palisade built by Legazpi in 1565 to protect the Spaniards from pirate raids, Fort San Pedro has some Spanish cannons still in place. Through the centuries it has served many functions: a prison for rebels under Spanish rule, a school during the Commonwealth period, a Japanese refuge during World War II, and a hospital during the battle for liberation.

Taoist temple. This paragon of pagoda architecture — a maze of winding staircases, shrines, and tongue-lashing dragons — perches on a ridge overlooking the exclusive residential district of Beverly Hills. You climb 93 steps to the main shrine to light a joss stick and receive divine advice from a priest who consults wooden blocks and oracle sheets. Another 49 steps brings you to an outlook over city and ocean.

Cottage industries. At ukulele and guitar factories on Mactan Island, where visitors are welcome, coconut shells are transformed into 4-string ukuleles, inlaid with mother-of-pearl, and red and-yellow stained jackfruit wood is carved into guitars. Nearly every child in Cebu has one of these instruments, which he learns to play in school.

You are also welcome at a furniture workshop where apprentices learn to make chairs out of midrib, the center of the palm frond. The Mehitabel rattan factory, open to visitors by appointment, has a windowed room from which visitors can observe craftsmen heat rattan with torches to bend it into shapes for chair backs and seats. Other crafts made in Cebu are shell items, woodcarvings, and woven goods.

On the water. Within a day's range of the city, divers find year-round sites with steep drop-offs and rare shells and marine life. Boats and equipment are available for rent. If beachcombing and snorkeling are more to your taste, spend a day at Santa Rosa by the Sea. Reached via motorized *banca* (outrigger canoe) from Mactan Island, the resort has sandy, palm-shaded beaches, swimming, fishing, and horseback riding.

MINDANAO

The mountainous island of Mindanao, second largest in the Philippines, lies at the southern end of the archipelago, its southwestern tip closer to Indonesia and Borneo than to Manila. You'll notice a strong Muslim influence, particularly in the western part of the island, where domed mosques are more evident than church steeples. The island's main destinations are Davao and Zamboanga.

Getting your bearings

You can fly to Davao and Zamboanga from Manila. Flights are scheduled four times daily to Davao, a 1¾-hour trip, and twice daily to Zamboanga, a 2½-hour trip. Flights also come in from Iloilo and Cebu, and ships out of Manila dock at both ports.

Geological extremes distinguish Mindanao. It boasts the country's highest point — 2,954-meter/9,690-foot Mount Apo — and its lowest — the Philippine Deep, descending to 10,802 meters/35,440 feet off the Surigao coast to the north.

The Cotabato coastal range, enclosing much of the island's southern coast, is home of the Tasaday tribe. Discovered in the early 1970s, the tribespeople lead a primitive existence, collecting food rather than cultivating plants and using stone axes as their main tool. The government has created a jungle reserve to protect the tribe's way of life.

Davao for tropical ambience

Located on the southwest coast of Mindanao, Davao is the island's largest city. Representing all of the ethnic groups and dialects in the country, its population renders the city an instant Philippines for visitors, a quality borne out in the variety of ethnic handicrafts seen in the markets.

Davao attracts those seeking the relaxed tropical life that prevails at resorts such as the Davao Insular Inter-Continental Inn, which basks on the shores of the Davao Gulf 8 km/5 miles north of the city. Muslim architecture and manicured gardens make it a city attraction. Sailboats and outrigger canoes are available for day excursions. Downtown Davao has the Cuison Hotel, with a casino, and the Apo View Hotel.

Lon Wa temple. Noteworthy for its Chinese architecture and gold, bronze, and marble altars, this Buddhist temple, the largest on Mindanao, houses the Buddha with the Thousand Hands. A monk is on hand to read your fortune from slips of paper, determined by a numbered stick you pick from a container.

Shopping. You'll find brass trays, zigzag-patterned mats, and other Muslim handicrafts at the Aldevinco Shopping Center, where bargaining lowers a price from reasonable to a steal. Chinatown's stores have the best prices in town. Seek out the downtown fruit stands for a surfeit of luscious fruits. If you're adventurous, try the spiny-skinned durian, foul smelling but marvelously tasty. A monument to this fruit stands downtown.

Mount Apo National Park. A 2-hour drive from the city, the park harbors some unusual wildlife, namely the mouse deer and the monkey-eating eagle, the world's largest eagle. Mountain slopes bloom with giant ferns, pitcher plants with tall pitchers, and the *waling-waling*, reputedly the most beautiful orchid in the world. Hikers take 3½ days to reach the top of the mountain, a trek best attempted during the relatively dry period from April through June.

Aguinaldo Pearl Farm. A 45-minute boat trip across Davao Gulf to Samal Island brings you to this pearl center. In the laboratory, guides explain the culturing process that requires frames of oysters be suspended underwater for 2-year periods.

Exotic Zamboanga

Situated at the tip of the Zamboanga Peninsula, bathed by the waters of the Sulu Sea and the Moro Gulf, the seaport of Zamboanga blends a variety of cultures with a cloak-and-dagger history. The smuggling of goods from Borneo was once a primary activity here.

Ethnic heritages are patent. The *Moros* (Filipino Muslims) worship in domed mosques and live in stilt-supported houses; yet the patron saint of this Spanish-founded city is a Catholic saint, and the spoken dialect is strongly Castilian. Known as the City of Flowers, Zamboanga glories in orchids, bougainvillea, and poinsettias, each flourishing along roadsides and in yards.

The city's hotels offer a contrast in style. At the Hotel Lantaka by the Sea, set immediately on the waterfront, you can sip a drink on the terrace while watching children dive for coins, or bargain for shells from the *Badjaos* (sea gypsies) on bobbing rafts just off the seawall. The Badjaos spend their lives aboard their bright-sailed *vintas* (outriggers). At the Zamboanga Plaza, you survey city and bay from the hotel's hillside viewpoint in Pasonanca Park. The hotel has a casino that accommodates 1,000 players.

Pasonanca Park. This expanse of botanical gardens overlooking the city has several swimming pools fed by mountain streams. At the park's south end, a one-room tree house, equipped with electricity and running water, sits in a large tree. Honeymooners can stay here free of charge.

Fort Pilar. Built by the Spanish in 1635 as a fortress against Muslim pirates, this fort on the southern edge of Zamboanga has also defended the city from Dutch, Portuguese, and British marauders. It holds the Shrine of our Lady of Pilar, Zamboanga's patron saint.

Markets. Downtown Zamboanga centers on the waterfront public market — a clamor of bargaining voices and a maze of covered stalls displaying brightly-colored Indonesian batiks, woven cloths called *malongs* (a piece of material that is wrapped around the body to form a dress), mats, brassware, pieces of coral, and fresh seafood. Dockside in the early morning, you'll see fishermen unloading their catch.

Next to the public market, behind a chain link fence, is the Barter Trade Market. Awning-covered stalls hold imported goods from around the world — Japanese parasols, French perfume, Russian caviar, and bolts of fabric of every imaginable color and design.

Shopping for seashells. One of Zamboanga's natural resources is seashells, which come in an array of colors and shapes. You can bargain for them from the Badjaos along the waterfront or delve into the displays at the Rocan Shell Shop just outside town. Its factory-showroom exhibits prize shells and sells cowries, cones, turbos, and many others. Shell jewelry set in sterling silver is also for sale.

Santa Cruz Island. Small motorboats depart from the waterfront at the Hotel Lantaka for the 10-minute ride to the island's shores for swimming, snorkeling, and shelling. Sand of crushed coral gives the beach a pink tinge. For local color, visit the small Muslim cemetery, its graves marked by wooded figures, and the fishing village, where you can bargain for shells.

KNOW BEFORE YOU GO

Here is some basic information to help you in planning your trip to the Philippines.

Entry/exit procedures. You can visit the Philippines for up to 21 days without a visa, but to enter you must show a passport and proof of onward passage. With a visa, you may stay for a maximum of 59 days. Visas, valid for a 3-months stay, are issued at the Philippine embassy in Washington, D.C., and its consulates in San Francisco, Los Angeles, Seattle, Chicago, New York, New Orleans, and Honolulu.

If you are arriving from an infected area, you must have a yellow fever inoculation. The U.S. Public Health Service suggests you have typhoid, tetanus, and gamma globulin shots. Beyond the urban areas, there is a malaria risk in many parts of the Philippines.

When leaving the country, you are charged a P10 security fee and a P15 departure tax.

Customs. You may bring into the country duty-free two liters of liquor, 200 cigarettes, 50 cigars, a camera, and a reasonable amount of film.

Currency. The Philippine peso is the official monetary unit, and the rate of exchange is U.S. $1 to P7.90. (Coins are in centavos.) There's no restriction on the amount of U.S. currency you bring into the country, but the amount you take out must not exceed it. No more than 500 Philippine pesos may be brought in or taken out of the country. Receipts from the Central Bank of the Philippines, obtained when you exchange dollars for pesos, are required for reconversion of pesos into dollars.

Traveler's checks and major credit cards are accepted at hotels, stores, and restaurants. It's advisable to have your passport on hand when you cash traveler's checks.

Health conditions. Medical facilities are good in Manila and other major cities, but limited in rural areas. Over-the-counter medicines and personal necessities are available in most hotels and drugstores. The water in Manila and environs is safe to drink, but boiled or bottled water is recommended in outlying areas.

Tipping. A service charge is added to the bill in major hotels, so further remuneration is optional. In restaurants, you should tip 10 percent if the service charge has not been included in the total. At the airport, the rate per bag is set at one peso. Taxi drivers are generally not tipped.

Weather and what to wear. The Philippines is a tropical country with warm to hot temperatures, high humidity, and much sunshine. Though the temperature averages 26.7°C/80°F and can rise to 32.2°C/90°F, steady sea breezes relieve the heat, particularly in the evening. Most rain falls from May through October, with typhoons occurring from July through October, if at all. The best time to visit Manila and the northern islands is from November through February; prime season for the southern islands is from January through March.

You will be most comfortable in informal cotton clothing or wash-and-wear garments. In the evening, more formal outfits are appropriate in the better restaurants. Men can wear the long-sleeved native *barong tagalog* (loose fitting embroidered shirt) or a coat and tie, and women wear either a long or a short cocktail dress. Women should also carry a light sweater or shawl.

Time. There is a 15-hour difference between the U.S. west coast and the Philippines. When it is noon Sunday in Manila, it is 8 P.M. Saturday in San Francisco.

For more information. The best source of information about travel in the Philippines is the Philippine Ministry of Tourism (MOT). Contact the MOT's Philippine headquarters at P.O. Box 3451, Manila or their head office in the United States, located at 3325 Wilshire Boulevard, Los Angeles, CA 90010. Branches are in New York, San Francisco, and Chicago. Philippine Airlines, a source of a handy guidebook of mini-tours as well as its domestic schedules, has offices in San Francisco, Los Angeles, Chicago, and Washington, D.C. Consulates are located in San Francisco, Los Angeles, Seattle, Chicago, New York, New Orleans, and Honolulu. The Philippine embassy is in Washington, D.C. In Manila, the American Embassy is located on Roxas Boulevard.

THAILAND

An exotic travel experience — wats dotted with golden spires; graceful silk-clad dancers; a capital city sliced by canals; beaches fringed with palms; teak-covered mountains, home to colorful tribespeople and toiling elephants

Thailand is an exotic, varied land. At its heart is Bangkok, both capital and main port of entry. Here visitors will find all those things one expects to find in a modern, fast-growing city — a rapid pace, traffic-clogged streets, garish billboards, neon-lit discos, and concrete and steel office blocks.

Beyond this modern facade is another Bangkok—the Bangkok of quiet backwater *klongs* (canals) lined with simple stilt houses. Bangkok's water people depend on the klongs for transportation, food, and bathing. In Bangkok (as well as the rest of Thailand), towering, gold-leafed *wat* (Buddhist monastery) spires provide visible evidence of the Thai peoples' devotion to Buddhism. Behind wat walls, saffron-robed men lead a monastic life of prayer and meditation.

South of Bangkok is a tropical world of deserted, palm-fringed beaches, coral islands, and fishing villages. Northern Thailand's jungle-covered mountains are home to Thailand's colorful hill tribes and Chiang Mai's artists and artisans. Ruins of Thailand's ancient cities — Ayutthaya, Pimai, Sukhothai—lie scattered across the country's rice-growing central plain north of Bangkok. They provide a visible reminder of Thailand's ancient civilizations and their architectural achievements.

This is a country of Thai silk, resplendently gowned Thai dancers, lush green flatlands covered with rice fields, orchids that literally grow like weeds, lumbering water buffaloes, giant elephants, clear mountain streams, tumbling waterfalls, and best of all, the friendly Thai people. Proud and nationalistic, the Thais call their country *Muang Thai* — "the land of the free." Unlike other nations of Southeast Asia, Thailand has never been subject to colonial rule by a Western nation.

A TROPICAL HEARTLAND

Thailand's tropical kingdom lies in the heart of Southeast Asia. Somewhat larger than California, it covers an area of about 518,000 square km/199,950 square miles.

It shares borders with four other Southeast Asian countries: Burma on the west, Laos on the north and northeast, Cambodia (Kampuchea) on the southeast, and Malaysia on the extreme south. The southern part of Thailand shares a narrow peninsula with Burma. The eastern shore of this finger of land is washed by the waters of the Gulf of Thailand and the western shore by the waters of the Andaman Sea. Small islands are sprinkled along Thailand's 2,615 km/1,625 miles of coastline.

Plains and mountains

Bangkok — the country's capital — sits in the middle of a broad central plain, irrigated by the Chao Phraya River and its tributaries. This area is the nation's rice bowl — a rich, verdant land of lush rice fields. Throughout Thailand's history, this large plain has been the site of the nation's political development.

In the north, broad valleys separate lofty mountain chains, which are carpeted with forests of teak. Thailand's southern peninsula features expansive beaches, tiny fishing villages, jungle-covered hills, rubber plantations, and tin mines.

Lavished with warm sunshine and abundant rain, Thailand is rich in colorful vegetation including bougainvillea vines, flame of the forest trees, and rose bushes. Most famous of its floral offerings is the orchid. This remarkable plant grows wild in jungle forests throughout the country. There are hundreds of varieties in numerous shapes, colors, and sizes. Since not all varieties bloom at the same

Gilded statue *of* kinnari, *half-woman, half-bird, looks toward* chedi *at Wat Phra Keo in Bangkok.*

Motorized rafts *on River Kwai take tourists upriver from notorious bridge, made famous by World War II movie.*

time, you're bound to see some blossoms during your Thailand touring. They add delicate color to local gardens and are sold in village markets.

A variety of wildlife

Thailand's waters and forest lands (nearly half the country is still covered by jungle) teem with wildlife.

Bears, tigers, leopards, black panthers, wild boar, and several varieties of wild buffalo and deer live in Thailand's jungles. Monkeys and civet cats share trees with honeysuckle birds. Many kinds of snakes, including the poisonous cobra and banded krait, slither across the jungle floor. The forest overflows with insects — including some 800 species of butterflies and moths — and small creatures, such as bats and gecko lizards.

Edged by mangrove swamps and warm, shallow waters, the Thailand peninsula provides a haven for crocodiles, crabs, fish, rock lobsters, prawns, and the amphibious pigtailed monkey. In the Gulf of Thailand, fishermen harvest mackerel, herring, mullet, pomfret, sole, bass, anchovies, and sharks. Inland rivers, marked by fishing traps, nets, and bamboo fishing poles, enrich the farmer's diet with fresh minnow, carp, catfish, and dappled murral.

A LONG, LONG HISTORY

Little is really known about Thailand's ancient history. However, recent archeological findings near Ban Chiang in northeastern Thailand indicate that there may have been a thriving Bronze Age culture in the area over 5,000 years ago. The story of this early civilization has yet to be unraveled.

It is believed that the original Thai people began to migrate to Thailand from south-central China between the 5th and 7th centuries. In the 13th century, Kublai Khan's forces drove a large number of the Thais that remained in China into the Thailand area. In 1238, the Sukhothai kingdom was founded. Under its most important ruler, King Ramkamhaeng, the Thai alphabet was created and Buddhism adopted.

Ayutthaya's rise and fall

In 1350, the center of power shifted to Ayutthaya. This new kingdom, which became known as Siam, grew strong and prosperous. In the 15th century, its ambitious warlords were involved in a series of long and indecisive wars. Invading Khmer territory, they captured Angkor but failed to hold it. Wars also developed in Chiang Mai—then a Lao state—and later Burma.

The Burmese marched on Ayutthaya in 1767. After capturing the city, they demolished it, destroying most evidence of Thai culture and art. All the city's records and written history were burned and some 1,200 bronze and gold Buddha images were left in ruins. These images were rescued and eventually restored with lacquer and gold leaf. Today they can be seen in Bangkok's monasteries; the largest collection is at Wat Po.

A surviving general, Taksin, organized a new army and drove the Burmese out of Thailand. The capital city was established at Thon Buri across the Chao Phraya River from present-day Bangkok. Taksin served as king for a brief period.

In 1782, the capital was moved to Bangkok's current location. King Rama I ascended the throne, and the Chakri Dynasty was founded. Thailand's current king is the ninth ruler of this dynasty.

Colonial influences

In the 16th century, the Portuguese became Thailand's first European visitors. They set up trading posts at Ayutthaya. In the 17th century, the Dutch and English also established trading posts in Thailand.

The French, hoping to convert Thailand to Christianity, soon followed with missionaries, ships, and soldiers. Troubled by the problems these new visitors caused, Thailand expelled most of the foreigners in the late 17th century and closed its doors to the western world for more than a hundred years.

By the mid-19th century, Thailand developed an enlightened line of absolute kings who retained political independence and initiated programs of partial modernization. King Mongkut, crowned in 1851, reopened Thailand to western trade and introduced western learning and science.

The first United States trade treaty with Thailand was signed in 1833.

Wartime occupation

Japan occupied Thailand at the outset of World War II. A short time later, Thailand declared war on Great Britain and the United States. However, Thailand tried to make it clear that this alliance with Japan was one of necessity; the country's real sympathies were with the West. Many Thais who opposed the Japanese established an underground. This organization was so effective that it won the country moderate treatment by the Allies after the war. In fact, the United States refused to acknowledge Thailand's war declaration.

As a member of the United Nations, Thailand serves as a regional center for various UN agencies.

Thailand today

Thailand became a constitutional monarchy in 1932; previously it had been an absolute monarchy. Its present ruler is King Bhumibol Adulyadej, officially known as King Rama IX. The king was born in Cambridge, Massachusetts (where his father was engaged in public health research), and received his education in England.

The prime minister, chosen by an elected parliament consisting of a House of Representatives and a Senate, is the chief executive of the government.

Responsibility for local government rests with the Ministry of Interior, which appoints governors for each of Thailand's 72 changwads (provinces). These changwads are subdivided into amphoes (districts) governed by nai amphoes (district officers). The number of districts each province has depends on its population. Each district has villages governed by headmen and commune councils. The government representative at the village level, the pu-yai-ban, reports to the district officer.

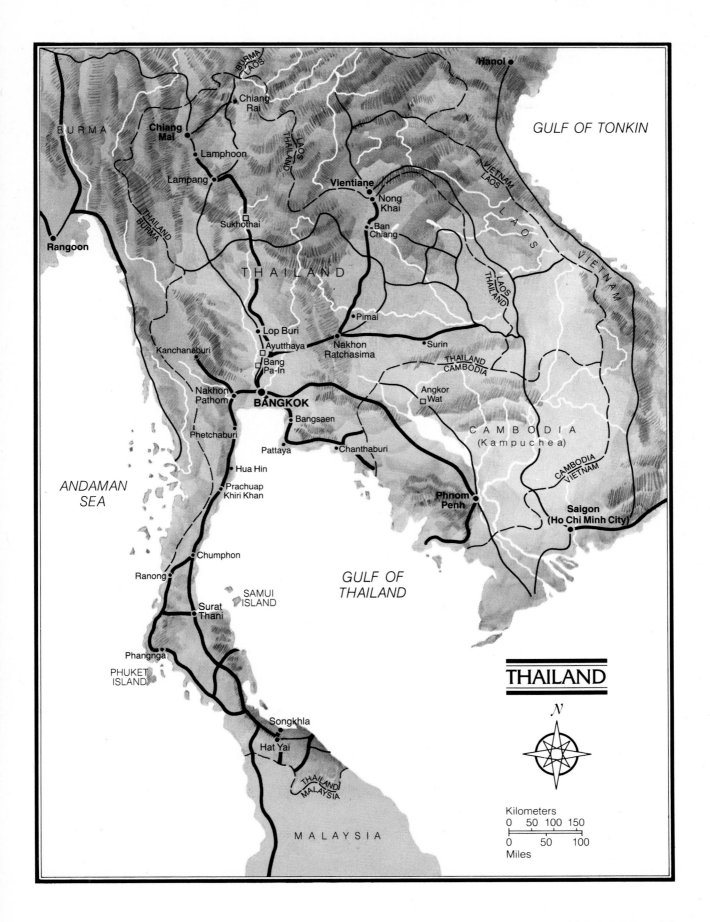

BURMA

Rangoon

ANDAMAN
SEA

Chiang
Rai

Chiang
Mai

Lamphoon

Lampang

Sukhothai

THAILAND

Lop Buri

Ayutthaya

Bang
Pa-In

Kanchanaburi

Nakhon
Pathom

BANGKOK

Phetchaburi

Bangsaen

Pattaya

Hua Hin

Prachuap
Khiri Khan

Chumphon

Ranong

Surat
Thani

SAMUI
ISLAND

Phangnga

PHUKET
ISLAND

Songkhla

Hat Yai

THAILAND/
MALAYSIA

MALAYSIA

Vientiane

Nong
Khai

Ban
Chiang

Pimai

Nakhon
Ratchasima

Surin

THAILAND
CAMBODIA

Angkor
Wat

Chanthaburi

CAMBODIA
(Kampuchea)

CAMBODIA
VIETNAM

Phnom
Penh

GULF OF
THAILAND

Hanoi

GULF OF TONKIN

LAOS

VIETNAM
LAOS

LAOS
THAILAND

VIETNAM

Saigon
(Ho Chi Minh City)

THAILAND

N

Kilometers
0   50 100 150

0   50   100
Miles

In moment *of quiet meditation, saffron-robed Buddhist monk at Wat Sraket resembles gleaming golden statue of Buddha.*

Towering spires *and stepped roofs of Bangkok's mile-long Grand Palace were once glimpsed only from river bank; tourists now enter arched gate, wander through temples, pavilions, and courtyards.*

PEOPLE OF THAILAND

The Thai people—descendants of those who migrated to Thailand from south-central China many centuries ago—account for almost 90 percent of the country's 47 million people. Generally small, slight, and delicately built, the Thais are a hospitable people with gracious manners and friendly smiles.

The largest minority group is Chinese—some 3 million people. More than half of Bangkok's population is Chinese; for centuries this group has dominated Thailand's commerce and retail trade. Other minorities in Thailand include Indians, Pakistanis, Khmers, Vietnamese, and almost a million Malays, clustered near the southern border of the country.

In the hills and mountains surrounding northern Thailand's Chiang Mai live tribespeople who differ from the Thais in culture, costume, language, and tradition. Though the origins of these mountain people are uncertain, anthropologists believe that the original tribespeople migrated from southern China, some arriving in Thailand as recently as a hundred years ago. The six main tribal groups are the Meo, Karen, Akha, Lisu, Lahu, and Yao. Each tribe has its own language and observes many primitive ancestral customs.

An agrarian society

Thailand is basically an agricultural society. Over 85 percent of its people live in rural areas in or near small towns or villages. Rice is the principal crop, grown both for local consumption and export. Other exported items include textiles, teakwood, rubber, and tin. Fishing is a growing industry.

Thailand's rural people dress in a cool and comfortable fashion. Thai men wear loose cotton shirts and trousers and wide straw hats. Their most indispensable item is a *pakaoma* (a piece of cotton cloth used as a bathing robe, decorative waist sash, or all-purpose bundle wrapping). Country women wear the traditional *pasin* (a colorful piece of cloth wrapped tightly around the hips and draped to the mid-calves).

Unlike their country cousins, the people of Bangkok and other urban areas prefer western clothes and the latest continental fashions.

The importance of religion

More than 90 percent of Thailand's people follow Buddhism. You'll also find Muslims, Hindus, Sikhs, Christians, and, in the hill tribes, those who practice animism and ancestor worship.

Buddhism, adopted by the Thais in the 13th century, provides inspiration for Thai art and literature. Through Buddhism's influence, Thais have developed a carefree attitude, a flexible nature, and a lack of tension—qualities characterizing their national image.

As part of their religious practices, the Thai Buddhists pay respect to their country's 28,000 *wats* or monasteries (sometimes called temples). Devotees purchase gold leaf and apply it to the thousands of Buddha images. Buddhists also venerate roadside shrines (spirit houses) with flowers, incense, and candles. You'll find that no Thai home, office, or shop is considered secure without a "spirit house" on its grounds. These small temples, set atop posts, accommodate the spirits of the land who were displaced by the construction of a building.

Young Thai Buddhist men, regardless of their social status, are expected to spend a minimum of 3 months as a *bhikkus* (monk) in the Brotherhood of Monks. This period in a young man's life usually occurs before he marries and starts raising a family. During their stay in the monastery, these lay monks must adhere to the ways of the Buddhist monk. They shave their heads, don saffron robes, and go out in the streets early each morning for their daily meal. Monks do not beg for food. Buddhists believe that the filling of a monk's rice bowl is a privilege—a deed that helps the donor earn a reward in the Thai Buddhist "merit system."

TRIP PLANNING AIDS

Thailand can be reached by air from points throughout the world. It's about 8,300 air miles from the west coast of the United States to Thailand. More than 30 international carriers, including Thai International and Thai Airways (Thailand's regional carrier), serve Bangkok's Don Muang Airport, the country's main international gateway. Chiang Mai in northern Thailand also has an international airport. Cruise ships and cargo/passenger liners call at Songkhla on the Thailand peninsula and at Bangkok's port of Klongtoey, 32 km/20 miles south of the city.

You can also travel by rail between Singapore and Bangkok. Departing from Singapore, you travel north along Malaysia's west coast to Kuala Lumpur, where you change to an express train. You then continue your journey northward, passing through Butterworth and the Thailand peninsula, to Bangkok. The trip from Singapore takes about 48 hours. Malaysia's east coast trains make connections with Bangkok-bound trains at the border town of Sungai Kolok.

Accommodation choices

Thailand has accommodations to suit a wide range of tastes and pocketbooks. Many new hotels have gone up in Bangkok during the past decade, and several of the older ones are undergoing remodeling. At the other major tourist destinations, you'll find luxury hotels and small resorts. Pattaya Beach offers both high-rise hotels and beachside bungalows. You'll find small local hotels in towns and cities throughout the country.

Amenities at the country's first-class hotels usually include air conditioning, shopping arcades, gourmet restaurants, and swimming pools. The beachside resorts offer guests an array of water sport opportunities and have rental equipment available. At the small local hotels you may only have a fan to keep you cool and cold water to wash with, but the prices are reasonable and you'll have a greater opportunity to mingle with the local people. Knowing a little of the Thai language is helpful in these local establishments.

All hotel prices are subject to a 10 percent service charge and a 16½ percent government tax.

Thailand's peak tourist season is from November to March. It is important to make room reservations well in advance for visits during this period.

Local transportation tips

The best ways to travel in Thailand are by air and rail. If you are on a limited time schedule, air transportation will allow you to see Thailand's far-flung sights in a short period of time. Thai Airways, the country's regional carrier, provides frequent air service to Thailand's major towns and cities. Be sure to book your reservation well in advance.

If time permits, you might want to do some traveling by train. It's a great way to see Thailand's beautiful countryside. The State Railway of Thailand has 4,000 km/2,486 miles of track. From Bangkok's two main terminals, Bangkok Railway Station and Bangkok Noi (in Thon Buri), there's daily service to important destinations throughout the country. You can book tickets 20 days in advance, either at the train station or through a local travel agent.

Other local transportation. Public bus lines provide service between Bangkok and main provincial towns. Many coaches are air-conditioned.

If you are planning to travel by car in Thailand, it's best to hire a chauffeur along with your rental vehicle. Most of the road signs are in Thai and traffic can careen along at an unnerving pace. If you do plan to drive yourself, you'll need an international driver's license. In Thailand, traffic moves on the left.

Tours. Thailand's tour operators offer a wide variety of tours by road (usually in an air-conditioned bus), rail, boat, or air to most of Thailand's major attractions. There are tours including Bangkok city sights, important destinations near Bangkok, Pattaya, Phuket, Songkhla, Chiang Mai, and Chiang Rai.

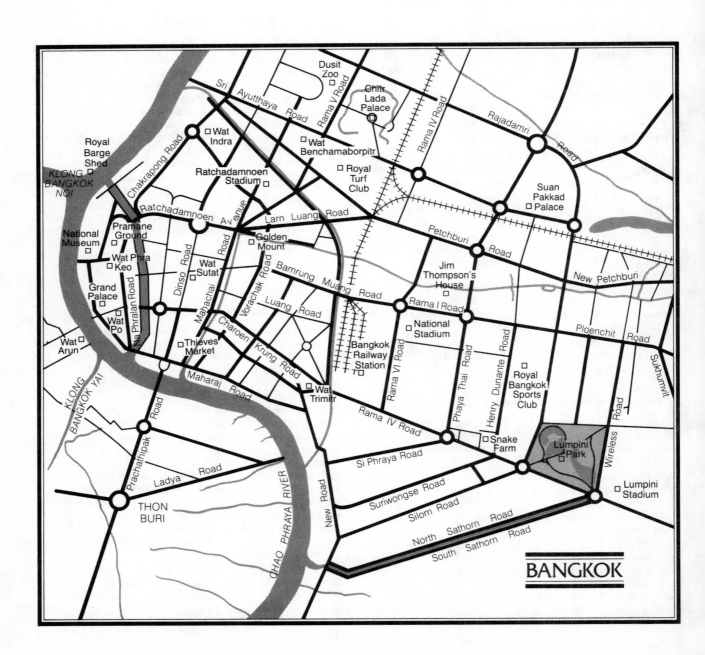

THE ESSENTIALS/**BANGKOK**

Here are a few basics to help you in planning and taking a trip to Thailand's capital city, Bangkok.

Getting there

Bangkok is served by air, rail, bus, and sea transportation.

Air. International service to and from Bangkok is by Thai International and foreign flag carriers.

Domestic flights by Thai Airways link Bangkok with other major Thailand cities and towns. Thai Airways also has flights between Bangkok and Penang, Malaysia.

Don Muang International Airport is 24 km/15 miles, about an hour's drive, from downtown Bangkok. A limousine service provides transportation to major hotels. There's also taxi and local bus service.

Rail. Train routes link Bangkok with Malaysia, Singapore, and Thailand cities and towns.

Bus. Local buses provide service between Bangkok and Thailand towns.

Sea. International cruise and cargo/passenger ships call at Klongtoey, 32 km/20 miles south of Bangkok. Transportation into Bangkok is by taxi or bus.

Where to stay

Bangkok offers visitors a wide range of accommodations. All the major hotels offer rooms with private bath and air conditioning; many have restaurants, shopping arcades, and swimming pools.

Major hotels include the Amarin, Ambassador, Asia, Dusit Thani, Erawan, Rama Tower, Indra Regent, Mandarin, Montien, Narai, Oriental-Bangkok, President-Regent of Bangkok, Rajah, Sheraton Bangkok, and Siam Inter-Continental.

For the tourist on a limited budget, the city offers a number of smaller hotels and guest houses. A list of these can be obtained from the Tourism Authority of Thailand. There's also a YMCA and YWCA.

Getting around Bangkok

Bangkok transporation includes taxis, *tuk-tuks* (three-wheeled motor scooters), and buses. You must negotiate the fare before you depart in a tuk-tuk or a taxi; local taxi drivers don't use their meters. Most major hotels have their own taxi service with fixed fares for different destinations.

Ferryboats and speedboats provide transportation across and on the Chao Phraya River and neighboring klongs.

Tours

Half and full-day tours take in city sights, a floating market (see page 62), Ayutthaya and Bang Pa-in (page 64-65), the Ancient City (page 62), River Kwai (page 65), and Pattaya (page 67).

Dining out

Bangkok's major hotels and city restaurants offer a wide variety of cuisine—Thai, Chinese, Vietnamese, Indian, Korean, Japanese, Indonesian, and European. You'll also find many restaurants offering Thai-style dinners. In its traditional form, Thai food, with its many chile peppers, can be very hot to the uninitiated. However, Thai restaurants catering to visitors (including hotels and restaurants featuring Thai classicial dance performances) offer less spicy Thai dishes.

If you want to try some authentic national dishes, here are two of Bangkok's popular Thai restaurants:
• Baan Keo Ruen Kwan at 212 Soi, Sukhumvit Road is popular with Thais.
• Jit Phochana, also catering mainly to Thais, has two locations. The restaurant at 1082 Phahonyothin Road is a multistory building seating hundreds. The original, smaller version is located at 62 Soi, 20 Sukhumvit Road.

Cultural offerings

Bangkok also has many theater-restaurants where you can enjoy a tempered (less hot) Thai dinner and Thai cultural entertainment—classical folk dancing, music, and sword-fighting. Better-known theater-restaurants include Baan Thai, 7 Soi, 32 Sukhumvit Road; Phinam, 46 Soi, 49 Sukhumvit Road; Sala Norasingh, Soi 4, South Nana Road; and Sukhothai, Dusit Thani Hotel, Saladaeng Circle.

The Oriental Hotel stages outdoor cultural performances of Thai boxing, sword fighting, and classical and folk dancing on the lawn on Thursday and Sunday at 11 A.M.

On a half-day excursion out of Bangkok, you can see the Rose Garden's show, with demonstrations of dancing, boxing and sword fighting. The Ancient City also features Thai dancing.

Night lights

After dark, Bangkok offers entertainment to suit every taste. The city's major hotels, restaurants, and nightclubs offer a choice of local performers and international shows. Bangkok also has a gaudy array of discotheques, small nightclubs, bars, and massage parlors. As in many Asian cities, a number of Bangkok's nightclubs provide hostesses.

For more information

The Tourism Authority of Thailand's head office at 4 Ratchadamnoen Avenue in Bangkok has maps, brochures, and other tourist information on Bangkok and other points of interest in Thailand.

City transport. Popular forms of local city transportation are taxis, *tuk-tuks* (three-wheeled, passenger-carrying motor scooters), and pedicabs. These bicycle-powered trishaws are banned from Bangkok's streets, but they're popular in other cities.

When using any of these vehicles, it's important to negotiate the price of the trip with the driver in advance. This policy applies to metered taxis as well. (The meters are never used.) If you are unsure of how much the trip should cost, check with your hotel receptionist. Some hotels have their own taxi services; you pay in advance according to an established rate schedule. The price of the trip can be more, but you avoid the haggling.

It's also advisable to have your hotel receptionist write out your destination in Thai; many drivers can't speak English. Be sure you also have the name of your hotel written in Thai for your return trip.

Bangkok and other major cities also have city bus service.

Dining Thai-style

Influenced by Chinese, Indian, and Malay cookery, Thai cuisine achieves a unique blending of flavors. Thai food is never bland. You'll find it sweet, sour, salty, or hot and spicy. Thais love to add hot chile peppers to nearly everything they cook. These small red and green peppers have brought tears to the eyes of many a Western diner; to smother the burning sensation, take a spoonful of rice or sugar rather than water. Other favorite Thai ingredients are coconut milk, coriander, ginger, turmeric, lemon grass, mint, basil, and cardamom.

You will find hotel dining establishments and other tourist-oriented restaurants offer westernized versions of Thai cuisine. To experience real Thai food, you'll have to visit a local Thai restaurant, preferably in the company of Thais. Menus are not always in English.

A typical Thai meal consists of rice, four or five side dishes, and *khong waan* (a dessert) or fruit. Local dishes you might try are *dom yam gung* (a hot and spicy soup with shrimp, chicken, or fish); *khao pat* (fried rice flavored with bits of crab, chicken, pork, onion, egg, and saffron); *kai dom kha* (chicken curry with cashew nuts); and *gang pet* (a hot, curried sweet-tasting dish made from pork, chicken, beef, fish, or prawns). Almost every meal contains one of the dozens of Thai curries. Based on chicken, beef, or shellfish and frequently flavored with coconut milk or lime juice, a Thai curry can range from sweet or sour to hot and peppery. Frequently used condiments are garlic, *nam puk* (hot and spicy shrimp paste), and *nam pla* (an amber-colored, salty fish sauce).

Thais end their meals with some of Thailand's succulent fruit—mangoes, oranges, melons, bananas, rambutans, and papayas—or a sweet khong waan, which may resemble jello, cake, custard, or pudding. National drinks include the full-bodied Singha beer and Mekong whisky. Many visitors adopt the pleasant oriental custom of drinking tea with the meal.

The entertainment scene

Thailand's urban areas have a remarkably large number of nightclubs, discotheques, cocktail lounges, and hostess bars. Hotels, theater restaurants, and supper clubs feature local and international shows, with music provided by Thai bands.

However, for many visitors, Thailand's most fascinating entertainment is the Thai classical dance-drama, characterized by intricate steps and gestures. Dressed in heavily embroidered silk costumes, dancers express varying emotions by the delicate movements of their hands; many performers wear long brass fingernails.

In one form of classical dance, the *khon* (masked play), dancers don brightly painted masks and act out scenes from the Ramayana. The Thais have taken this Indian epic—well known throughout Southeast Asia (see "The Story of Ramayana," page 137)—and adapted it to their culture. The Thai version is called the Ramakian. Shadow plays with leather puppets also dramatize stories from the Ramakian.

In contrast to classical dance, the key to local folk dances, usually performed during festivals, is simplicity. Costumes include sarongs and long-sleeved tops. Beautiful flowers adorn the hair of the female performers.

One of the best ways to see both classical and folk dancing is to attend a folklore show in Bangkok. In Chiang Mai, you can see the folk dances of the hill tribespeople.

Shopping around

In Thailand you'll have the opportunity to buy a great variety of locally produced items. Prices are fixed in department stores and some other larger shops, but it's customary to bargain at small shops and local markets. Friendly bargaining is part of the game of shopping Thai-style—a pleasant smile can help you get your price.

Most stores are open from 8:30 or 9 A.M. to 6 P.M. Monday through Saturday. Some souvenir shops and hotel shopping arcades remain open until 8 P.M. or later and reopen on Sunday.

The Tourism Authority of Thailand's handy "Official Shopping Guide" includes a list of recommended shops. You'll recognize these shops by the blue decals in their windows.

Things to buy. Thai silk is the most popular tourist purchase. An American, Jim Thompson, brought this soft, handwoven fabric to the attention of leading fashion designers just after World War II. Stores and shops sell silk in a variety of colors, patterns, and weights. You can buy ready-made (or custom-made) Thai silk suits and dresses or silk and Thai cotton by the yard for draperies and wall hangings. Though lacking the sheen and glamour of silk, Thai cotton is popular for dresses, blouses, and suits.

Thai jewelry is another favorite purchase. You can get some good buys on precious and semiprecious stones, including zircons, sapphires and star sapphires, and rubies. In the unique, cone-shaped princess ring, nine stones (diamond, cat's-eye, ruby, emerald, sapphire, topaz, moonstone, garnet, and zircon) are set in concentric tiers—a setting reminiscent of the ornate headpiece worn by a Thai classical dancer.

Other locally made products are nielloware (silver inlaid with a black alloy), Thai celadon (a high-fired stoneware reproduction of pottery made in northern China more than 2,000 years ago), bronze tableware, silverware, lac-

Congested waterways *create traffic hazard at Damnoen Saduak outside Bangkok. Get up early to watch floating-market vendors hawk wares; action is over by 10 A.M.*

No garages needed *in Thailand; boats replace many autos, tie up in "front yards" along watery highways.*

WHAT IS A WAT?

Thailand has thousands of *wats*. Their spired buildings add a dramatic touch to both city and country panoramas. A Buddhist wat is actually a monastery, a compound where saffron-robed monks reside and pray. The buildings within the compound — a pleasant blending of multi-tiered roofs, curved gables, and soaring, gilded spires — reflect a mixture of Indian, Khmer, Burmese, and Chinese architecture. The result is something wonderfully and uniquely Thai.

Within a wat complex is always found a *bot*, the main temple that houses an image of Buddha. Because the bot is the most sacred part of the wat, special ceremonies such as ordinations take place here. A smaller chapel, the *viharn*, serves as the place for public devotion. It, too, has an image of Buddha. You may find several viharns within the wat complex. The tall, sharply pointed spires atop bell-shaped bases are called *chedis*. The thick, somewhat tapered stone columns with rounded tops are *prangs*. Both of these house sacred objects.

When visiting a wat, you should follow certain rules of etiquette: Dress modestly and remove your shoes before entering a bot or viharn. Women should refrain from standing too close to a monk, touching him, or looking him directly in the eye. All Buddha images, even those in disrepair, should be regarded as sacred objects to be treated with respect.

querware, small brass and bronze temple bells, Thai dolls dressed in elaborate dance costumes or folk dress, *khon* masks, intricate teakwood carvings, rattan and bamboo products, leather shadow play puppets, handpainted silk or paper umbrellas, and temple rubbings (motifs in bas-relief).

Things not to buy. The United States restricts the import of products made from animals and plants it has officially listed as endangered or threatened. Even though these items are sold abroad, they will not be allowed into the United States. For more information, see page 9.

Thailand has restrictions on the exportation of Buddha and deity images as well as other religious art. Before buying any of these items, check with Bangkok's National Museum.

THE SPORTS SCENE

Thailand offers visitors a host of spectator sports to enjoy; some of them are unique to Thailand. In addition, there are recreational opportunities for tennis players, golfers, and water sports enthusiasts.

Sports to watch

Many of Thailand's sports involve a form of fighting that requires agility, skill, and endurance. One of the most popular is Thai-style boxing. For more information on this high-kicking sport, see page 72.

Other sports that test the skill and agility of the participants are kite flying (a duel to see which person's kite can remain airborne in spite of attacks by the opponent's kite); fish fighting (large-finned, Thai fish are pitted against one another in a small glass bowl); bull fighting (unlike Spain's sport, this one really is between two bulls); cockfighting (the bloodless variety); and sword fighting.

The latter sport is derived from a form of Thai martial arts practiced 2,000 years ago. The wielding of the heavy sword or swords (sometimes the player carries a blade in each hand) takes physical coordination and concentration. The contestant judged the most skilled wins the competition.

One of the leading national team sports is *takraw* (a game played by two teams using a hollow, braided rattan ball). Team members keep the ball in the air by kicking or hitting it with their feet, heads, or shoulders — using any part of the body except the hands.

More familiar to Westerners are the popular spectator sports of soccer, badminton, basketball, rugby, and volleyball. Horse racing also has a big following.

Recreational possibilities

The country's more than two dozen golf courses are plush and rich in vegetation. Most clubs have caddies (usually girls), and greens fees are inexpensive. The Thais prefer playing with a crowd, rather than a foursome, giving rise to the term "alligators" — a string of six, seven, or more golfers teeing off together.

Tennis players will find courts at most big hotels and in most major cities and resort areas. Water sports abound at Thailand's southern beach resorts. There's good diving in the Gulf of Thailand and off the western shores of Thailand's southern peninsula with coral reefs in abundance as far north as Pattaya. Water-skiing, para-sailing (parachute sailing with the help of a speedboat), sailing, and windsurfing are also popular.

EXOTIC BANGKOK

Bangkok—Thailand's capital and center of business, industry, and transportation—sprawls along both banks of the curving Chao Phraya River some 32 km/20 miles inland from the Gulf of Thailand. Called *Krung Thep* (City of Angels) by the Thais, Bangkok is brightened by many gleaming wat spires, walled palaces, and a network of boat-filled klongs.

Present-day Bangkok had its beginnings in 1782 when Siam's seat of government was moved from Thon Buri on the west side of the river to the eastern bank. In those early days, the city's mud flats supported a few Buddhist wats and a Chinese trading community. Along the river were moored Thai houseboats.

From these humble beginnings, a modern and prosperous city has developed. It's a city of distinct contrasts: Thai and western-style architecture and ways juxtaposed. Sleek glass and concrete office buildings rise above ancient Buddhist wats with golden towers. The city's exhaust-clouded avenues are jammed with traffic; yet just behind these main thoroughfares are calm residential streets, laced with small watery klongs and narrow *sois* (lanes). Moving through the city, you'll glimpse cool tropical gardens splashed with flowering bougainvillea, garish billboards, rows of concrete block buildings where swamp and jungle once were, and pastoral scenes of fishermen dipping their nets into murky roadside klongs. Of the city's more than 4½ million inhabitants, fully one-fifth live on or near the water.

A brief orientation

To get an idea of Bangkok's layout, imagine the city as an upturned left hand with its fingers spreading northeast and east. The Chao Phraya River flows from north to south, running from the tip of the thumb and curving across the wrist. The palm holds the city's proliferating center, and the radiating fingers represent the main avenues reaching out toward Bangkok's northeastern and eastern regions.

The northern section of Bangkok is marked by broad tree-shaded avenues, meandering klongs, and modern houses brightened by small gardens. Ratchadamnoen Avenue, a Thai adaptation of Paris's Champs Élysées, leads north to the Dusit Zoo, magnificent palaces, and public parks.

Many of the city's new hotels, elegant shops, embassies, office buildings, and shopping centers are located in the eastern section of Bangkok, bounded by New Petchburi Road on the north and Rama IV Road on the south. Some of the city's wealthiest residents live on the sois that branch off Sukhumvit Road.

Because Bangkok's major attractions are scattered throughout the sprawling city, it's wise to first experience Bangkok on an organized tour. You can then take a taxi or local bus to the places you want to explore more thoroughly; Bangkok is not a city easily seen on foot.

Start with the palace

First stop for most visitors is the Grand Palace in Bangkok's oldest section. The early kings lived within the walls of this compound, which was a complete, self-contained world—

SPEAKING THAI

Thailand's language, phonetically related to some Chinese dialects, uses written characters derived from the Khmer alphabet, which in turn is based on the ancient Sanskrit of India. When the Thai language is written in Roman script, multiple spellings abound.

In Thailand's main cities English is understood and spoken by some, especially the professional and business people. To help you communicate with those who can't speak English, here are a few phrases:

The universal greeting is "Sawaddee," meaning "hello," "good morning," "good evening," or "goodbye." Thais accompany this salutation with the *wai*, made by placing the hands together in a prayerlike gesture, raising them to the face, and bowing slightly. Thais seldom shake hands.

Please— "Karuna"
Thank you— "Khopkhun"
Yes— "Chai"
No— "Mai" or "Plao"
How are you?— "Sabaidi ru?"
Very well, thank you— "Sabaidi, khopkhun"
I don't understand— "Chan mai kao jai"
Please speak slowly— "Poot cha-cha noi"
Please drive slowly— "Proad khap loht cha-cha"
How much is this?— "Raka tao-rai?"
Excuse me— "Kah-thot"
Where is the toilet?— "Hong nam yu ti nai?"

Stone Buddha images *commune with nature among ruins of Ayutthaya, former Thai capital sacked by Burmese in 1767. Some of city has been restored; other parts are still undergoing excavation.*

the symbolic center of Bangkok and Thailand. Thrust into the 20th century, the city moved away from the palace, and so did the king. (The reigning monarch, Rama IX, lives in the Chitr Lada Palace, across from the zoo on the east side of Rama V Road.) Yet the Grand Palace remains the ceremonial center of Bangkok: all great occasions of state are held here.

Covering a square mile on the east bank of the Chao Phraya River, the Grand Palace's grounds are entered from Na Phralan Road. Once inside the walled compound, you'll discover that the palace is a fabulous city within a city — a world of glittering spires, painted in gold or studded with chips of colored glass; spacious pavilions and buildings, decorated with mother-of-pearl inlay and lacquerwork and topped by tile roofs with upturned eaves; and carved gateways, guarded by monsterlike statues. Each of the Chakri sovereigns who has lived at the Grand Palace has added his own architectural touches to the palace.

A major Grand Palace attraction is the Amarindra Vinichai Hall, a T-shaped structure used as the coronation hall. Within are ornate golden thrones, richly colored walls, and red and gold ceilings. Other palace attractions are Chakri Hall, an unusual mixture of European and Thai architecture, and Dusit Palace. Used as a state reception hall, Chakri Hall features a marble façade, a red and green tile roof with curving eaves, spires, and a central balcony. The Dusit Palace's ornate building is topped with four graduated tile roofs crowned at their corners by gilded spires. It was built by King Rama I as an audience hall.

You can visit the Grand Palace daily from 9 A.M. to noon and 1 to 4 P.M. The throne halls are closed on holidays. Visitors to the palace are asked to dress modestly, no shorts or T-shirts.

Not far from the Grand Palace complex lies Pramane Ground. This 32-acre grassy oval is the sight of the annual Ploughing Ceremony (see "Festival Time," page 64) and Bangkok's New Year celebration. The Weekend Market is also held here (see page 60).

Wat wandering

Bangkok has over 400 *wats* (Buddhist monasteries), many of them fine examples of Thai architecture. To better acquaint yourself with the components and customs of a wat, see "What is a wat?," page 56. The following are some of the city's most important wats.

Wat Phra Keo. The Monastery of the Emerald Buddha is located in the northeast corner of the Grand Palace compound. Focal point of this wat is the central *bot* (temple). Within this multistoried building with its golden, three-tiered roof is the Emerald Buddha, Thailand's most venerated Buddha image. The 79-cm/31-inch statue, carved from translucent green jasper, sits atop a tall golden altar. Several times a year, the king changes the Buddha's gem-encrusted garments in a special ceremony. Frescoes depicting the earthly life of Lord Buddha decorate the interior of the bot.

Wat Po. The Monastery of the Reclining Buddha, located just south of the Grand Palace, is Bangkok's most extensive wat. Surrounded by a low wall, the complex is known for its four large *chedis* (sharply pointed spires atop bell-shaped bases) and 394 images of the seated Buddha.

However, the main attraction of the complex is the massive statue of the Reclining Buddha, stretching 49 meters/160 feet long and rising 12 meters/39 feet high. Resting on its right side, the Reclining Buddha is overlaid with gold leaf except for the soles of the feet, which are inlaid with mother-of-pearl.

Wat Arun. The Monastery of the Dawn stands in Thon Buri on the west bank of the Chao Phraya River, almost opposite the Grand Palace. Its dominant feature is the 82-meter/269-foot *prang* (a round-topped, cylindrical spire on a sculptured base), surrounded by four smaller prangs. The brick prangs, covered with stucco and imbedded with colorful chips of porcelain and glass, were built by Rama II in 1809. From the balcony of the central prang, reached by a narrow flight of steps, you have a view of the boat-clogged river and the city beyond.

The Wat Arun presents an impressive picture at dawn. Standing on the east side of the river, you'll see sculptured spires, at first silhouetted against the early morning sky, then glimmering in the first light of day.

North of Wat Arun, housed in the Royal Barge Shed, are some 30 ornate barges, once the main transportation of Bangkok's royalty. The largest of the barges, *Suvannahong*, is over 30 meters/100 feet long and requires at least 60 oarsmen to propel it. This red and gold barge sports a carved prow resembling a sacred bird of Thai mythology. On ceremonial occasions, there are still royal barge processions on the Chao Phraya River.

The Golden Mount. This artificial hill, near Vorachak Road just east of the old city wall, is part of Wat Sraket. Its upper platform, built atop a pile of brick rubble, is some 79 meters/260 feet high and has a gilded chedi in the center. The platform, a good spot from which to view Bangkok, can be reached by a circular staircase. When completed in 1868 by King Mongkut, the Golden Mount was the highest point in extremely flat Bangkok.

November is the time of the Wat Sraket Fair. At this time pilgrims climb the steps to pay homage to a relic of Lord Buddha enshrined atop the hill.

Wat Benchamaborpitr. The Marble Monastery, on Sri Ayutthaya Road north of the Golden Mount, was built in 1899 by Rama V. One of the finest examples of Thai architecture, it is constructed of white Italian marble and houses a famed collection of 52 life-size bronze Buddha images.

Across the klong from the bot are the monks' quarters, frequently guarded by young boys selling caged birds. For a few cents, you can purchase a bird—setting it free brings good luck.

Wat Trimitr. The Monastery of the Golden Buddha, located on the edge of Chinatown not far from Bangkok Railway Station, houses a literally priceless 5½-ton solid-gold Buddha. The beauty and worth of this Buddha image was discovered by accident. In 1953, when the image was being transferred from an abandoned monastery to Wat Trimitr (also spelled "Traimit"), the crane hook holding the heavy image gave way. The Buddha image fell to the ground where it remained overnight. In the morning, a monk began cleaning the image, mud-splattered and wet from the night's heavy rain, and glimpsed something glittering through a crack in the plaster. It is believed that the gold Buddha image was cast during the 13th century and later was covered with plaster to conceal its true worth from invading armies.

Wat Indra. A 33-meter/108-foot Buddha stands in front of Wat Indra on Visukasat Road. Construction began on this huge statue over a century ago. It's still not totally completed.

Wat Sutat. This wat, located on Dinso Road, is noted for its giant, red-lacquered swing. Located in a square opposite the wat, the swing used to be part of annual wat festivities.

The wat itself features beautiful carved wooden doors whose designs depict scenes from the Ramayana. Wat Sutat's bot houses an image of Buddha, plus statues of Buddha's disciples.

Museums and galleries

In addition to Bangkok's excellent museum, there are several other opportunities to view Thailand's antiques. The work of modern Thai artists, most of whom concentrate on Thai subjects, is found in local galleries. For artistic works of nature, you can tour Bangkok's Shell Museum.

National Museum. Occupying a former 18th century palace off Na Phrathat Road on the west side of Pramane Ground, this extensive museum recalls the nation's history and past glories.

Here you'll see a wide collection of traditional Thai paintings as well as exhibits of antique porcelain, coins, weapons, textiles, royal thrones, traditional garments and dance costumes, and elaborate cremation chariots. There's even a full-scale model elephant dressed for battle. You can also see some of the Ban Chiang archeological finds including 5,000-year-old pottery.

The museum is open Tuesday through Thursday and Saturday and Sunday from 9 A.M. to noon and 1 to 4 P.M. There are guided tours of the museum during the morning hours. Check with your hotel to find out on which days English-speaking tours are given. At the museum entrance, you can purchase a handy museum guide book.

Jim Thompson's House. This building, located at 6 Soi Kasemsan 2, north of Rama I Road, is actually a composite of six traditional Siamese houses. The houses were dismantled in Ayutthaya, brought downriver, and rebuilt to form Thompson's main home and servants' quarters.

The interior of the home, which sits in a garden next to a tree-shaded klong, has floors, ceilings, columns, wall panels, and roof timbers made of teak; Italian marble paves the entrance hall. Antique green Chinese tiles—originally brought from China as ballast on rice boats—were used for the terrace parapet.

Jim Thompson, the man who popularized the Thai silk industry, loved antique art and collected many valuable pieces during his Southeast Asian travels. Thompson's house contains some fine stone and bronze statues, porcelains and paintings, beautiful chinaware, and Thai furnishings.

Mr. Thompson mysteriously disappeared in the 1960s while on a hunting trip in Peninsular Malaysia; since that time, a special trust has maintained the house.

It is open to visitors Monday through Friday from 9 A.M. to 4 P.M.

Suan Pakkad Palace. Located at 352 Sri Ayutthaya Road, this palace is also a composite of old Thai houses. Highlight of the palace, owned by Princess Chumbhot, is a formal garden with a lacquer pavilion brought from Ayutthaya. The pavilion walls are decorated with gold leaf and carvings depicting the life of Buddha. Inside the palace are paintings, carvings, and Siamese furniture dating from the 17th century.

The palace is open daily except Sunday from 9 A.M. to noon and 1 to 4 P.M.

Shell Museum. Shells from all over the world are displayed in this museum at 124 Sukhumvit Road. Catalogued and arranged by species, exhibits include specimens of conus, cowrie, murex, and harp shells.

The Museum is open from 9 A.M. to 5:30 P.M. Friday through Sunday.

Shopping around

Best buys in Bangkok include nielloware (products of silver inlaid with a black alloy), Thai celadon pottery, bronze tableware, silverware, lacquerwork, dolls in traditional Thai dress, Thai cotton and silk in fabric lengths and garments (both ready-made and custom tailored), and precious and semiprecious stones.

In this widely dispersed city, there's no defined shopping district, but the city does have several large, air-conditioned shopping complexes. Most hotels have shopping arcades, and you'll find additional stores on New Road and Suriwongse and Silom roads. The huge Central Department Store on Silom Road has a special section featuring Thai handicrafts. Another place to shop for handicrafts is the government-run Narayanaphand on Larn Luang Road.

Most shops are open from 8 A.M. to 9 P.M. daily; department stores are open from 10 A.M. to 7 P.M. Bargaining is expected, except in the larger, fixed-price stores.

Chinatown and a Thieves' Market. Like the rest of the city, Chinatown rose from mud flats. Encompassing a maze of narrow lanes in the southern part of central Bangkok, Chinatown today stretches along New Road and Yaowarat Road.

It is a beehive of squat, century-old shops selling tea, jewelry, rattan, cure-all medicines, and household items such as pots and pans. Streets are jammed with honking cars, overloaded trucks, and noisy motor scooters. Narrow sidewalks are flooded with throngs of people.

The Thieves' Market spreads over the north end of Chinatown. Once, it was primarily an outlet for stolen goods. Today you'll find shops selling industrial machinery (power and hand tools, air compressors, pumps), Chinese character stamps (called *chops*), polished bronze incense bowls, and reproductions of Thai antiques. Experts occasionally unearth a genuine piece of antique sculpture, bronze, or porcelain.

Other markets. One of the best ways to learn a little about local life styles is to wander through a public market. The Weekend Market, one of Asia's largest, occurs each Saturday and Sunday at Pramane Ground near the Grand Palace. Here, under colorful canvas roofs, you'll stroll narrow aisles past stalls cluttered with an assortment of goods — sarongs, antiques, cold drinks, leather belts, fighting fish, fighting cocks, transistor radios, umbrellas, sun hats, and crockery. In the market's food section are live crabs, red and green chile peppers, shrimp paste, and a colorful array of durians, mangoes, oranges, and rambutans. A kaleidoscope of smells and sounds greets your senses: the appetizing aroma of satay sizzling on a charcoal brazier or noodles frying in a wok, vocal myna birds chattering from their cage perches, and housewives and vendors engaging in the fine art of haggling. The Weekend Market is open from 9 to 6 Saturday and Sunday.

Other markets include the Pratunam Market on Petchburi Road (similar to the Weekend Market with produce, fish, electrical goods, and spices); Bangkrak Market off New Road (flowers and items for traditional Chinese festivals); and Pahurat Road Indian Market (silk, laces, and cotton). All of these markets are open daily.

Outdoor sights

Bangkok also offers visitors a zoo in a parklike setting, an interesting snake farm, a beautiful park, and a living folk museum.

Dusit Zoo. Containing some 61 hectares/150 acres, Dusit Zoo is noted for its large boating lagoon and network of connecting canals. Tree-shaded paths border the water. Most of the animals, birds, and reptiles living in this parklike setting are from Asia. You can also see the royal white elephants, a special type of elephant revered by Thai Buddhists.

The zoo, a favorite weekend destination of Bangkok families, also has a children's playground and various souvenir and snack stalls. Located adjacent to the National Assembly Hall, Dusit Zoo is entered from Rama V Road. It's open from 8 A.M. to 6 P.M. daily.

Saowapa Snake Farm. This farm, located on Rama IV Road, is part of the Thai Red Cross Institute. Twice weekly at 11, attendants extract venom — used for vaccines — from the cobras, king cobras, banded kraits, vipers, and other snakes in residence. The farm is open daily except on public holidays.

Lumpini Park. You'll find Bangkok's largest park on Rama IV Road opposite the Saladang traffic circle. The park's tree-shaded green is a popular weekend spot for local Bangkok residents, who come to enjoy its picnic areas, scenic lakes, lakeside and floating restaurants, and open-air concert bowl. Be sure to look for its pagoda-style clock tower.

TIMland (Thailand in Miniature). Visitors with little time in Thailand can get a capsulized view of Thailand's culture by spending an afternoon at TIMland.

You'll see how rice is planted and harvested, and how various craft items like pottery, lacquerware, and colorful umbrellas are produced. Girls demonstrate the delicate art of Thai silk weaving, and elephants display their agility at teak log rolling. There's also Thai dancing, both classical and folk.

Open afternoons daily, TIMland is located near the Don Muang International Airport.

The sports scene

Thais love spectator sports. Thai boxing events (see page 72) are scheduled every Tuesday, Friday, and Saturday evening at Lumpini Stadium and every Monday, Wednesday, and Thursday evening at Ratchadamnoen Stadium. Thai sword fighting (see page 56) can be viewed at the Rose Garden's Thai village (see page 62) or, on occasion, at the Ratchadamnoen and Lumpini stadiums. During the windy months (February through April), you can observe kite fighting (see page 56) on the Pramane Ground.

Horseracing enthusiasts can watch the horses run at the Royal Bangkok Sports Club on Saturdays and at the Royal Turf Club on Sundays. Other popular events for spectators include polo matches held at the Royal Bangkok Sports Club and soccer games at the National Stadium.

Golf is a popular recreational pursuit in Thailand, and you'll find ten 18-hole courses in the Bangkok area. Other golf courses include Bangkok Sports Golf Course and the Navy, Army, and Royal Thai Air Force golf courses.

CRUISING THE WATERWAYS

Thailand's waterways are a dominant feature of the country, serving as its highways and, in times past, its lines of communication. When King Rama I designed Bangkok, he included a complete network of *klongs* (canals). These klongs — manmade branches of the Chao Phraya River — formed the city's first streets.

Not until the 1840s, when horse-drawn carriages entered the city, did Bangkok start filling in some of its klongs, turning them into tree-shaded avenues. With the coming of the automobile, more and more klongs were filled to accommodate this new form of transportation. Though many of the original klongs are only remembered in street names, others still survive.

For a memorable look at Bangkok and its water people, take a waterway excursion. There are both organized tours and public transportation.

Short excursions

Bangkok's waterways offer visitors a kaleidoscope of water life. You'll see sampans powered by straw-hatted women, broad rice barges pulled by slow-moving tugs, and commuter-packed ferry boats propelled by noisy, chugging engines. Roaring between the slower moving traffic, are sleek, long-tailed motorboats, *hang yaos*, which leave sprays of water behind them. The hang yao's propeller is mounted on the end of a long movable shaft, making this boat ideal for use in shallow and deep water.

Not far from the city's modern office complexes, simple stilt houses line backwater klongs, and fishermen catch their evening meal from their front porches. People who live along these klongs shop at the floating market — a collection of sampans brimming with fruits, vegetables, and kitchen utensils.

Organized tour. On a 3-hour afternoon tour, you'll explore Bangkok's rural klongs by hang yao, stop at a farmhouse on the outskirts of the city, and then return to your departure point on a converted rice barge. The tour starts at 3 P.M. at the Prakanong Bridge on the south side of downtown Bangkok.

Exploring on your own. In addition to taking an organized tour, you can sample river and klong life on public transportation. Chao Phraya River express boats carry commuters between Krung Thon Bridge (Thanon Tok) and Krung Thep Bridge (Nonthaburi) daily between 6 A.M. and 6 P.M., stopping at some 30 wharves along the way. Sights you'll pass include Wat Arun, Wat Po, and the Grand Palace. There's also regular ferry service across the river between Wat Po and Wat Arun and between Tha Prachan and the Royal Barge Shed.

Hang yaos ply the waters of Bangkok's klongs on a semiregular basis, making stops at landings along the way. You'll find these fast-moving boats at Chao Phraya River wharves near the entrance to Klong Bangkok Noi and Klong Bangkok Yai. When you want to return, get off at the next landing and wait for a return boat. You'll find the most frequent boat service is during early morning and late afternoon.

For more information on klong and river public transportation contact the Tourism Authority of Thailand.

A Thai dinner cruise. A converted teak barge makes evening dinner cruises along the Chao Phraya River, departing from the Oriental Hotel pier at 6 and 8 P.M. Resplendent with carved and oiled teak paneling, polished bronze fittings, and handwoven fabrics, the *Tahsaneeya Nava* has a rich and traditional Thai look.

Aboard the "queens"

Still other members of Bangkok's cruise fleet are the *Oriental Queen* and *Orchid Queen*. Departing from the Oriental Hotel pier, these sleek, air-conditioned cruisers make day tours to Bang Pa-In, a departure point for the ancient ruins of Ayutthaya.

Two tours are available. On one tour you travel by cruiser up the Chao Phraya River to Bang Pa-In (see page 65) where you board an air-conditioned bus for Ayutthaya (see page 64). After touring the ruins, you return by bus to Bangkok. The other tour reverses the schedule, leaving the city by bus for Ayutthaya and Bang Pa-In. You board the boat at Bang Pa-In for the leisurely return trip to Bangkok.

Market, temple, and garden

One of the more popular day trips out of Bangkok travels by tour bus to Damnoen Saduak to visit a floating market on a rural klong, stops briefly at Nakhon Pathom to view its chedi, and concludes with lunch and a cultural show at the Rose Garden, a resort near Nakhon Pathom.

Floating market. Damnoen Saduak, located about 97 km/60 miles southwest of Bangkok, presents an alternate to the capital's crowded, commercial floating market. At the Damnoen Saduak boat landing, you board a hang yao for the short ride to the small side klong where the floating market is located.

Lining both sides of the klong are open-fronted shops,

built atop stilts, which sell a variety of household merchandise, clothing, and handicrafts. A series of boardwalks connect these buildings. From these boardwalks you have a good view of the river activity.

Dozens of sampans glide back and forth; from each, a vendor hawks wares to the shoppers above. Thai women, dressed in blue tunics and sarongs and shaded from the sun by conical straw hats, sell a diverse array of fresh fruits, vegetables, fish, poultry, and meats. The market's busiest time is from 7 to 10 A.M.

Nakhon Pathom. After the floating market, your trip continues by bus to a snake farm and then on to Nakhon Pathom, about 58 km/36 miles west of Bangkok. You can also reach Nakhon Pathom on your own by bus or car.

Dating from 150 B.C., Nakhon Pathom is historically important because here Buddhism was first introduced to Thailand. Thailand's largest and oldest pagoda, the 116-meter/380-foot Phra Pathom Chedi is located here. Resembling a huge inverted golden bowl, the chedi is covered with glazed gold and brown tiles brought from China. English-speaking tour guides, versed in the history of the chedi, are available for hire at the entrance.

During the early part of November, Buddhist devotees flock to Phra Pathom Chedi to pay homage to Buddha. The area takes on a carnival atmosphere complete with food vendors, fortune tellers, and musicians.

Rose Garden. A short distance east of Nakhon, 32 km/20 miles west of Bangkok, is the 20-hectare/50-acre Rose Garden Country Resort — the last stop on your full-day tour. The resort features a replica of a Thai village, where you'll see craftspeople at work spinning silk, painting umbrellas, and making pottery.

Included in your tour is a Thai cultural show, presented daily in the afternoon. The 90-minute performance, presented in a large thatch-roofed, open-air theater, includes demonstrations of a Thai wedding ceremony, Thai dances, cockfighting, Thai-style boxing, sword fighting, and the hauling of teak logs by elephants.

You can also take a half-day tour out of Bangkok to the garden or travel on your own by car or bus. Rose Garden visitors can stay overnight in a modern, high-rise hotel or in a traditional Thai-style bungalow. The resort, nestled in a gardenlike setting rich in fragrant rose bushes, features two floating restaurants, a lounge, swimming pool, shopping facilities, 18-hole golf course, tennis courts, and a river for water-skiing.

NEARBY EXCURSIONS

Within a day's travel from Bangkok are a capsulated version of Ancient Siam, ruins of an ancient city, a royal retreat, an infamous World War II bridge, a beautiful national park, and remnants of the Khmer civilization.

Many of these sights are included in half-day and full-day tours from Bangkok, or they can be visited independently.

Ancient Siam revisited

Rising from former rice fields southeast of Bangkok is a re-creation of Ancient Siam complete with temples,

Take your choice *of pool or sea at popular Pattaya Beach on Gulf of Thailand. Modern, air-conditioned hotels line white sand beaches; para-sailing is only one of many water sports.*

Boatman plies craft *along southern Thailand's west coast where rugged mountains, descending abruptly to meet shore, poke up again to dot Phangnga Bay.*

FESTIVAL TIME

In Thailand nearly every week brings holiday festivities. Many of the colorful festivals are religious in nature, associated with the life of Lord Buddha. Since some of the country's festivals are regulated by the lunar calendar, they occur on different days each year. When you arrive in Thailand, check with the Tourism Authority of Thailand or look in the Bangkok newspapers for current dates.

Here are some annual festivals and events.

New Year celebration. The Thais celebrate the new calendar year with parades, religious ceremonies, and private get-togethers. In Bangkok bells toll, gongs sound, and there are games and displays at Pramane Ground. The Chinese New Year is celebrated in February.

Phra Buddhabaht Festival. This 3-day February ceremony, held at the Shrine of the Holy Footprint in Sara Buri, features religious rites, dance-dramas, folk music performances, and a bazaar.

Makha Bucha. This event commemorates the meeting of Lord Buddha with 1,250 disciples. During the full moon in February, there are candlelight processions and worshippers fill Buddhist temples.

Chakri Day. Every year on April 6 ceremonies take place honoring the first king of the Chakri Dynasty, Rama I, who established Bangkok as the capital of the country.

Songkram Festival. This 3-day event, April 13–15, is Thailand's New Year holiday. Water and perfume are sprinkled on images of Buddha. Throughout the country, water throwing (meant to wash away evil spirits) becomes very energetic, often drenching bystanders. Bangkok celebrates with folk dancing, singing, and music.

Royal Ploughing Ceremony. A traditional May ritual, this ceremony begins the rice planting season. The King and Queen preside at Pramane Ground for the ritual ploughing and sowing of the furrows.

Visakha Bucha. Held on the full moon day in May, this event commemorates Buddha's birth, enlightenment, and nirvana. Candlelight processions herald the event.

Loi Krathong. In November the rivers, streams, lakes, and canals of Thailand glitter with thousands of tiny floating *krathongs* (banana leaves supporting flowers, candles, and incense).

The event honors Mae Khonka, goddess of the waters. There are special fairs at Golden Mount (Wat Sraket) in Bangkok and Phra Pathom Chedi in nearby Nakhon Phathom.

King's Birthday. December 5 is a national holiday; public buildings are illuminated and full dress ceremonies occur at the Grand Palace.

---

palaces, gardens, waterways, rural villages, and markets. This new Ancient City is about 33 km/21 miles (a 45-minute drive) from Bangkok. Half-day tours from Bangkok feature the Ancient City.

The 87-hectare/216-acre site is shaped roughly like the country of Thailand, and buildings are situated to correspond with their location (or former location) in the country. More than 50 major structures, representing architectural styles of different periods of Thai history, have been reproduced here. Some of them are copies of existing buildings; others are modeled after structures now in ruins or long since destroyed. Most are three-fourths of the original size, though some are smaller; a few are full-scale replicas.

Through the Ancient City's reproductions, you will perceive some of Ayutthaya's grandeur before it was destroyed. One of the complex's finest buildings is the model of Phra Sri Sanpetchaya, Ayutthaya's throne room. It sits majestically on an island—a white jewel gleaming under an ornate roof with curved eaves.

On the north side of the complex, Thais from various parts of the country live in villages composed of typical Thai houses. Craftspeople demonstrate such skills as silk weaving, woodcarving, and umbrella making.

The Ancient City is open daily from 8:30 A.M. to 6 P.M.

Ayutthaya, former royal capital

Ayutthaya, 88 km/55 miles (a 1½-hour drive) north of Bangkok, served as Thailand's capital for 417 years. Founded in 1350, the city soon became one of the most prosperous trading centers in Southeast Asia. The city, located on a bend in the Chao Phraya River, encompassed 13 square km/5 square miles of canals, palaces, temples, and magnificent houses. In 1767, the Burmese invaded and destroyed all this grandeur.

Today, much of Ayutthaya remains in ruins—a crumbling mass of walls, brick foundations, pillars, archways, and chedis. Some of the city's ruins have been restored; others are being excavated by archeologists.

In spite of their deteriorated state, many of the wat complexes are still being used by worshippers. You'll find ancient Buddha images inside and outside these places of worship. Wats of interest include Wat Phra Monkhon Bophit with its huge, seated bronze Buddha; Phanan Choeng Temple with its golden Buddha image; and Phu Khao Thong Temple with its 80-meter/262-foot chedi.

Ayutthaya's Chao Sam Phraya National Museum has 13th and 14th century Buddha images, 6th and 7th century stonecarvings, and carved wooden door panels from the 17th and 18th centuries. Still another sight to see is the old Elephant Kraal. This expansive area, enclosed by a teak log fence, was used to capture wild elephants.

From Bangkok you can reach Ayutthaya by car, bus, train, or boat. A full-day tour by bus and boat (see page 62) includes Ayutthaya and nearby Bang Pa-In. Once at Ayutthaya, you can explore the widespread ruins by taxi or bus. Many of the major sights are near the Royal Palace.

Bang Pa-In, royal retreat

The former summer home of Thai kings, Bang Pa-In, lies downriver from Ayutthaya. It was built in the 1600s as a hideaway for Ayutthaya's royalty. After Ayutthaya was destroyed, Bang Pa-In was left unused until the reign of King Mongkut in the 1800s. Now it is used mainly for special royal parties and state visits.

The Royal Palace complex contains a wide variety of architecture: Greek-style buildings, a replica of a Peking Palace, a small Gothic church (really a wat), a Renaissance-style hall, and, in the middle of a lake, a Thai-style pavilion.

Bang Pa-In is a part of Ayutthaya tours out of Bangkok. You can also reach it by car, train, or boat. The palace complex is open daily except Monday from 8:30 A.M. to 3 P.M.

Bridge on the River Kwai

Made infamous by a book and movie of the same name, this seldom-used, one-track bridge is located near the town of Kanchanaburi about 129 km/80 miles (a 2-hour drive) northwest of Bangkok. Though the film was shot in Sri Lanka (Ceylon), the subject of the World War II story was the Allied soldiers, prisoners of the Japanese, who perished in building this "death railway" bridge across the River Kwai.

(Continued on page 67)

ROUNDING UP THE ELEPHANTS

Elephants have been important to the Thais for centuries. Throughout Thailand's history, many invaders have been repelled by warrior kings mounted on battle-trained elephants. The Thai national flag and Thai coins used to have an elephant figure on them, and many old monasteries are decorated with carved elephant figures.

Today, the elephant is a worker, friend, and even pet to the Thai people. In many parts of Thailand, you'll see these massive beasts hauling teak logs from the forest as they have for several hundred years. They are carefully trained for this task at the Young Elephant Training Center at Lampang south of Chiang Mai (see page 70). The special training takes 4 to 5 years.

If you're in Thailand the third week of November, you'll have chance to see the country's massive pachyderms in action during the annual "Elephant Roundup" that takes place in Surin, about 451 km/280 miles northeast of Bangkok. Visitors see how elephants are captured and trained and then watch some compeling performances: elephant races, obedience and agility demonstrations, a tug of war between a mature elephant and 100 men (the elephant usually wins), an elephant soccer match, and a war-elephant parade. Other roundup activities include colorful folk dances and elephant rides.

A specially chartered, all-sleeper express train with dining car transports visitors from Bangkok to Surin in 8 hours for this event. For more information on the Elephant Roundup, contact the Tourism Authority of Thailand. Since the event is a popular one, it's wise to book early.

Handpainted *floral sprays decorate jewel-toned silk umbrellas from handicraft shop at Borsang, tribal village outside Chiang Mai.*

Baby elephant *tags along with family for day of hauling logs. Working elephants still bring out teak from forests in northern Thailand.*

. . . Continued from page 65

Major points of interest near Kanchanaburi include the bridge (reconstructed since the war), the Allied cemeteries, and Neolithic burial sites anthropologically linking Thailand and Malaysia.

Out of Bangkok, you can take 1 to 4-day tours to the Kanchanaburi area. The State Railway of Thailand runs 1-day excursions to Kanchanaburi on weekends. You'll find accommodations at the River Kwai Village, about 80 km/50 miles from the bridge. Hotel amenities include air conditioning, a restaurant, and a swimming pool.

Khao Yai National Park

This jungle recreation area is 209 km/130 miles (a 4-hour drive) northeast of Bangkok. You cross a broad plain of rice fields, then climb through wooded green hills toward the distant mountains. The park's southern entrance is located at the small town of Khao Yai, between Lop Buri and Nakhon Ratchasima.

Narrow, jungle-shaded roads twist through the park's 2,168 square km/837 square miles. Dense teak forests cover the mountainsides. Hiking trails follow mountain streams and penetrate the jungle. Often you'll see native birds and animals. On weekends, the park is very popular with Bangkok residents.

Park facilities include overnight accommodations, a restaurant, wildlife viewing towers, swimming lagoons, and a golf course.

You can reach Khao Yai National Park on your own or on a full-day tour out of Bangkok.

Pimai ruins

Thailand's version of Angkor Wat— the Pimai ruins — are located 306 km/190 miles northeast of Bangkok (5 hours by road) near the town of Korat. The Khmers, who occupied the Korat area during the 11th century, are believed to have built Pimai between 1002 and 1049. Pimai was linked to Angkor, the Khmer Empire's capital, by road and prospered until the 13th century.

The Pimai ruins give testimony to the great skill of Khmer builders and artisans. You can still see the towers and beautifully carved stone galleries, traces of the stone walls that framed the 5-square-km/2-square-mile city, the wall's four gateways, and the restored main temple, a fine example of classical Khmer architecture. Pimai's open-air museum displays pieces of Khmer art, including ancient statues, friezes, and lintels.

There are 1 and 2-day tours to Pimai from Bangkok. You'll find overnight accommodations at Khao Yai National Park and Nakhon Ratchasima.

In addition to Pimai, there are Khmer ruins at Lop Buri, 153 km/95 miles (a 3-hour drive) north of Bangkok. You can see them on a full-day tour out of Bangkok.

GULF OF THAILAND RESORTS

Along the coast of the Gulf of Thailand south of Bangkok are several scenic beach resorts, with tiny offshore islands and coral reefs within exploring distance. The two best known— Bangsaen and Pattaya— are on Thailand's eastern Chonburi Peninsula, within easy reach of Bangkok.

Bangsaen, a local retreat

Bangsaen Bay, with its calm blue waters and white sandy beaches dotted with swaying palm trees, is a favorite holiday retreat for Bangkok residents. It's only 105 km/65 miles (a 1½ -hour drive) southeast of the capital city.

Popular resort activities include swimming, sunbathing, water-skiing, sailing, and fishing. The challenging 18-hole Bangphra Golf Course, nestled among wooded hills that overlook the Gulf of Thailand, is only a 15-minute drive from Bangsaen.

Most visitors stay at the Bangsaen Beach Hotel, which includes a main building and an additional 150 bungalows in a garden setting of lawns, trees, and flowers. The hotel complex is separated from the bay and beach by a palm-lined promenade.

Pattaya, a bustling resort

Within the last 15 years, Pattaya has grown from a quiet fishing village to a booming resort, catering to guests from around the world. Located 137 km/85 miles southeast of Bangkok, Pattaya can be reached in about 2½ hours by road. There's convenient air-conditioned bus service between Bangkok and Pattaya several times daily, or you can travel to the resort on a 1 or 2-day tour out of Bangkok.

Large modern hotels including the Asia Pattaya Beach, Holiday Inn, Pattaya Palace, Nipa Lodge, Ocean View, Orchid Lodge, Regent Pattaya, Royal Cliff Beach, Royal Garden, Siam Bayshore, Tropicana, Chiang Inn Pattaya, and Wongse Amatya offer a full range of resort facilities. There are opportunities for tennis, horseback riding, golf, boating, fishing, water-skiing, scuba diving, yachting, para-sailing (using a parachute), and pedal boating. Guests have a wide choice of restaurants, supper clubs, and other night spots.

Just offshore from Pattaya are several islands, ideal for picnicking, swimming, snorkeling, or coral viewing. They can be reached by speedboat or fishing boat.

From Pattaya you can take a day trip into the teak forests near Sriracha to watch working elephants. Another excursion is the overland tour to the sapphire mines in Chanthaburi, 177 km/110 miles away, with stops en route at waterfalls and botanical gardens.

EXPLORING SOUTHERN THAILAND

Southwest of Bangkok, Thailand consists of a narrow section of land that reaches south to the border of Malaysia. It's an area of rubber plantations, coconut groves, rice fields, tin mines, dense jungle, lush mountain scenery, tumbling waterfalls, quiet fishing villages, and numerous pristine beaches washed by crystal clear waters. With the Gulf of Thailand on its east side and the Andaman Sea on its west, this section of Thailand offers sun and sea lovers more than 2,000 km/1,243 miles of mainland coast and hundreds of offshore islands to explore.

Though off the main tourist track, southern Thailand is easily accessible. The highway south from Bangkok to the Malaysian border (about 1,328 km/825 miles) is completely paved. Thai Airways has service to several areas of interest, and the express trains of the State Railway of Thailand are excellent. A number of Bangkok tour operators run luxury coach service between Bangkok and Malaysia and/or Singapore.

The weather varies between the east and west coast of southern Thailand. The east coast's rainy season is from October through January. The west coast's rainiest months are late May through September.

Down the east coast

Thailand's National Route 4 runs along the peninsula's eastern coast, paralleling the Gulf of Thailand for about 322 km/200 miles. Separating this coastal area from the Peninsula's west coast is a chain of mountains that parallels the Burmese border. (Thailand shares the northern section of the peninsula with Burma.)

Along Route 4 are several interesting attractions including an antique palace, Thailand's oldest beach resort, and beautiful offshore islands.

Phetchaburi. Located 126 km/78 miles southwest of Bangkok, Phetchaburi is noted for the palace of King Mongkut, built on a hill overlooking the town. A cobbled road, lined with thick tropical foliage, winds up the hill past roadside stables, a guardroom, and a guest hall. The palace, built in neoclassical style and surrounded by colonnaded arcades, is open to the public. The palace affords a good view of the town and its temples, as well as vast rice fields and palm groves.

Worth visiting are the area's limestone hills riddled with caves, some of which have Buddhist shrines. The largest is Khao Luang, best visited at midday when a shaft of sunlight illuminates the cave.

You can reach Phetchaburi by car, train, or bus from Bangkok. Though Phetchaburi has no adequate accommodations, you can find a place to stay 106 km/66 miles to the south in Hua Hin.

Hua Hin. Thailand's oldest beach resort is Hua Hin, 231 km/144 miles southwest of Bangkok. Once a small fishing village, Hua Hin became Thailand's summer social center when King Rama VII built his summer palace here in 1920. Thailand's present king still spends part of the year in Hua Hin, and prominent Bangkok families maintain spacious beach bungalows along the shore.

Hua Hin offers visitors miles of white sandy beaches, an 18-hole seaside golf course, tennis courts, and good fishing opportunities. Fishing is an important industry in the area. Just north of town at the port, you'll see fishing nets drying in the sun against a colorful backdrop of anchored fishing boats.

Overnight guests can stay at the Railway Hotel complex; some of the rooms in the main building and in the bungalows under the trees overlook the sea. The town also has a number of small hotels and bungalows. Enjoy Thai and Chinese-style dishes, which include seafood specialties, at Hua Hin's small restaurants.

From Bangkok, you can reach Hua Hin by train, car, or bus.

Prachuap Khiri Khan. Only 55 km/34 miles down the coast from Hua Hin, Prachuap faces a large, semicircular bay edged by miles of unspoiled beaches. Nearby are wooded mountains and lacy waterfalls.

Prachuap's nearness to Hua Hin makes it ideal for a day's outing of swimming, sunbathing, and picnicking. You can even hire a boat to cruise to one of the offshore islands or go fishing. Accommodations are limited in Prachuap.

You can reach Prachuap, 287 km/178 miles southwest of Bangkok, by road or rail.

Samui islands. This enchanted group of islands, lying off southern Thailand's east coast 780 km/485 miles south of Bangkok, offers a refuge of quiet and solitude. Coconut palms sway above white sand beaches and warm blue waters.

On the main island of the group, Samui, are coconut plantations, deserted beaches, and rock rimmed coves. Samui's port and principal town, Tambon Ankthoug, has four small hotels; the most popular is the Sea View.

Samui Island is accessible from Bangkok by a 12½-hour rail trip (on the southern express from Bangkok to Surat Thani) and a boat ride across the gulf. Surat Thani is south of Chumphon off National Route 41.

West coast touring

At the small, provincial town of Chumphon, National Route 4 turns west, twisting across wooded mountains to Ranong on the western coast and continuing south to the Malaysian border. The highway follows the coast but at times jogs inland to parallel mountain streams. Once inland, you catch glimpses of waterfalls and vast rubber plantations. Like the east coast, the west coast of the peninsula offers visitors quiet retreats and beautiful sandy beaches.

Ranong. This provincial town, its buildings marked by an architectural style mixing Chinese and Portuguese influences, is located 564 km/350 miles southwest of Bangkok.

The Hotel Thana, in a hilly, wooded setting a few minutes south of town, is the best place to stay. From the hotel you can make interesting side trips into the mountains, to nearby beaches, and to offshore islands.

South of Ranong you'll see tin mines—some still active, others long abandoned.

Phuket Island. Plans are on the drawing board to develop this scenic haven, 917 km/570 miles southwest of Bangkok, into one of Thailand's major beach resort areas. However, at the moment, Phuket Island is still a relatively undeveloped island of thickly forested mountain slopes, tumbling waterfalls, sprawling rubber and coconut plantations, offshore coral reefs, and miles of unspoiled beaches—a haven for skin divers, sunbathers, and seekers of peace and solitude.

Lying off the west coast, 538-square-km/208-square-mile Phuket Island is connected to the mainland by a bridge at its northern end. The major population hub, Phuket City (45,000 people), is a few miles inland from the Andaman Sea on the southern end of the island. Here you'll find restaurants, accommodations, and good shopping for pearls and shells.

Among the island's historic sights are three wats: Wat Cha-Long, an ancient temple with a sacred image; Wat Pra-Thong, with a Buddha image half-buried in the ground; and Wat Monkon, containing a beautiful golden

Buddha image dating from the 13th century.

Phuket accommodations include the Patong Beach Hotel, Pearl Hotel, Phuket Island Resort, Phuket Merlin Hotel, and Thavorn Hotel. Hotels not on the beach offer transportation to nearby beaches. All the hotels have swimming pools and restaurants. The Phuket Island Resort also has facilities for golf and tennis.

Thai Airways has daily service to Phuket. You can also reach the island by bus, car, or train (as far as Surat Thani where you transfer to a local bus). There are also 4-day tours out of Bangkok to Phuket.

Phangnga Bay. The most popular sightseeing tour from Phuket Island visits nearby Phangnga Bay, an area of spectacular mountain scenery, unusual rock formations, and caves. Journeying around the beautiful bay in a hang yao, you'll glide past strange rock outcroppings eroded by the water and covered with trees and thick vegetation. Crescents of white sand fringe some of these small mountain islands; others rise abruptly from the water in sheer cliffs. Caves and grottos abound, some cutting deeply into the mountain islands. One cave—Thum Lod—is large enough for boats to enter.

Sights on your bay excursion may include some of the islands, such as Phingkan, made famous because it was used as the setting for the James Bond movie *The Man with the Golden Gun.* Still another fascinating island is Khao Tapu, marked by its slender, eroded rock pillar. Built on stilts in the bay is the Muslim village of Panyi. Though fishing is its main concern, the village has a small school, open-air shops, and even flocks of quacking ducks swimming beneath the houses. Many tours make this village their luncheon stop.

At the tip of Thailand

Just north of the Malaysian border are the region's two largest cities: Hat Yai, with a population of 240,000, and Songkhla, with a population of 850,000. The influences of nearby Malaysia can be seen in this part of Thailand. You'll find domed mosques rather than Buddhist temples, and many people speak Bahasa Malaysia. You can reach the area by road, rail, or air.

Hat Yai. Only about 80 km/50 miles north of the Thailand/Malaysia border, Hat Yai is a popular city with Malaysians who are attracted to its mountain scenery, shopping opportunities (especially for Thai silks and cottons), and active night life. On the last Saturday and Sunday of each month, visitors can see Thai-style bullfights (between two bulls) starting at 10:30 A.M.

The town has some 50 hotels including the Nohra, President, and Sukhontha.

Songkhla. Though Hat Yai is an important rail and commercial center, it's Songkhla—about 32 km/20 miles northeast—that proves more interesting. Facing the Gulf of Thailand, Songkhla abuts Samila Bay and salt-water Songkhla Lake, a body of water covering almost 1,295 square km/500 square miles.

Nearby sights include fishing villages, a quaint lakeside early-morning fish market, and the beautiful white sand beaches of Pinetree and Samila, usually deserted except for local picnickers and swimmers. Day ex-

cursions take visitors to Bird Island, famous for its birds' nests collected for Chinese soup; to the top of 610-meter/2,000-foot Mount Tang Kuan; offshore to visit Cat and Rat islands; and to a potters' village.

You can travel between Hat Yai and Songkhla by long distance taxi. You'll find accommodations at air-conditioned Samila Beach Hotel, offering such amenities as a restaurant, swimming pool, tennis courts, and a 9-hole golf course.

INTO THE NORTH

The cool, forest-covered mountains of northern Thailand provide a pleasant change from the hot, flat rice fields surrounding Bangkok. It is here Thailand had its beginnings. Migrating from China, the first Thais settled here and began to lay the foundations of Thai culture.

The heart of northern Thailand is Chiang Mai, the country's second largest city and center of traditional folk arts and crafts. The people of this city are warm and friendly; the pace is leisurely, a contrast to the feverish activity of Bangkok.

To the northeast of Chiang Mai is Chiang Rai, with its interesting hill tribes. Southeast of Chiang Mai are the ruins of Thailand's first capital—Sukhothai.

City of roses

Because flowers—especially roses—grow profusely in its temperate mountain climate, Chiang Mai is called "City of Roses." Residential flower gardens present a riotous array of colorful roses, hydrangeas, and rhododendrons.

Chiang Mai sits on a wide mountain plateau over 305 meters/1,000 feet above sea level. Surrounding the city are soaring mountains including 1,676-meter/5,500-foot Mount Doi Pui and 2,591-meter/8,500-foot Mount Doi Inthanon. The city's cool mountain climate makes it an ideal retreat from the heat of Bangkok. The coolest months are October through January, when daytime temperatures are in the 20s°C/70s°F and nights even cooler.

To get to Chiang Mai, you can make the 805-km/500-mile journey by bus or private car, on an overnight rail trip, or on the 50-minute flight north from Bangkok. Chiang Mai's international airport is also served by international air carriers from the Orient. Bangkok tour operators run several-day tours to Chiang Mai.

Accommodations include the Chiang Inn, Poy Luang Hotel, Railway Hotel, Rincome Hotel, Sri Tokyo Hotel, Garnet Chiang Mai, and Hotel Suriwongse. Most are air-conditioned and have restaurants. Local Chiang Mai transportation includes taxis, *samlors* (three or four-wheeled mini-vehicles), and buses.

A note of history. Though its early history is obscure, ancient records indicate that Chiang Mai was founded in 1296. It was the seat of an independent kingdom called Lanna until the mid-16th century, when Burmese war lords conquered the city. Chiang Mai then became the center of a tug of war between Burma and Thailand.

Built nearly seven centuries ago as a fortress protected by walls and a moat, Chiang Mai still retains intact portions of the original walls and moat. The old walled city stands on the western bank of the Mae Ping, separated by the river from the newer part of the city on the eastern bank.

Wat wandering. Chiang Mai's streets are interspersed with some 117 wats. Many of them reflect both Thai and Burmese architectural influences. Ancient and weathered, they have colored tiled roofs stepped in two or three levels that overhang low teak side walls. Most of them house huge Buddha images covered with gold leaf.

Four important wats are located within the walls of the ancient city. Wat Phra Singh, built in 1345, is the city's largest temple and an important monastery housing the most venerated Buddha image in the north. The wat is on Lamlap Road.

Chiang Mai's oldest temple, Wat Chiang Man, dates from 1297. Located on Ratchaphakhinai Road, Wat Chiang Man was formerly the home of Chiang Mai's founder, King Mengrai. It houses an important Buddha image covered with precious stones.

Wat Chedi Luang, one of Chiang Mai's most important monasteries, contains an 8-meter/26-foot-high Buddha image. This wat, on Phra Poklao Road, was once the home of the famous Emerald Buddha, now housed in Bangkok's Wat Phra Keo.

Wat Suan Dork, built in 1383, contains Buddha relics and ashes of members of the Chiang Mai royal family. The wat's viharn contains a 500-year-old bronze Buddha image. Wat Suan Dork, located on Suthep Road, is the site of important religious ceremonies during the Songkram Festival in April (see "Festival Time," page 64).

Outside the walls are several other important temples: Wat Papao, built in the Burmese style; Wat Mahawan, with fine woodcarvings; and Wat Chiang Yuen, with its chedi decorated with dragons, tigers, and Chinese porcelain motifs. Wat Phrathat Doi Suthep sits on the lower slopes of Mount Doi Pui, 25 minutes from Chiang Mai. You reach the wat—at an altitude of 1,067 meters/3,500 feet—on a tortuous road. The view from the top of the wat makes the mountain drive and the climb up the wat's 300 steps all worthwhile.

Other sights. Though Chiang Mai itself offers many attractions, you should travel into the countryside to visit tribal villages, experience rural Thai life, and see some of the north's industrious craftspeople. Local tour companies conduct half-day and full-day excursions into the surrounding countryside. Take along a sweater; temperatures can be cool at higher elevations. Jungle trips and cruises on the Salween and Mekong rivers are also available.

On a full-day tour from Chiang Mai, you penetrate the deep jungle on the upper slopes of Mount Doi Pui to see Poo-Ping Rajanive, winter palace of Thailand's royal family. Fridays through Sundays, except when the family is in residence, you can stroll through gardens lush with flowering plants. The surrounding mountain vista is breathtaking. This tour also includes a stop at Wat Phrathat Doi Suthep.

Traveling to Lampang, 164 km/102 miles south of Chiang Mai, you can visit a unique Young Elephant Training Center. Visitors see some elephants being bathed, others being trained to drag, push, and stack enormous teak logs with their trunks and tusks.

Young elephants are brought to the training center at age 4 or 5. They spend the first month getting to know their *mahouts* (keepers and drivers). They then continue their lessons for 4 years, learning how to kneel, pick up things, and drag, pull, push, and carry heavy logs. Northern Thailand's teak forests supply the world with much of its teak lumber.

Other Lampang attractions include numerous old temples decorated with mother-of-pearl, ivory inlay, or cut glass. Two of the more famous temples are Wat Phra Keo Don Tau and Wat Phra Sang, located on opposite banks of the Wang River. You can tour Lampang in quaint horse-drawn carriages.

Other tours include visits to the Chiang Dao Caves north of the city, and to 483-meter/300-foot-high Nam Tok Mae Klong waterfall, considered one of Thailand's most scenic. Doi Intanon National Park is also located south of Chiang Mai.

Crafts and music

Chiang Mai is the center of traditional Thai handicrafts. On city excursions and countryside tours, you can see craftspeople at work. Chiang Mai is also the home of northern folk entertainment.

Handicraft treasures. Handspun and handwoven Thai silks and cottons of the Chiang Mai region are made in a variety of designs, weights, and colors. Other handicraft items include Thai celadon pottery and native pottery, silver items, teak woodcarvings, costume dolls, temple bells, lacquerware, paper umbrellas, embroidery, and basketry.

Craftspeople at work. Different areas of Chiang Mai are dedicated to different cottage industries. You'll find silversmiths, lacquerware artisans, and woodcarvers along Wua Lai Road and near Chiang Mai Gate. On road No. 108, about 5 km/3 miles from town, is the center of pottery production, and on road No. 107 are most of the celadon potters.

Colorful parasols are created and handpainted in Borsang, east of Chiang Mai. Just beyond, in Sankamphaeng, girls weave Thai silk. Lamphoon, 24 km/15 miles south of Chiang Mai, is also noted for its silk weaving. Farther south is Pasang, known for its handwoven cotton fabrics.

Local tours feature visits to craft villages.

Cultural performances. While in Chiang Mai don't miss attending a *khantoke*, a northern-style Thai dinner, served at low tables and featuring a variety of spiced dishes accompanied by glutinous rice. At the Old Chiang Mai Cultural Center the khantoke includes music and dance by costumed hill-tribe members. Old Chiang Mai Cultural Center also has shops—designed like Thai-style houses—selling handicraft items of Chiang Mai. These include woodcarvings, cotton, and silk.

Some Chiang Mai hotels also feature khantokes on a weekly basis.

Hill tribespeople

Amid the hills and mountains surrounding Chiang Mai live tribespeople who differ from Thais in culture, costume, language, and tradition. The six main tribal groups are the

In Sukhothai, *grinning boy seems about to be plucked by hand of giant golden Buddha. Sparkling flakes are gold foil, pressed on by worshippers.*

Like mother, *like daughter—Meo woman from Thai hamlet of Doi Pui teaches child art of embroidery. Hill tribes from mountains of Chiang Mai differ from Thais in culture, costume, language, tradition.*

THAI BOXING — A HIGH-KICKING SPORT

The high pitched wail of Javanese flutes and the resounding beat of drums signal the start of a Thai boxing match. From their respective corners, the gloved fighters appear. They first kneel and pray and then do a slow motion dance mimicking the fighting gestures of Thai box-

ing (elbow jabs, hooks, and kicks). Each fighter tries to prove his prowess to the other during this dance.

Then the true battle begins. The boxer in blue trunks unleashes a high kick. "Thump!" The blow is quickly followed with a series of snapping elbows, thrusting knees, and short jabs to the body, head, thighs, and kidneys. The fighter in the red trunks responds with his own form of jabbing and kicking. The 3-minute rounds seem to last an eternity, the 2-minute breaks flash by, and five rounds prove physically damaging and tiring to even the most skilled fighters.

Thai boxing dates from the medieval ages when bows and arrows, and swords and pikes decided a battle. For close-in fighting, the military devised a method of turning an unarmed soldier into a human battering ram, using all his skills and contact points to disable an enemy. In 1560, King Naresuen, captured by the Burmese, regained his freedom by defeating that country's best fighters with his Thai boxing skills. Upon returning to Thailand, the king became a hero, and Thai-style boxing a national sport.

Throughout the country, 1,500 training camps teach Thai boxing. In Bangkok you can attend boxing matches Monday through Saturday at either Ratchadamnoen or Lumpini stadiums.

Meo, Karen, Akha, Lisu, Lahu, and Yao; each tribe has its own culture.

You can visit a Meo village on a day trip from Chiang Mai. Until recently, the Meo tribespeople cultivated opium poppies; now they grow rice, corn, coffee, and lichees. They also raise various domestic animals and make handcrafted souvenirs including handsome silver bracelets, belts, neck rings, bowls, boxes, and candlesticks.

The Meo people, who believe in spirits, live in primitive thatch-roofed wooden huts. They dress in black shirts and trousers decorated and trimmed in red or white. Their wealth is displayed in the form of silver neck rings and silver ornamented clothing.

Before visiting a village, you may wish to tour the Tribal Research Center at the University of Chiang Mai. The center, established in 1965, is involved with the socio-economic research of the country's hill tribes and includes a museum of tribal culture. You'll also want to explore the university's 202-hectare/500-acre campus with its golden-roofed buildings, lake, gardens, and trees.

Side trip to Chiang Rai

Chiang Rai, deep in the mountains at the very northern tip of Thailand, lies not far from the borders of both Burma and Laos. The area's major attraction is its colorful hill tribes.

Located near the town of Mae Chan, 29 km/18 miles north of Chiang Rai, is a group of tribal villages, part of the Mae Kam Community Development Center set up to train the hill tribespeople in various agricultural practices.

Area villages includes those of the Yao and Akha. Yao women are noted for their colorful turbans trimmed with fanciful red ruffs. Akha women wear black dresses decorated with vivid embroidery, bright beads, and silver coins; they also wear heavy silver jewelry. Other villages includes those of the Lisu, Karen, Muhsur, and Meo.

Like the hill tribespeople around Chiang Mai, the hill people of Chiang Rai are noted for their beautiful handicrafts, including intricate embroidery work, basketware, and silver jewelry. You can shop for these items at the Hill-Crafts Foundation in Chiang Rai.

Still another interesting side trip out of Chiang Rai takes you to Chiang Saen. Here, on the banks of the Mekong River, you'll see the ruins of King Mengrai's 13th century capital.

You can reach Chiang Rai by bus or air from Chiang Mai. There's also air service from Bangkok. Chiang Rai accommodations include the Vieng Inn, Suk Nirand, Krung Thong, Ruang Takhon, and Rama. All are air-conditioned.

Ruins of an ancient city

The ruins of Sukhothai, Thailand's first capital, lie 603 km/ 375 miles north of Bangkok (366 km/227 miles southeast of Chiang Mai). During the 13th century, this ancient city was the center of Siamese civilization. The center of power switched to Ayutthaya in the mid-14th century, and eventually Sukhothai became a ghost town.

Until 30 years ago, the ruins of this once great city were hidden by jungle growth. Excavation of the crumbled palaces and temples is now in progress, and the scattered pieces of many re-constructed. In old Sukhothai's Ramkanbaeng National Museum, you'll see bronze and stone Buddhas and ceramic artifacts of the Sukhothai periods.

Headquarters for a visit to Sukhothai is the town of Phitsanulok, an hour's drive from the Sukhothai ruins. Here you'll find accommodations at the Hotel Amerintr Nakorn. From Bangkok or Chiang Mai, you can reach Phitsanulok by air, bus, and rail service.

Phitsanulok has several interesting wats. Other area sights include a national park.

KNOW BEFORE YOU GO

Here are some practical details to help you plan your trip to Thailand.

Entry/exit procedures. You may visit Thailand for up to 15 days without a visa, but you need a valid passport and proof of onward passage such as an airline ticket. For longer stays, apply for a tourist visa at the nearest Thailand consulate or embassy.

You will need an international health certificate showing inoculation against yellow fever if you are coming from an infected area. The U.S. Public Health Service recommends you have typhoid, tetanus, and gamma globulin shots. If your plans include travel beyond the urban areas, check with your doctor for antimalarial treatment. There is a malaria risk.

On departure, you pay an airport tax of 50 baht.

Customs. Visitors are allowed to bring into the country, duty-free, 200 cigarettes, 250 grams (8 ounces) of tobacco, one liter of wine or liquor, five rolls of film, and one still or one movie camera.

Currency. The rate of exchange of the Thailand baht ("baat") is B20 to U.S. $1.

Health conditions. Although tap water is chemically treated in Bangkok, it's best to drink only bottled water. Drink boiled water in the countryside.

Tipping. Most hotels and restaurants add a 10 percent service charge. Additional tipping is optional; if done, light tipping is the rule. Baggage porters at airports and train stations can be tipped lightly. Taxi drivers do not expect tips, but may be given one if they are especially helpful.

Time. The time difference between the U.S. west coast and Thailand is 15 hours. When it is noon Sunday in Bangkok, it is 9 P.M. Saturday in San Francisco.

Weather and what to wear. Thailand's weather is tropical — with cool, hot, and wet seasons. But persistently high humidity is the greatest climatic reality. In Bangkok the best time to visit is November through February, the so-called "cool, dry season," when daytime temperatures average 29°C/84°F. The hot and humid weather lasts from March through June, when temperatures soar to 38°C/100°F. The rainy season starts the middle of May and lasts through October. During this period, monsoon rains are sporadic, often torrential, and usually occur in the afternoon and evening.

Chiang Mai, at a higher elevation than Bangkok, is cooler and a little less humid during the hot season. Sea breezes temper the heat and humidity at the beach resorts.

Because of the hot, humid climate, you will be most comfortable in lightweight clothing. Bring a sweater or jacket for air-conditioned buildings and the cooler climate of the north. Some restaurants and supper clubs require men to wear ties. Other useful items include mosquito repellent, an umbrella, sun hat, sunglasses, and suntan lotion.

Some local customs. When sitting opposite someone, it is rude to cross your legs or to point your foot at them. The head is considered the most sacred part of the body, so don't pat anyone (including children) on the head. Any show of disrespect for the Royal Family, who is shown great respect by the Thais, can have severe consequences — even a possible jail sentence.

For more information. Get in touch with the Tourism Authority of Thailand (TAT), 4 Ratchadamnoen Avenue, Bangkok, Thailand or their U.S. offices: 3440 Wilshire Boulevard, Suite 1101, Los Angeles, CA 90010, and 5 World Trade Center, Suite 2449, New York, NY 10048. In Thailand there are regional tourist offices in Chiang Mai, Kanchanaburi, Nakhon Ratchasima, Pattaya, Phuket, and Songkhla.

Sunset's rays *illuminate golden dome and striped minarets adorning magnificent Ubudiah Mosque in Kuala Kangsar, north of Kuala Lumpur.*

Tropical palms bend *toward warm waters of Batu Ferringhi shores, only one of many tropical beaches edging protected coves around resort island of Penang.*

MALAYSIA

A land of many contrasts — sun-drenched beaches
and cool mountain highlands, noisy cities and quiet
villages, Moorish mosques and Chinese temples,
modern shopping arcades and colorful country markets

Malaysia greets its visitors with a kaleidoscope of contrasting images: gold-domed mosques and white-steepled Anglican churches; peaceful *kampongs* (villages) built on stilts, and bustling cities projecting sky-piercing high-rises; humid rain forests thick with tangled vegetation, and cool highlands neatly planted with tea.

Contributing to this impression of contrast are the people — a cultural and racial mix of Malays, Chinese, Indians, Europeans, and Malaysian tribespeople. With this diversity of people comes a diversity of life styles, religions, festivals, languages, foods, and modes of dress.

Early European colonists left their mark in Malaysia. In Malacca, salmon-colored buildings such as Christ Church and the Stadthuys stand as reminders of Dutch occupation. A single gate, though, is all that remains of a Portuguese fort that guarded Malacca prior to the Dutch invasion. The mark of British rule can be seen in the colonial-style government and commercial buildings found in cities throughout the country.

You can visit Malaysia simply by driving the few miles across the Johore Causeway from Singapore, but there's so much more: Kuala Lumpur, the capital; the resort island of Penang and numerous other offshore island retreats; historic Malacca; the hill stations; the rural east coast with its miles of quiet, unspoiled beaches; and the Borneo states of Sabah and Sarawak.

SOME GEOGRAPHIC FACTS

Bathed by the Indian Ocean and South China Sea, Malaysia is really two separate geographic areas. Peninsular Malaysia occupies the lower half of the Malay Peninsula, while the states of Sabah and Sarawak are 966 km/600 miles to the east, across the South China Sea on the island of Borneo. It's surprising, then, that the total land area of this far-flung nation covers only 329,748 square km/127,823 square miles—slightly larger than the state of New Mexico.

Only a few degrees north of the equator, Peninsular Malaysia borders Thailand on the north and is joined by the Johore Causeway to the island nation of Singapore on the south. On the island of Borneo, east of Peninsular Malaysia, Sabah and Sarawak share borders with Indonesia's Kalimantan.

A lush, verdant land

Except for the alluvial plain along the west coast of Peninsular Malaysia, most of the country is mountainous. Malaysia's highest peak is Sabah's Mount Kinabalu, rising 4,101 meters/13,455 feet. On the peninsula, 2,190-meter/7,184-foot Gunung Tahan is the highest peak.

Adding to the scenic beauty of the rugged country are rivers and streams that course through steep gorges and plummet over cliffs in magnificent waterfalls. Where these rivers slow to meet the sea, tangled mangrove swamps have developed. The three largest rivers on the Malay Peninsula are the Perak, emptying on the west coast into the Strait of Malacca, and the Pahang and Kelantan, draining into the South China Sea on the east coast. The numerous rivers of Sabah and Sarawak are often the principal means of transportation and communication in these two states.

Tropical forests. Dense tropical forests, estimated to be nearly 100 million years old, cover three quarters of Peninsular Malaysia and most of Sabah and Sarawak. While the rest of the Northern Hemisphere shivered through the Ice Age, the jungles of Malaysia remained untouched. Today's jungles harbor a triple canopy of growth. Tall banyan trees soar to over 30 meters/100 feet. Beneath their protective cover grow shorter trees, lacy ferns, twisted lianas, and fragile orchids.

Abundant plant life. The country has more than 15,000 species of plants, many of them decorated with colorful blooms. Pride of the country is the hibiscus, Malaysia's national flower, blossoming in red, pink, white, yellow, or orange. Still other flowers providing bursts of color are the morning glory, yellow allamanda, and bougainvillea. Malaysia even has the largest flower in the world — the rafflesia. This unusual red flower has no true leaves or stem, but grows on a woodlike vine on the forest floor. Tulip trees and yellow flame trees add warm color to country roads and town parks, while flame of the forest trees add a splash of orange-red to the hillsides.

Elusive wildlife

Wildlife abounds in the rain forests of Malaysia. A list of Malaysia's animals is impressive: tigers, leopards, panthers, elephants, bears, tapirs, deer, wild oxen, crocodiles, wild goats, squirrels, rhinoceroses, and orangutans (the last two nearly extinct because of overhunting). Most animals mainly roam the deep, remote jungle areas, though, and aren't easily seen by the casual visitor. Those you'll probably hear (if not see) during jungle walks are monkeys and gibbons.

Over 130 species of snakes inhabit both the jungle and the sea. All of the sea snakes and 16 varieties of the land snakes — including the king cobra and pit viper — are poisonous. Sharing the trees with some of the snakes are frogs and lizards and flying lemurs.

Most of the country's 600 species of birds hide amid the luxuriant jungle growth. Those easily spotted or heard include orioles, swallows, mynas, magpies, and robins.

THE PATH OF HISTORY

Malaysia's history dates back more than 40,000 years to a time when Stone Age people dwelled in gigantic limestone caves in Borneo. Archeological findings indicate that these first residents were Negroid with characteristics similar to those of the Aborigines of the Philippines, Indonesia, New Guinea, and Australia. Descendants of these primitive people, still living in Malaysia's Perak Hills and other isolated areas, show little change from their Stone Age level of civilization.

Ancestors of Malaysia's present-day Malays, however, were Mongoloids who migrated into the area from southwest China between 2,000 and 250 B.C. Possessing a more advanced civilization than the first cave dwellers, these immigrants—called Proto-Malays—lived in wooden houses, cultivated crops, and domesticated their animals. Later arrivals — known as Deutero-Malays — came to the Malay Peninsula and contributed a knowledge of metalwork to the Proto-Malay culture. Eventually these two groups merged, and their descendants are the Malays of today.

Foreign influences

During the early Christian era, trading ships sailing between India and China brought still other people to the Malay Peninsula. These early Indian and Chinese traders explored the coastal area for tin and jungle products. Some stayed to set up trading posts.

In A.D. 200 gold was discovered on the Malay Peninsula and the rush began. Soon fortune-hunting seafarers from China, India, and as far off as Rome flocked to Malaysia's shores in search of riches. Those that stayed married local women. About this time, Hinduism was introduced to the native aristocracy and, by A.D. 500, Hindu river states had emerged, each ruled by a Malay sultan and his court.

In the 8th century, the entire Malay Peninsula fell under the domination of the Sailendra Hindu rulers of the Sri Vijaya kingdom (based in Sumatra). This government lasted until the 14th century when the peninsula came under the influence of the Majapahit empire of Java.

Malacca Sultanate. A Sri Vijaya prince, fleeing the Majapahit rule, founded Malacca in 1403. Because of its location on the Strait of Malacca at the crossroads between China, Southeast Asia, and India, the town soon became a rich seaport and hub of shipping and trading activity. The town's opulent sales pavilions were filled with both aromatic and visual delights—cloves from Molucca, perfume from Persia and Arabia, sandalwood from Timor, and cloth from India and China. The prince and founder of this wealthy port soon became Sultan of Malacca. During this period Islamic merchants and missionaries traveling the Malaccan trade route brought their religion with them. Malays began to convert to Islam, which eventually became the national religion of Malaya following its independence from Britain in 1957.

The golden age of the Malacca Sultanate lasted only about a century. The Portuguese, craving the riches of Malacca for themselves, attacked in 1511. The Sultan's massive war elephants and fighting men armed with poisoned arrows were no match for Portuguese cannons. But Portuguese domination of Malacca lasted little more than a century. In 1641, the Dutch besieged Malacca, took control, and dominated the area for the next 180 years.

The British presence. In 1786 Britain obtained permission for a naval base in Penang, and established its first foothold in Malaya. In 1824 the Treaty of London defined Dutch and British spheres of influence in Southeast Asia. Malacca was transferred to the British; the Dutch East Indies (Indonesia) remained under the Dutch.

Two years later the British East India Company incorporated Penang, Malacca, and Singapore as the Straits Settlement, later making them a British Crown Colony. Sarawak and Sabah (both in northern Borneo) became British protectorates in 1882. During the next three decades, British suzerainty was extended over the remaining states of the Malay Peninsula; a series of treaties induced all the Malay states to accept British advisers.

World War II. In December, 1941, the Japanese Army landed at Kota Bharu on the northern Malay Peninsula. In tanks and on bicycles they proceeded southward down the peninsula to Singapore, seizing the city in March, 1942. Many of Malaya's residents were imprisoned or sent to

Siam to work on railway construction. The Japanese occupied Malaysia and Singapore until 1945.

An independent country

After the war, the British continued to administer the country amidst economic uncertainties and terrorist attacks by Communist guerilla fighters. In 1948 a state of emergency was declared that lasted until 1960.

Politically, the British attempted to establish a union of Malay states to replace the prewar arrangements and to dissolve the former colony. Resentment against the union plan resulted in Britain's establishment of the Federation of Malaya.

Final independence of the Federation of Malaya was granted on August 31, 1957. Singapore, Sabah, and Sarawak joined the Federation to form the nation of Malaysia in 1963. Two years later, Singapore seceded from the Federation and became an independent republic.

Today, Malaysia is a constitutional elective monarchy, composed of 13 states: Sabah, Sarawak, and 11 other states of the former Federation of Malaya. Hereditary Malay sultans who rule nine of the Malay states elect the *Yang di-Pertuan Agung* (supreme head of state) from their royal group within the Conference of Rulers. The Conference also includes the nonroyal governors of Penang, Malacca, Sarawak, and Sabah. Upon election, the royal monarch relinquishes his functions as ruler of his own state, but remains head of that state's Muslim religion.

National executive power is vested in a prime minister and cabinet appointed by the Yang di-Pertuan Agung. A 58-member Senate has 32 members appointed by the Yang di-Pertuan Agung and 26 elected members. The 154 members of the House of Representatives are elected by popular vote.

MALAYSIA TODAY

Malaysia is a multiracial society. Nearly half the country's 13 million inhabitants are Malays and other indigenous people, including the aboriginal Orang Asli and tribespeople of Sabah and Sarawak (Ibans, Bidayuhs, Kadazans, Bajaus, Muruts, and Kedayans). Malaysia's Chinese number about 4 million, Indians and Pakistanis account for another million, and Eurasians and Europeans — mostly British — make up most of the balance.

Diversity of life style

This racial and cultural mix generates a fascinating variety of life styles. Many Malays, preferring the quiet of a country *kampong* (village) to the bustle of the city, live in wooden houses perched on stilts and tend the rice fields nearby. Other Malays, though, have ventured to the cities for jobs. Many Chinese and Indians live in the cities in two-story shophouses. Many of them work as merchants or moneychangers.

In contrast, many tribespeople of Sarawak live in longhouses with thatched roofs, and grow hill rice and pepper. Blackened skulls hanging from rafters present a grim reminder that once these were a head-hunting people. Still more removed from civilization are the Orang Asli — aboriginal tribespeople descended from early cave

dwellers — who live in the deep jungle and hunt for their food with blowpipes and poison spears.

Dress. Malaysia's varied cultures are also reflected in the colorful clothing worn by her people. Western influences have affected clothing styles, especially in the cities, but you can still find Malay village women dressed in the fitted *kebaya* (tunic) and skirtlike *sarong*. Malay men often dress western-style, in shirts and trousers, though on festive days they may wear the Malay shirt, called a *baju*. Some men also wear sarongs. Indian women drape themselves in flowing *saris*; and Chinese women sometimes wear the tightly fitted *cheong-sam*, slit to the thigh, or *sam foo*, a loose tunic and trousers.

Religion. Islam is the state religion of Malaysia, and most Malays are Muslim. Five times daily in towns throughout Malaysia, the wail of the muezzins calling faithful Muslims to pray can be heard from mosque minarets.

Islam isn't the only religion in Malaysia, though. The country enjoys complete religious freedom. Most of Malaysia's Chinese adhere to Buddhism, though many are Christians or Taoists. Most Malaysian Indians are Hindus. The indigenous tribespeople are mainly animist, though many have embraced Islam or Christianity.

Backbone of tin and rubber

Malaysia's economy was built on tin and rubber. The country is the world's leading supplier of both. Tin mining, mainly in the Kuala Lumpur area, is one of Malaysia's oldest industries, dating back to A.D. 900. With the advent of the auto age, large rubber plantations were created. Today, neat rows of high-yield rubber trees dot much of Peninsular Malaysia's western coastal plain.

Still other Malaysia acreage is planted in oil palms, coconut trees, pineapple, pepper, and rice.

TRIP PLANNING AIDS

Located in the heart of Southeast Asia, Malaysia is easily reached from points around the world. (It's about 8,000 air miles from the west coast of the United States to Malaysia.) Some 20 international airlines, including Malaysian Airline System (MAS), fly into Malaysia. The main entry point is Kuala Lumpur's international airport at Subang, a 25-minute drive from Kuala Lumpur. Kota Kinabalu and Penang also have international airports. In addition, a number of cruise ships and cargo/passenger liners include Malaysian ports on their Southeast Asia and Orient itineraries.

Posh and simple accommodations

Malaysia's accommodations suit a range of tastes and pocketbooks. You'll find modern, first-class hotels in the larger cities and in mountain and seaside resort areas.

Elsewhere rest houses owned and operated by the government provide inexpensive accommodations. Reservations should be made in advance for rest house accommodations; for more information contact the Tourist Development Corporation of Malaysia in Kuala Lumpur (see page 105).

(Continued on page 78)

. . . Continued from page 77

Other accommodation possibilities include staying at a village longhouse (see page 102) and camping in a national park alpine hut. The country also has youth hostels and YMCA and YWCA facilities.

Local transportation tips

Malaysian Airline System (MAS) provides frequent daily air service to Malaysia's major towns. For the budget-minded, there are special discount night flights between Kuala Lumpur and Penang, Kota Kinabalu, Johore Bahru, Kota Bharu, and Kuching.

Taking the train. The Malayan Railway's main line — between Butterworth Station (opposite Penang Island), Kuala Lumpur, and Singapore — features day and night express train service in air-conditioned, first-class coaches. At Butterworth Station, you can board the International Express for Bangkok.

There is also daily train service between Gemas, in Peninsular Malaysia's mountainous interior, and Tumpat, on the east coast north of Kota Bharu, with continuing service into Thailand. In Sabah, rail service is offered by the government-operated Sabah State Railways.

Tourists with passports can purchase special 10 or 30-day rail passes either in Malaysia or Singapore. Check with the local tourist office or railway station for information.

Traveling by bus. Main cities and towns on Peninsular Malaysia are connected by a well-developed network of roads. Long-distance, air-conditioned express buses travel these roads on a regular basis. There's also daily bus service between Kuala Lumpur and Singapore. Because of less-developed roads on Sabah and Sarawak, bus service in parts of these areas may be provided by four-wheel-drive vehicles.

Malaysia's major cities also have regular local bus service.

A taxi ride. You can arrange to share a taxi ride between Malaysian towns. It's faster than a bus ride and only slightly more expensive, so many local people travel this way. In Malaysia's main towns, you arrange for a "share taxi" at special, long-distance taxi stands where drivers call out their destinations. When they have a full load (four persons), they depart.

In addition to these long-distance taxis, all large towns have *teksis* (taxis) that you can hire on a per-mile tariff or by the hour. These teksis are required to have meters. For short trips around town, the bicycle-powered trishaw provides a leisurely way to view local sights.

Driving a car. Peninsular Malaysia's extensive road system makes it one of the best areas of Asia to tour by rented car. Main roads on the more developed west coast can be congested with both auto and truck traffic; but the less developed east coast is ideal for a leisurely driving excursion. Roads are not as well developed in Sabah and Sarawak.

The country has over a half dozen rental car agencies with offices in major towns. Some agencies allow you to drive a car from Singapore into Malaysia and leave it without a drop charge.

Traffic moves on the left side of the road in Malaysia. You'll need an international driver's license.

Tours. Malaysia's tour operators offer a wide variety of tours, from overnight trips out of Kuala Lumpur to several-week excursions covering the entire country. There are tours of Penang and Peninsular Malaysia's west coast; cultural trips featuring craft villages along the east coast; tours to Sabah and Sarawak with a stay at a longhouse; and wildlife safaris into one of Malaysia's national parks.

Ethnic food specialties

Food in Malaysia reflects the multiracial mix of its people. You'll find an interesting range of Malay, Chinese, Indian, and western cuisines.

Favorite local dining spots are the outdoor food stalls. At dusk in towns throughout Malaysia, clusters of food stall carts appear in parking lots, along public esplanades, and in market places. The carts arrive completely equipped with charcoal cooker, wok, food, folding tables, and chairs. Walking from stall to stall, you can gather a delicious meal of Malay, Chinese, and Indian specialties.

Local dishes. *Satay* — Malaysia's national dish — is a food stall specialty also found in restaurants. Slender skewers of mutton, beef, or chicken are grilled over a charcoal fire then served with a spicy peanut sauce. Accompanying this is *ketupat* (steamed rice wrapped in coconut palm leaves) and sliced cucumbers and onions.

Malay curries, based on beef, chicken, fish, or vegetables, have a distinctive flavor derived from such ingredients as coconut, chile pepper, and lemon grass. Indian restaurants offer spicier curries of mutton and vegetables served on banana leaves and eaten with the fingers. Chili crab with its hot chili sauce, and *ipoh kwei-teow* — chicken soup with prawns, chicken pieces, fine noodles, and spring onions — are other local favorites.

The entertainment scene

Malaysia's diverse cultures have left an impact on the entertainment scene as well as the cuisine.

Throughout the country, you can enjoy colorful, graceful Malaysian folk dances that tell stories of local life. Many of these folk dances reflect strong foreign influences. The *ronggeng* with its catchy rhythm and many variations is believed to have come from the early Portuguese. Arabian traders perhaps influenced the slow, graceful moves of the *hadrah*. Malaysia's dances are usually accompanied by the music of a traditional orchestra which includes a *gendang* (two-headed barrel drum), a *tawak-tawak* (deep-rimmed gong), and a *rebab* (three-stringed spike fiddle).

On the east coast of Peninsular Malaysia, you might see a *wayang kulit* (shadow play). One of the most ancient forms of theater in Southeast Asia, this play is normally performed in villages during festivals or on special occasions. Visitors to the east coast may also see a wayang kulit performance during an organized tour of the area.

In various towns during Chinese festivals, or on special occasions, touring road shows give open-air presentations of Chinese opera, with its heavy grease paint and brilliant costumes.

Crowds throng *giant stairway leading to Batu Caves, sacred shrines deep in limestone cliffs. Thousands of Hindu faithful make annual pilgrimage during Thaipusam.*

Muslim ladies *in traditional Malaysian attire form vivid contrast to austere modern walls of National Mosque in Kuala Lumpur.*

Handicraft treasures

Malaysia is blessed with a wealth of skilled artisans who produce a wide range of handicrafts. Many are part of small cottage industries in villages along Peninsular Malaysia's east coast. Touring this area, you'll see them at work (see page 100).

You'll find handicraft items for sale throughout Malaysia in hotel shopping arcades, department stores, handicraft centers, and at local public markets. Fixed prices prevail in larger stores, but expect to bargain in smaller shops and at the public markets.

You can purchase colorful batik fabric in lengths, or fashioned into shirts, dresses, ties, tablecloths, and napkins. Another famous Malaysian fabric is *kain songket* or "cloth of gold." On a hand loom, gold or silver thread is woven with silk thread to create a richly decorated length of cloth usually made into a formal sarong.

Malaysia's pewter consists primarily of locally mined tin. Fine pewter articles range from candlesticks to tea sets. Similar items are also manufactured locally out of brass or silver. Web-fine, silver filigree jewelry is another beautiful craft product.

Other handicrafts include pottery in a variety of designs and colors, mats and purses woven from pandanus leaves, and woodcarvings made by the tribespeople of Sabah and Sarawak and the Orang Asli.

For duty-free items, you'll find shops in both Kuala Lumpur and Penang.

What not to buy. The United States restricts the import of products made from animals and plants it has officially listed as endangered or threatened. Even if these items are sold abroad, it does not mean that they will be allowed into the United States. For more information on this, see page 9.

Store hours. Open hours vary from town to town. Take note that Friday is a weekly holiday in the states of Perlis, Kedah, Kelantan, Trengganu, and Johore; Sunday is observed as the day of rest in other states.

For the sports enthusiast

Malaysia offers the visitor a variety of opportunities to enjoy sports, both as spectator and participant.

Sports to watch. Looking more like ballet than karate, *bersilat* is Malaysia's traditional art of self-defense. Moving to the sounds of an orchestra, carefully trained youths perform slow, graceful moves, yet deliver lightning-fast punches, chops, and kicks. Once a form of combat, bersilat today is considered an artistic form of physical exercise and is often demonstrated at weddings and other ceremonial occasions. Exhibitions are most easily seen on Peninsular Malaysia's east coast.

Throughout Malaysia, young people play *sepak raga*. The object of the game: to kick a ball—made of rattan strips — high into the air and to keep it there for as long as possible by passing it from player to player. The ball can be propelled by feet, thighs, shoulders, and heads, but not by hands. With fast footwork and high jumping, the ball can sometimes be kept in the air for hours.

Still other popular pastimes are kite flying and giant top spinning (see page 89), badminton, soccer, basketball, cricket, and rugby.

Recreational activities. In Malaysia you can play golf in the highlands at a place like Fraser's Hill or in the lowlands, perhaps at the Royal Selangor Golf Club near Kuala Lumpur. Highland play features temperate weather from dawn to dusk, whereas lowland golf courses are best played in the early morning or late afternoon to avoid the noonday heat. Malaysia has over 50 golf clubs, and visitors can arrange to play at many of them. For more information on golf, write the Honorable Secretary, Malaysian Golf Association, c/o Royal Selangor Golf Club, P.O. Box 1051, Kuala Lumpur.

Tennis enthusiasts have over 500 courts (lawn, asphalt, or cement) to choose from in Malaysia. Many major hotels have tennis facilities. For more tennis information contact the Secretary, Lawn Tennis Association, 11, Jalan 6/18, Petaling Jaya.

Malaysia is crisscrossed by a system of rivers and streams well stocked with fish. In addition, waters off Peninsular Malaysia's east coast teem with game fish: Indian trout, catfish, sailfish, barracuda, sea bass, and black marlin. The best time for fishing is May through October.

COSMOPOLITAN KUALA LUMPUR

Clean, green Kuala Lumpur is set against a backdrop of jungle-clad hills often hidden by billowing white cumulus clouds. Familiarly known as KL, this city of a million people is located about halfway down Peninsular Malaysia near the west coast.

The most vivid quality of this 100-year-old city is its heterogeneous mixture of races, religions, and cultural influences. It includes a fascinating mélange of ornate temples, Moorish mosques, and sleek Western skyscrapers; Malay girls in sarong-kebayas and sari-draped Indian women; and food stalls offering Chinese noodles, Malaysian satay, and Indian curry.

A federal territory similar to Washington, D.C., Kuala Lumpur is Malaysia's administrative capital and rapidly growing center for education and industry. Yet it maintains a leisurely pace. It's a pleasant, spacious city with wide streets and plenty of well-tended parklands.

Getting your bearings

City center lies to the east of the Klang River. To the west are the parklands and attractions of Lake Gardens. New multistory banks and commercial office buildings are rising north and east of city center, and to the south is old Chinatown with its two and three-story shophouses.

You'll find that Kuala Lumpur can be easily explored on foot or by taxi or minibus. The best—coolest—times for strolling are early morning or late afternoon.

City maps are available at your hotel or a tourist information center (see "The Essentials," page 85). When reading a map, note that *Jalan* is Malay for "street."

Mosques: Moorish and modern

Minareted mosques—Islamic temples of worship—dominate city skylines throughout Malaysia. Most mosques,

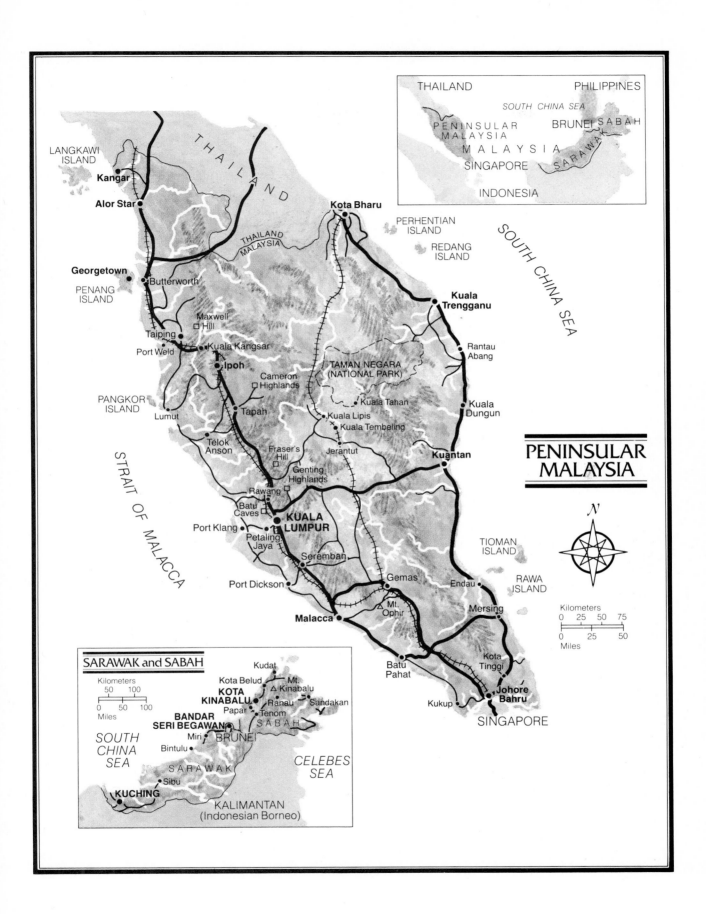

PENINSULAR
MALAYSIA

Main map labels:

LANGKAWI ISLAND
Kangar
Alor Star
THAILAND
THAILAND MALAYSIA
Georgetown
PENANG ISLAND
Butterworth
Maxwell Hill
Taiping
Port Weld
Kuala Kangsar
Ipoh
PANGKOR ISLAND
Cameron Highlands
Lumut
Tapah
Telok Anson
Fraser's Hill
Genting Highlands
Rawang
Batu Caves
Port Klang
KUALA LUMPUR
Petaling Jaya
STRAIT OF MALACCA
Seremban
Port Dickson
Gemas
Mt. Ophir
Malacca
Batu Pahat
Kukup

Kota Bharu
PERHENTIAN ISLAND
REDANG ISLAND
SOUTH CHINA SEA
Kuala Trengganu
Rantau Abang
TAMAN NEGARA (NATIONAL PARK)
Kuala Tahan
Kuala Lipis
Kuala Tembeling
Jerantut
Kuala Dungun
Kuantan
TIOMAN ISLAND
RAWA ISLAND
Endau
Mersing
Kota Tinggi
Johore Bahru
SINGAPORE

Inset map (top right):
THAILAND
PHILIPPINES
SOUTH CHINA SEA
PENINSULAR MALAYSIA
BRUNEI SABAH
MALAYSIA
SARAWAK
SINGAPORE
INDONESIA

Inset map (bottom left): SARAWAK and SABAH
Kilometers 50 100
Miles 0 50 100
SOUTH CHINA SEA
Kudat
Kota Belud
KOTA KINABALU
Mt. Kinabalu
Ranau
Sandakan
Papar
Tenom
SABAH
BANDAR SERI BEGAWAN
Miri
BRUNEI
Bintulu
SARAWAK
CELEBES SEA
Sibu
KUCHING
KALIMANTAN (Indonesian Borneo)

N

Kilometers
0 25 50 75
Miles
0 25 50

Priest packs *trunk of car outside pink Christ Church in center of historic Malacca. Tombstones inside church tell tales of hardship.*

Cameron Highlands *offers respite from tropical heat. Cool hill station was formerly British planters' retreat.*

including Kuala Lumpur's Masjid Jame, are of traditional Moorish design with gently curving domes.

One exception is KL's National Mosque with its contemporary shapes and precise lines, but even this mosque has a traditional minaret. In times past, muezzins had to climb the spiral staircases of these minarets or towers five times daily to call Muslims to prayer. Today, loudspeakers and microphones in many mosques have made the job easier, and the arduous climb is no longer necessary.

Masjid Jame. Located at the junction of the Klang and Gombak rivers, the city's oldest mosque (built in 1909) is surrounded by graceful palm trees. The pale-blue, onion-shaped domes and minarets banded in red and white create fairy tale images from the *Arabian Nights*. It's open to visitors from 9 A.M. to noon daily.

National Mosque (Masjid Negara). Southwest of Masjid Jame, and in dramatic contrast with it, is an ultramodern place of worship that seems to float up out of its 5 hectares/13 acres of fountained pools and vast lawns. It's the National Mosque which, since its opening in 1965, has become a landmark with its grand yet simple lines executed in concrete, marble, and tile. Dominating the main dome is a graceful spire that rises 75 meters/245 feet. Everywhere, tranquil pools and well-polished floors mirror the mosque's enormous pillars and graceful angles. Fountains twinkle with sunlight, and wherever you stand the sky and trees are visible.

Visiting hours are from 9 A.M. to 6 P.M. Saturday through Thursday and 2 to 6 P.M. on Friday.

Other noteworthy buildings

Still other Kuala Lumpur structures illustrate the blend of traditional and modern architecture.

Of Moorish design. Diagonally opposite the sleek, modern National Mosque is KL's Railway Station. It's a prime example of Kuala Lumpur's Moorish-style architecture with its intriguing profusion of pinnacles, pointed domes and towers, porticos and arches, and nooks and crannies. The Railway Station was built in 1910—about 24 years after the first train puffed into town from Port Klang.

The federal Secretariat, on Jalan Raja in the heart of town, is another example of elaborately designed Moorish architecture, complete with a 40-meter/130-foot central clock tower. Across the cricket green from the Secretariat, is the Tudor-style Selangor Club.

Wisma Loke. Former home of Towkay Loke Yew, one of Malaysia's rich Chinese merchants, this house (built in 1904) includes sweeping archways, jade ballustrades, and a Chinese "moongate." Standing in the shadow of high-rise buildings on Jalan Medan Tuanku just off Jalan Tuanku Abdul Rahman, Wisma Loke was the first home in KL to be powered by electricity. Today, it's a music conservatory and art gallery.

Parliament House. Malaysia's Senate and House of Representatives meet in this very modern, white rectangular building at the northernmost edge of Lake Gardens. An adjacent 18-story tower houses governmental offices. When Parliament is in session, visitors may obtain passes to the public gallery by telephoning the parliamentary secretary at 27781 or 28231.

Some museums

Two museums in Kuala Lumpur feature the life style of Malaysia's people and the art they create.

Muzium Negara (National Museum). Located on Jalan Damansara at the south entrance of Lake Gardens, this museum deserves a visit of at least several hours. Its well-designed displays depict Malaysia's history, culture, and natural history—a synopsis of Malaysian life both past and present.

The current museum building, completed in 1963, is one of the most stunning buildings in Kuala Lumpur. Based on traditional Malaysian architecture, it consists of high, sloping roofs and walls decorated with two huge mosaic murals illustrating Malaysia's history and crafts.

Within the building, displays further tell the story of Malaysia. There are shadow play exhibits, artifacts of the Orang Asli, ruby-studded daggers worn by rich sultans, royal dance costumes, musical instruments, and an old Chinese Malaccan house complete with bridal chamber.

The National Museum is open daily from 9 A.M. to 7 P.M., except on Fridays, when it is closed between noon and 2:30 P.M.

National Museum of Art. On Jalan Ampang, northeast of the central district, this gallery of art has an excellent collection of works by Malaysian artists. Its exhibition hall frequently displays work by international artists as well. The museum is open Monday through Sunday from 10 A.M. to 6 P.M. It, too, is closed on Friday from noon to 2:30 P.M.

Shopping around

Since Kuala Lumpur has no specific shopping district, you'll have to move around a bit to do your purchasing. But half the fun of shopping in KL is discovering its little shops with their fascinating goods — local and international. Local bargains include batik, silver, pewter, woodcarvings, and pottery.

You'll find a host of intriguing shops on the city's main streets — Jalan Tuanku Abdul Rahman, Jalan Raja Chulan, Jalan Ampang, Jalan Tun Perak, and Jalan Bukit Bintang. On narrow Jalan Petaling in Chinatown, you'll find Chinese porcelain, jade figurines, antiques, and jewelry. While in the area, be sure and visit the See Yeah Chinese Temple — the city's oldest — tucked in among the shops and alleys off Jalan Rodger near the Central Market.

Department stores, hotel arcades, and shopping centers also make shopping a pleasure.

In search of handicrafts. KL's Tourist Development Corporation's handicraft center—a series of chalet-style shops —lies off Jalan Raja Chulan, halfway up the green slopes of Bukit Nanas (Pineapple Hill). Once you climb the flight of stairs to the seven center shops, you'll find all kinds of goods for sale: batik, pandanus and mengkuang woven-leaf products, woodcarvings, ceramics, and copper, silver, and brass works.

For Selangor pewter, visit the Pewter Showroom and

Demonstration Center, housed in a 1930s-style Malaysian bungalow at the junction of Hot Spring Road and Jalan Genting Klang. There you can watch demonstrations of pewter production, and shop for items ranging from beer mugs to coffee and tea sets. Most tours to the KL countryside visit this center.

At Kampong Batik near the Batu Caves, you can see demonstrations of how batik fabric is made. Silver artisans reveal their skills at Syarikat TABA in Selayang Baru 14 km/9 miles north of Kuala Lumpur.

Local markets. A visit to one of the local markets gives you a glimpse of what KL citizens buy and how they go about it. The Sunday Market (held on Saturday nights) on Jalan Rajah Muda Musa in Kampong Bharu, a Malay section of town, offers pictures on bamboo, batik paintings and cloth, and tempting Malaysian food, all under bright lights. The Chinese night market on Petaling Street offers everyday items like clothing and shoes and a good sampling of local produce. For the hungry, it also has food stalls stocked with noodles and Chinese soup.

Outdoor pleasures

There's a feeling of spaciousness in Kuala Lumpur, due in large part to the city's many parks. KL has 33 of them, ranging from tiny, grassy havens on corner lots to expansive Lake Gardens. Not far from the city, still other parklands give you a taste of Malaysia's jungle.

The city and its environs also offer many places where visitors can pursue recreational activities or watch others do so.

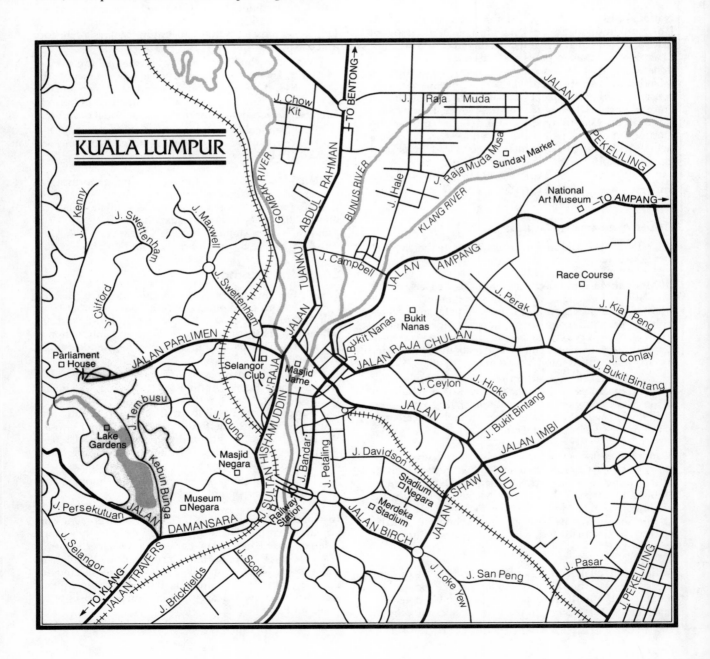

Lake Gardens. Largest of Kuala Lumpur's public greens, Lake Gardens—on the west side of town—includes neat flower beds, natural forest, and twin lakes surrounded by rolling manicured lawns. Local residents love to stroll the park's many paths, enjoy weekend picnics on its lawns, and row boats on the calm lakes. On Sundays, shows in the park's pavilion feature everything from local popular singers to groups performing traditional folk dances.

At the north end of the park, you can see the National Monument, a massive sculpture honoring Malaysia's free-dom fighters. The monument's seven bronze figures — created by the designer of Washington, D.C.'s Iwo Jima Memorial, Felix W. de Weldon — is surrounded by a fountain-studded pool.

Bukit Nanas (Pineapple Hill). This jungle-clad hill sits in the center of urban Kuala Lumpur. You can journey to the top of the 229-meter/750-foot slope either by bubble-canopied gondola or chairlift. Either way, a view of the city will greet you, both en route and at the top. Once you reach

THE ESSENTIALS/**KUALA LUMPUR**

Malaysia's capital city of Kuala Lumpur (KL) is well endowed with all the comforts a traveler could wish.

Getting there

Kuala Lumpur is served by air, rail, bus, and sea transportation.

Air. International service to and from KL is by Malaysian Airline System (MAS) and foreign flag carriers. Domestic flights by MAS link KL with other major Malaysian cities and towns. The international airport at Subang is about a 25-minute taxi ride from downtown. Buy taxi coupons from special airport booths.

Rail. Train routes link KL with Singapore, Thailand, and Peninsular Malaysia towns.

Bus. Buses provide service between KL and Singapore, and between KL and other Peninsular Malaysia towns.

Sea. Cruise ships and cargo/passenger ships call at Port Klang, 43 km/27 miles west of Kuala Lumpur.

Accommodations

Many of Kuala Lumpur's hotels are concentrated along Jalan Sultan Ismail and other streets south of the Selangor Turf Club. Larger hotels include the Equatorial, Federal, Holiday Inn Kuala Lumpur, Kuala Lumpur Hilton, Merlin, and Regent of Kuala Lumpur.

Smaller hotels and motels include the Fortuna, Furama, Majestic, Malaysia, Shah's Village Motel, Southeast Asia Hotel, and the motel and cottages at Mimaland Tourist Complex.

All these hotels are air-conditioned, with a full range of services.

Getting around

Taxis and mini-buses are good ways to travel around Kuala Lumpur. Taxis are metered or you can arrange ahead to hire them by the hour. Rental cars are also available.

Tours

Half and full-day tours take in city sights, countryside offerings, Fraser's Hill (see page 92), Port Dickson (see page 91), and Malacca (see page 86).

Dining out

You'll find a wide variety of Asian and European foods in KL's major hotels and city restaurants.

Malay dishes. Bintang Restoran, 44, Jalan Sultan Ismail; Chempaka, at the Holiday Inn; Yazmin, at the Ampang Shopping Complex.

Indian food. Akbar, Medan Tuanku; Bilal, 33, Jalan Ampang.

Chinese food. Imperial Room, Malaysia Hotel; Kum Leng, 119, Jalan Pudu; The Pines, 297, Jalan Brickfields.

Food stall dining. For local food and atmosphere, make an evening visit to the city's many food stalls, usually open between 6 P.M. and 1 A.M. It's a fun way to sample *satay* and other Malaysian favorites at a modest cost. You might try Jalan Campbell stalls or the Sunday Market (on Saturday night) on Jalan Raja Muda Musa.

Other cuisines. KL also has restaurants featuring continental, Korean, Japanese, and Taiwanese food as well as several fast-food restaurants selling hamburgers and French fries.

Night lights

Other than the evening markets, night life in KL is pretty much limited to hotel nightclubs. They provide music for dancing, and, in some cases, floor shows and cabarets. The young at heart will find discotheques at major hotels.

Cultural shows of native or local music and dance are held on a regular basis at Yazmin in the Ampang Shopping Complex and at the Paddock in KL's Hilton.

More information

There is a tourist information center on Jalan Tun Perak and at the Subang International Airport. *Kuala Lumpur—Penang This Month*, available at hotels, offers helpful activity hints plus informative maps.

the top, you'll find jungle paths through a forest reserve and a restaurant.

The lifts operate Tuesday through Sunday from 9 A.M. to 5:30 P.M. You can catch a gondola off Jalan Raja Chulan, and a chairlift off Jalan Ampang.

Mimaland. Located 18 km/11 miles northeast of KL on the road to Kuantan, this park contains gardens of native plants and jungle trails. The 40 hectare/100-acre complex offers recreational facilities for swimming, boating, hiking, golf, hunting, and fishing. A shopping arcade sells local arts and handicrafts.

Templer Park. Just 23 km/14 miles north of Kuala Lumpur on the north-south trunk road on the way to Rawang, you can experience a touch of Malaysia's jungle while hiking well-marked paths. Templer Park offers a pleasant retreat of tumbling cascades, towering trees, abundant wildflowers, colorful birds and butterflies, and cool lagoons and pools for swimming.

National Zoo and Aquarium. You can view a cross section of Malaysia's wildlife at this zoo, 13 km/8 miles southwest of KL on the road to Ulu Klang. Over 24 hectares/60 acres of green gardens, complete with a small lake, provide a pleasant home for brightly plumed birds, wild buffaloes, tapirs, crocodiles, gibbons, pythons, and tigers.

An aquarium contains tropical and fresh-water fish. Children can enjoy elephant, camel, and pony rides. The zoo and aquarium are open from 10 A.M. to 6 P.M. daily except Wednesdays.

Fun in the sun. The Royal Selangor Golf Club, east of city center, invites visitors to play at its two 18-hole and one 9-hole golf courses. Just make prior arrangements with the club secretary. Located on an extensive flat plain in a parklike setting, the golf club is the scene of the annual Malaysia Open Golf Tournament every March.

The 18-hole Subang Royal Golf Club and the Kuala Kubu Golf and Country Club with its 9-hole course also welcome visitors.

Sports to watch. Merdeka (Independence) Stadium, east of the Railway Station, is the site of KL's track, soccer, hockey, and other outdoor sports events. In this huge earthen amphitheater, Malaysians celebrated their independence on August 31, 1957.

Nearby Stadium Negara (National Stadium), on Jalan Davidson, is KL's indoor sports stadium featuring basketball and badminton contests. It also houses concerts and variety shows.

On weekends, cricket matches are held at the Selangor Club's green across from the Secretariat, and horses are raced at the Selangor Turf Club.

Other nearby attractions

There are several other attractions easily explored from Kuala Lumpur, either on your own or on an organized countryside tour.

Batu Caves. Just 13 km/8 miles north of KL on the road to Ipoh, a 122-meter / 400-foot limestone outcrop features a series of vast caverns. The largest contains the Hindu

shrine of Lord Subramaniam. It's a 272-step climb to this cavern and its shrine. A funicular railway helps make the journey easier.

Each February, the shrine at Batu Caves is the scene of a festival to celebrate Thaipusam, one of the most important events of Malaysia's Hindu community. On festival morning thousands of devout Hindus mount the 272 steps to the shrine cave. Penitents — their cheeks pierced with metal skewers — climb the steps in a painless, trancelike state. They bear *kavadis* — elaborate, flower-decorated frames supported by long silver spikes that pierce their backs and chests. At the shrine, priests remove these burdens and bless the penitents.

The caves are open to visitors from 9 A.M. to 4:30 P.M. weekdays except Wednesdays.

Rubber plantations and tin mines. These two industries form the basis of Malaysia's prosperity. You can see rubber plantations along the main roads out of KL as well as in other parts of Malaysia. On the road to the zoo, for example, about 8 km/5 miles north of the city, you pass through a plantation. By 6 A.M. each day, tappers start their rounds, tapping the latex from the orderly rows of trees. Around 11 A.M. the tappers return, collect the white latex from each tree, and bicycle or walk to the factory where the latex is processed into rubber sheets.

Opposite this rubber plantation and along the road to Batu Caves, you can see large open pits where tin is dredged.

HISTORIC MALACCA

Sightseeing takes a historic turn in Malacca, a city lying 154 km/96 miles south of Kuala Lumpur and 249 km/155 miles north of Singapore.

Founded by a Sri Vijaya nobleman in 1403, Malacca was once the greatest city in Southeast Asia. For centuries, it was the rendezvous port for sailing ships from many seafaring nations. Located on the Malacca River at the junction of the maritime route linking the Indian Ocean with the South China Sea, Malacca stood where the monsoon winds converge. Benefitting from these winds, ships carrying the rich spices and woods of the East — camphor, cloves, nutmeg, and sandalwood — unloaded in Malacca. Silks, carpets, and porcelain were also brought in from India, Arabia, and China for barter or exchange. It's easy to understand, then, why European merchants called at this port to purchase the riches of the Orient. It's also easy to understand why Malacca, so valuable and rich a seaport, was under many rulers during its history. The Portuguese, Dutch, and British all left their imprint here.

Getting there

From Kuala Lumpur, you can take a short side trip to Malacca, or you can stop there en route to Singapore. By car it's a 2-hour drive from Kuala Lumpur, which makes for an excellent overnight side trip. (The trip can be made in a day, but there's little time left for sightseeing.) Stops along the route can include Seremban and Port Dickson (see page 91). You can also reach Malacca by air or express bus, and many tours stop there as well.

(Continued on page 88)

Clothed in golden robe, *108-foot-long Reclining Buddha plays host to visitors at Penang's Wat Chayamangkalaram.*

Entranced visitor *reaches toward incense-lulled pit vipers, coiled around branches in vase at Penang's Snake Temple.*

. . . Continued from page 86

Once you've arrived in Malacca, the best ways to really explore this historic city are on foot or in a bicycle-powered trishaw. You can also take one of the half-day city tours. If you take a trishaw, be sure to negotiate the fare before you start.

A place to stay. Accommodations in Malacca range from small city hotels to beachside motels and government rest houses. Reservations are necessary, even though Malacca may seem off the beaten path. Downtown hotels include the Palace, the Regal, and the Straits Travel Inn Malacca. A favorite beach accommodation is Shah's Beach Motel with its chaletlike bungalows and swimming pool. It's on the beach road 10 km/6 miles southwest of town.

For more information. Maps and other information on Malacca are available at the Malacca Tourist Centre, Jalan Laksamana.

Historic landmarks

Malacca today moves at a slower pace. Gone are the hectic trading days and the romantic square-rigged sailing ships that once filled the harbor. Instead, cargo lighters are docked at the river quay, loaded with charcoal and freight from offshore vessels.

The city's past lives on, however, in its historic sights. In fact, Malacca still has a quaint air with its pastel-painted houses decorated with balconies and wooden shutters. Strolling the city's narrow streets, you'll pass antique buildings that bespeak former visitors and rulers.

The town square. One of the best places to start your tour of Malacca's historic sights is in this neat little square next to the Malacca River. Dominating the square is Stadthuys, believed to be the oldest Dutch building in the Far East.

SPEAKING BAHASA MALAYSIA

Bahasa Malaysia is Malaysia's national language, though you'll also find English widely spoken. Following are a few simple greetings and phrases in the national language.

Good morning — *"Selamat pagi"*
Good afternoon — *"Selamat tengah hari"*
Good evening — *"Selamat petang"*
Good-bye — *"Selamat tinggal"*
Thank you — *"Terima kasih"*
You're welcome — *"Sama sama"*
Excuse me — *"Maafkan saya"*
How much? — *"Berapa?"*
Too expensive — *"Mahal sangat"*
Where is the toilet? — *"Di-mana tandas?"*
Yes — *"Ya"*
No — *"Tidak"*

Built between 1641 and 1660, the salmon-colored Stadthuys features incredibly thick walls, massive hardwood doors, and windows with wrought iron hinges. Once the home of the Dutch governor, it is now used for government offices.

Churches. Christ Church, adjacent to Stadthuys in the town square, was built in 1753. This Dutch-designed building is made of pink bricks that were shipped from Holland, then faced with local red clay by Malacca masons. Possessing heavy wooden doors and a tiled roof, the church has windows topped by fan-shaped ornaments.

Not far from the town square, atop Residency Hill, the ruins of St. Paul's Church possess a commanding view of the Strait of Malacca. Though the tower has become a lighthouse and only the walls remain of this church built by the Portuguese in 1521, its interior is still lined with Dutch tombstones. In front of the church is a statue of St. Francis Xavier, who celebrated Mass in St. Paul's and was briefly buried here before his body was shipped to Goa.

St. Peter's Church, on the road north to the airport, is the Church of the Portuguese Mission under the Bishop of Macau. Built in 1710, the church is a mixture of eastern and western architecture. Inside, you'll see a life-size statue of Jesus Christ, as well as beautiful stained-glass windows and several old tombstones.

Other places of worship. You'll find Cheng Hoon Teng Temple on the north side of the Malacca River, on Temple Street, in the heart of Chinatown. Constructed in the 17th century by craftsmen from China, it's the oldest Chinese temple in Malaysia. The temple interior is intricately carved and features hardwood roof ridges and crossbeams decorated with mythical figures that are inset with colored glass and painted porcelain.

Several blocks west of the Chinese temple, Muslims pray at the Tranquerah Mosque on Jalan Tranquerah. Sumatran in architecture, this building with its wrought iron gateway was built 150 years ago. The Sultan of Johore — the man who signed over Singapore to Sir Stamford Raffles in 1824 — is buried within the mosque compound.

Ancient forts. Below the ruins of St. Paul's Church, a single gateway—Porta de Santiago—is all that remains of a once great Portuguese fortress, "A Famosa." Built in 1511, the fortress was a symbol of Portuguese supremacy. Behind its walls stood the palaces of Portuguese nobility, as well as hospitals, churches, and a school. The mighty fort withstood attacks until the Dutch bombardment of 1641. The British destroyed it in 1795.

East of town is St. John's Fort, originally built as a Portuguese chapel. It was the Dutch who converted it to a fort, and the steps leading to the top were once guarded by cannons. From here you can see the Strait of Malacca, the city, and the hillside Chinese cemetery on Bukit China (China Hill).

Bukit China (China Hill). In the 1400s, the Emperor of China sent his daughter to marry the reigning Sultan of Malacca. The 500 ladies-in-waiting that accompanied her were given this hill as their residence. Today, Bukit China— on the northeast side of town—is part of one of the largest Chinese cemeteries outside of China. Covering 65 hectares/161 acres, the cemetery includes weathered gravestones and some tombs dating back to Ming times.

GAMES MALAYSIANS PLAY

In some parts of the world top spinning and kite flying are child's play, but in Malaysia these two recreational activities are pursued seriously by adults. Both require a great deal of skill in creation and use.

To the rural Malay, top spinning is a highly skilled sport taking years to master. The carefully balanced top—in various shapes and sizes—is fashioned from special hardwoods and takes up to 6 weeks to make.

Top spinning is particularly popular along Peninsular Malaysia's east coast where top-spinning competitions between villages are held after the rice harvest, when men have more leisure time. Contests—many lasting all day—are an excellent excuse for a lively village get-together. Contests include "knock out," in which one team tries to topple the tops of their opponents, and "long spinning," the object of which is to see who can spin a top for the longest time.

Kite flying is also actively pursued by adults along Peninsular Malaysia's east coast. During the windy months of April, May, and June, villagers gather in fields to watch colorful, richly decorated kites dance in the sky.

As with top making and spinning, special skills are needed both to make kites and to fly them. Bamboo forms the kite's framework, and the shape can resemble anything from a cat or fish to a quail. The bamboo framework is covered with brightly colored paper and then cut-out paper designs are added. The whole kite-making process can take up to 2 weeks.

The kites are normally 2 meters/7 feet from tip to tail and 1.8 meters/6 feet across the wing. It takes two people to launch and land one. In a kite-flying competition, a kite is judged on how high it can fly, how skillfully it is handled, how ornamental it is, and how musical its hum is. (A special bow across the top of the kite's wing creates a humming sound.) As with top-spinning competitions, a kite-flying contest is a good excuse for a festive occasion.

In the past, top-spinning and kite-flying competitions were held on a spontaneous basis, but today many of the competitions are arranged through the local recreation departments. Visitors to Peninsular Malaysia's east coast are more likely to see top-spinning and kite-flying demonstrations on organized tours.

Malacca Museum. Displays illustrating Malacca's history are housed in a former Dutch home, more than 300 years old, on Jalan Kota. You'll see Portuguese costumes, Dutch weapons, Malay swords and shields, and Ming porcelain. You can visit the museum between 9 A.M. and 5 P.M.; no photographs are allowed within the museum.

Shopping around

Jalan Gelanggang (formerly Jonker Street) is Malacca's most interesting street for shopping and browsing. Its sidewalks are lined with shops offering everyday items and unusual gifts. Here's where you'll find the cobbler and rattan furniture maker, woodcarvers, and metal craftsmen.

Specialties made from local wood include canes and intricate woodcarvings, all at reasonable prices. You'll also find numerous antiques ranging from brass bedsteads to Chinese porcelain.

In addition to Jalan Gelanggang, you can shop at the city's night market near the waterfront on Jalan Taman. There you'll find local craft items as well as local seafood.

Outdoor adventure

Near Malacca you can explore a number of recreational retreats, from beautiful beaches to a breathtaking mountain.

Beaches. Both swimmers and beach walkers can enjoy the expansive stretches of golden beach west of town along the Strait of Malacca.

A legendary mountain. A 48-km/30-mile trip inland from Malacca takes you to Mount Ophir, called *Gunung Ledang* (the mountain with a legend) in Malay. Its cone-shaped summit seems much higher than 1,276 meters/4,187 feet because it rises so abruptly from the lowland rubber planta-

tions. According to legend, the mountain is the home of a fairy princess.

From the road near its base you can wander through gardens of tropical flowers and fruit trees and alongside clear pools of water brightened with silver and gold fish. Hikers wishing to try the trail to the summit should allow about 5 hours for the round trip.

Golf. At Ayer Kroh, 13 km/8 miles from Malacca, golfers can enjoy the two 9-hole courses at the Ayer Kroh Country Club. This championship course is laid out in a setting of lakes, rolling hills, and tall trees. Sand traps and water courses make for lively play.

MALACCA SIDE TRIPS

Endless vistas of forest, rice lands, and rubber and oil palm plantations characterize the Malay Peninsula both north and south of Malacca. The most direct route through this area (between Kuala Lumpur and Singapore) is the West Coast Highway. To the north of Malacca you travel through Seremban and can make a side trip to Port Dickson. To the south you turn inland at Batu Pahat, stopping at Johore Bahru before you cross the causeway to Singapore.

There is both bus and rail service north from Malacca to Kuala Lumpur and south from Malacca to Johore Bahru. You can drive the route yourself or travel by chauffeured car with a driver-guide. Organized tours cover the area en route to Singapore. There is also air service between Johore Bahru and Malacca, but you'll miss the scenery.

On the road north

Leaving Malacca and journeying north, you'll enter some of the richest rice country in Malaysia. Stately rubber trees give way to rice fields, coconut plantations, and numerous kampongs. Wooden Malay houses, invariably shaded by coconut palms and other trees, perch on stiltlike foundations above neatly swept yards of handpacked earth. Numerous paneless windows admit whatever breezes are available. Often the houses are decorated with carved wooden pillars, elaborate front steps faced in colored tiles, cheerful window hangings of checkered fabric or coarse lace, and a profusion of flowers.

En route to Kuala Lumpur, you'll find Seremban and Port Dickson are worth a stop.

Seremban. Capital of the state of Negeri Sembilan, Seremban is a typical Malay-Chinese town that sprang out of the tin-mining boom. Set in a valley 80 km/50 miles northwest of Malacca and 68 km/42 miles southeast of Kuala Lumpur, the town's one main street is a maze of cluttered arcades and tiny alleys. On the hillside above town, old colonial buildings house local government offices.

Places in Seremban worth a visit include the ultra-modern State Mosque overlooking Lake Gardens. Within the gardens is the State Museum, built in the style of the Minangkabau people with a curved roof resembling buffalo horns. Inside the museum you'll see exquisitely carved wooden panels, a Malay gong, Malay swords and knives, and a suit of chain mail that once belonged to a Bugis pirate. A traditional old Malay house — built without nails — also sits in Lake Gardens.

Accommodations in Seremban include the Carlton and Ruby hotels, and a government rest house.

Port Dickson. On the coast 40 km/25 miles southwest of Seremban, midway between Malacca and Kuala Lumpur, is Port Dickson — a favorite Malaysian seaside resort. Its sandy beaches, trimmed by feathery casuarinas and banyan trees, stretch 18 km/11 miles down the coast. As you might expect, its popular recreational activities include swimming, boating, snorkeling, deep-sea fishing, and tennis.

Beachside accommodations include the large Federal Hotel and the Si-Rusa Inn, as well as smaller motels, guest houses, and bungalows. Coastal roads both north and south of Port Dickson provide alternate routes between Malacca and Kuala Lumpur. A special Malayan Railway train makes Sunday excursions to Port Dickson from Kuala Lumpur.

South to Johore Bahru

The coastal road dead ends about 160 km/100 miles south of Malacca, but Singapore-bound traffic turns inland at Batu Pahat to pick up the main north-south route. From Malacca south, you pass rubber plantations, rice fields, and Malay farm houses set back from the road.

Malaysia's southernmost town, Johore Bahru, serves as a gateway to Singapore, to which it is joined by the Johore Causeway. The town is also the capital of Johore state. *Note:* In your travels you may see more than one spelling for *Johore (Johor)* and for *Bahru (Baru, Baharu, Bharu)* which means "new."

City sights. You first see Johore Bahru, backed by a row of hills, from the long coastal road sweeping into this seaside town along the Johore Strait.

Atop one hill is Bukit Serene, the sultan's private residence; its 32-meter/106-foot tower is a city landmark. Istana Besar in beautifully landscaped Istana Gardens is the former palace of the sultan. Now it's used for state banquets and royal ceremonies. Other features of Istana Gardens include an orchid garden as well as a Japanese garden complete with Japanese tea house.

Adjacent to Istana Gardens is the Johore Zoo. Once the sultan's private game reserve, the zoo features a few animals; the grounds are planted in bougainvillea, traveler's palms, orchids, and cannas. The zoo is open daily from 8 A.M. to 6 P.M.

High on a hill off Jalan Abu Bakar, stands the Abu Bakar Mosque — a spacious building with marble colonnades and floors, glimmering chandeliers, and space enough to hold 2,000 worshipers.

Johore Bahru accommodations include the Straits View, Regent Elite, Merlin Tower, and Orchid hotels. The Desaru Holiday Resort, on a beach 89 km/55 miles northeast of town, is a resort featuring swimming, boating, horse riding, and tennis.

Side trips. About 40 km/25 miles to the northeast — less than an hour's drive from Johore Bahru — are the Kota Tinggi Waterfalls and a favorite picnic area with self-contained chalets, eating stalls, and a restaurant. One waterfall plunges down a 37-meter/120-foot precipice into a pool ideal for swimming.

(Continued on page 92)

From tangle of color, *Malaysian woman weaves design into* mengkuang *mat at Cherating on Malaysia's east coast.*

...Continued from page 91

On a day-tour out of Johore Bahru, you can visit a plantation — Ulu Tiram Estate — located 26 km/16 miles inland. Here you'll see tapping of the rubber trees and harvesting of coconuts and oil palm fruit.

INTO THE HIGHLANDS AND BEYOND

North of Kuala Lumpur, you'll discover some of Malaysia's hill resorts. Originally patterned after the British hill stations in India, these resorts offer spectacular views, quiet jungle paths, a host of recreational activities, and a cool climate. Because of their elevation, they enjoy daytime temperatures averaging 21°C/70°F, while nighttime temperatures are about 16°C/60°F.

Two of the resorts — Genting Highlands and Fraser's Hill — are within a few hours drive of Kuala Lumpur. Cameron Highlands and Maxwell Hill are more easily reached en route to Penang. To really enjoy the relaxing atmosphere as well as the amenities of these resorts, it's best to spend at least one night.

Still another attraction north of Kuala Lumpur is Taman Negara (National Park).

Genting Highlands

Kuala Lumpur's closest hill resort is the Genting Highlands hotel-casino complex, just 51 km/32 miles northeast of town. Overlooking the jungle from atop 1,711-meter/ 5,614-foot-high Mount Ulu Kali, the resort is often shrouded in clouds and enveloped in mist. Close at hand is thick jungle greenery from which bird sounds break the stillness. When the clouds and mist roll away, you can see green valleys, the capital city, and the distant Strait of Malacca.

Genting Highlands is the country's newest hill station with the country's only licensed casino. Those wishing to tempt "lady luck" can play both western and oriental games of chance — roulette, blackjack, baccarat, keno, *tai sai* and, of course, the slot machines — for 24 hours a day.

Outdoor recreational facilities include an 18-hole golf course linked to the main part of the complex by a 2 km/1½-mile cable car system. Other resort amenities include a swimming pool, a manmade lake for boating, a bowling alley, and a movie theater.

Getting there. You can reach the complex by car in about an hour. There's also taxi and bus service from Kuala Lumpur. For a speedier trip, you can take a 10 to 15 minute ride by helicopter weekdays from both Subang International Airport and Segambut Helipad. Local Kuala Lumpur tour operators feature tours to Genting by coach or helicopter.

Accommodations. The Genting complex includes five hotels, a number of restaurants, and a nightclub.

Fraser's Hill

Once the hideout of adventurer Louis James Fraser, a dealer in opium and tin ore in the late 1800s, Fraser's Hill has been developed into a popular hill resort. Situated 103 km/65 miles northeast of Kuala Lumpur, low-key Fraser's Hill is 1,219 meters/4,000 feet high and offers its guests cool fresh air and peaceful jungle surroundings.

The main street of the resort is lined with stone buildings reminiscent of an English township. Well-kept flower gardens surround English-style bungalows and a small hotel. Paved roads, narrowed by encroaching jungle, lead to the guest bungalows, a restaurant, tennis courts, and a children's playground. One jungle walk, lined with bamboo and ferns, leads to Jeriau Falls with its swimming lagoon and picnic area. Nearby is an 18-hole golf course set in a sheltered valley with undulating fairways.

Getting there. By car, Fraser's Hill is a 2-hour drive from Kuala Lumpur. There's also bus and taxi service. By rail you journey as far as Kuala Kubu Bharu, then take a bus or taxi. The last 8 km/5 miles of the journey—from The Gap to the top of Fraser's Hill — are on a narrow, winding, one-way road. Traffic moves up the hill on certain hours and down the hill on others, so check locally for the traffic control schedule. There are also 1-day tours to Fraser's Hill from Kuala Lumpur.

Accommodations. At Fraser's Hill you can stay at the hotel or in a bungalow or chalet. The resort's peak seasons are April, August and December.

Cameron Highlands

Farther north, 225 km/140 miles from KL to be precise, is Cameron Highlands — a plateau surrounded by high mountains. The potential of the area was recognized by government surveyor William Cameron in 1885. Chinese tea planters soon found that the Highlands' climate was ideal for growing tea. The fertile soil and mild weather also proved productive for Chinese vegetable gardeners. A road was soon built to take their products to market. When wealthy rubber planters discovered the route they built weekend houses in the area.

Today the Highlands has three townships with a half dozen hotels. The main village of Tanah Rata—known for its clean air, streams, lakes, and mountain views—offers Swiss-style chalets, Chinese hotels, small cottages, restaurants, and an excellent steak house.

The 18-hole golf course features rolling fairways, a meandering stream, and tricky approaches to the greens. You can go swimming in the natural pool at Parit Falls. Other sporting activities include tennis and badminton.

Throughout the Highlands, well-marked jungle paths lead to hilltop vistas. The area is known for its many varieties of wild orchids, as well as colorful butterflies such as the Rajah Brooke.

Cameron Highlands is still a major tea-producing area, and local tours include a visit to one of the area's many tea plantations.

Getting there. It's a 4-hour drive from Kuala Lumpur to Cameron Highlands. There's also rail service to Tapah with bus or taxi service from there to the Highlands. From Tapah, the road becomes winding and weaves its way through the jungle, past waterfalls and rock-strewn streams. On occasion, you might see an Orang Asli native strolling along the road.

Accommodations. The Cameron Highland's peak months are April, August, and December. Accommodations include hotels and bungalows.

Maxwell Hill

Malaysia's oldest hill resort — Maxwell Hill — is located 9 km/6 miles east of Taiping. At 1,035 meters/3,396 feet, visitors enjoy a view of the town of Taiping with its famous Lake Gardens and the green residential districts beyond.

Flowers of every kind — roses, daisies, dahlias, petunias, and lupines — thrive in the mild resort climate. Guests can choose to stay in a rest house or bungalow.

You reach the resort by official four-wheel-drive vehicle; private cars are not allowed on the narrow winding road up the hill. It's about a 40-minute trip from the foot of the hill to the resort. The official vehicles normally run their shuttle service hourly from 8 A.M. to 6 P.M.

Taman Negara (National Park)

River roads cover the 4,345 square km/1,677 square miles of Taman Negara (National Park), a vast virgin rain forest 241 km/150 miles northeast of Kuala Lumpur. Rich in animals, birds, and plants, the preserve offers a memorable look at Malaysia's tropical wildlife. Wild orchids grow profusely, and multihued butterflies and exotic birds abound. There are jungle trails to hike, mountains to climb, fast-moving rivers to navigate, and even natural pools in which you can take a dip. Throughout the park, fresh-water anglers will find good fishing in the rivers, streams, and pools.

The park provides salt licks for the animals, and nearby "hides" or "blinds" for visitors from which they can get close-up views and pictures of the wildlife. Animals that may come within photographic distance include tapirs, barking deer, and wild pigs.

To reach the park from Kuala Lumpur, take a car or taxi to Jerantut, then another taxi to the park gateway at Kuala Tembeling. It's then another 3-hour boat ride to Kuala Tahan, the park headquarters. (There are 3 to 5-day organized tours from Kuala Lumpur to the park.) At Kuala Tahan, you'll find a rest house, chalets, a hostel, camping sites, and a restaurant. At several other points in the park, there are self-contained cabins. Camping equipment is also available for hire.

The best time of year to visit Taman Negara is April through October. It should be noted that the trip to the park takes some planning, and a stay there isn't a luxurious experience. But it will certainly give you a first-hand look at the Malaysian jungle.

PENANG, PEARL OF THE ORIENT

The evergreen island of Penang, Malaysia's popular holiday resort, marks the northern end of the Strait of Malacca. Located 3 km/2 miles off the northwest coast of Peninsular Malaysia, Penang is a small, hilly, tropical island just 24 km/15 miles long and 14 km/9 miles wide.

Penang is known for its miles of beaches edged by calm waters and backed by rolling hills of lush tropical vegetation. Its unspoiled scenery and peaceful pace have made it a favorite retreat. Year-round temperatures range between 24°C/75°F and 32°C/90°F during the day; nights are pleasant.

Named Pulau Pinang (island of the betel nut), Penang's history is based on trade. The British settlement at Georgetown on Penang was founded by Captain Francis Light in 1786, mainly as a base for the China opium trade. It was Light who suggested that Penang become a free port, and he served as its first superintendent until his death in 1796.

Today, Penang is no longer a free port, but it is still actively engaged in commerce. Its multiracial population numbers one million and is mainly Chinese, Malay, and Indian. But Europeans, Australians, Eurasians, Japanese, and Thais have also settled here. Each group has stamped its ethnic imprint on Penang's architecture, style of dress, cuisine, and life style.

Penang's city-port

Georgetown — Penang's only major city and busy port — occupies the island's northeast corner, facing the mainland town of Butterworth. It's a thriving city of a half million people. Narrow streets are lined with shuttered colonial-style buildings, ornate red-lacquered temples, domed mosques, and Chinese shops with red-tile roofs. Where there was once dense jungle, you now see Fort Cornwallis and the two-story, colonnaded City Hall. Bordering the fort and public buildings on the ocean side is the Esplanade, a sea-front road continuing some 3 km/2 miles further as Gurney Drive, a spacious tree-lined road edged with mansions set behind stone walls and ornate iron gates.

Penang's harbor pulses with activity. Along Weld Quay, yellow passenger ferries shuttle vacationers from the mainland. Small boats transport goods from anchored, ocean-going freighters to *godowns* (warehouses). South of the quay, Chinese fishermen, boatmen, and their families live their whole lives on clan piers in over-the-water wooden stilt houses. Each pier is restricted to a clan with a particular surname. These piers, similar to land villages, are complete with their own temples, stores, electricity, and running water. You'll see these piers if you arrive in Penang by ferry from Butterworth.

Getting your bearings

Penang's international airport at Bayan Lepas, 16 km/10 miles south of Georgetown, is served by daily flights on air routes between Bangkok, Singapore, and Hong Kong. Malaysian Airline System (MAS) also provides domestic service between Penang and Kuala Lumpur. The Malayan Railway has daily express service to Butterworth (opposite Penang Island) from Bangkok, Singapore, and intermediate Malaysian cities. From Butterworth, it's an easy 15-minute ferry ride to Penang's Weld Quay. Ocean freighters, cruise ships, and trading vessels also make frequent stops at Penang. In addition, Kuala Lumpur tour operators offer 3-day tours to Penang from KL.

Once you've arrived in Georgetown, the best way to see the city is by foot or trishaw. City taxis are metered. Taxis that travel around the island have a fixed rate per passenger. Be sure you agree on the price before you go.

Beyond Georgetown, you can tour the island by rental car, rental car with driver, or, if you are more adventuresome, by local bus. There are five local bus companies on Penang that provide inexpensive transport around the island as well as in town.

Local tour operators offer around-the-island tours, city/shopping tours, and hill/temple tours. All tours last about 3 to 3½ hours.

Where to stay. For many years Penang had only one good first-class hotel in Georgetown — the stately, ocean front Eastern & Oriental (E & O) Hotel. Today, though, Penang is blessed with a number of good hotels both in the downtown area and along the north shore beaches within 16 km/10 miles of town. Downtown hotels include the Ambassador, Central, Continental, Eastern & Oriental (E & O), Malaysia, Mandarin, Merlin, Oriental, Paramount, and Towne House.

Resort hotels along the beaches are particularly suited to visitors who prefer the leisurely life of sand, surf, and sun on uncrowded, palm-fringed beaches. Some of the hotels are the Bayview Beach, Casuarina Beach, Golden Sands, Holiday Inn, Lone Pine, Palm Beach, and Rasa Sayang. Penang Hill Hotel is the island's only hill hotel. The island also has low-cost bungalows and youth hostels.

Dining out. With Penang's multiracial heritage, you're assured of a wide range of cuisines. Local specialties include *laksa, enchee kabin, curry mee, satay,* and *nasi kandar.* You won't want to overlook Chinese steamboat cooking, either (see page 118), or Penang's notable fresh seafood.

Local food stalls offer the adventurous gourmet a real bargain in Chinese, Malay, and Indian foods — everything from satay to fresh crabs and prawns.

You'll find food stalls along Gurney Drive, on the Esplanade, on Padang Brown, and Gelugor Road. Food stalls are usually open from 6 P.M. to 1 A.M.

Entertainment time. Some of Penang's larger hotels have discotheques and nightclubs with floor shows. Some also have cultural shows of native music and dance.

Local festivals throughout the year also feature music, dance, and culture of Malaysia. One of note is Pesta Pulau Pinang, held in December. It features a month-long series of activities traditional to Penang — art, drama, dance, music. The Chingay Procession is a colorful Pesta Pulau Pinang event featuring an entertaining parade of acrobats, jugglers, trick cyclists, lion dancers, and men carrying brilliantly colored flags. Penang's International Boat Festival is also held during this period, and long, dramatically painted dragon boats from around the world come to compete.

For more information. The Penang Development Corporation's offfice is located in the Tuanku Syed Putra Building, Jalan Downing, Penang.

Some historic sights

In downtown Georgetown, several sights bring to mind the town's early days.

Fort Cornwallis. Guarding the northeast approach to Penang, Fort Cornwallis stands on the spot where Captain Francis Light first landed in 1786. Originally built of wood in the early 1800s, the fort was later rebuilt with stone. You can walk the ramparts and examine cannons that were never fired against an enemy.

St. George's Church. A British colonial officer, Captain R. Smith, designed this spired Anglican cathedral. Surrounded by banyan trees and adorned with white columns, it's located on Leboh Farquhar.

Penang Museum and Art Gallery. Located on Leboh Farquhar next to St. George's, the museum has exhibits depicting the history and cultural heritage of the island. You can view a 19th century Chinese bridal chamber, a room hung with paintings and etchings of old Penang, and a showcase of jeweled *krisses* (daggerlike Malay weapons). The Art Gallery upstairs displays batik paintings, as well as oils, graphics, and Chinese ink drawings. The museum and gallery are open Monday through Saturday from 9 A.M. to 5 P.M.

Places of worship

Penang has an impressive collection of places of worship— temples, mosques, wats, clan houses, churches. Many of these buildings are worth a visit.

Kek Lok Si Temple. Located above Ayer Itam village 8 km/5 miles southwest of Georgetown, Kek Lok Si is the largest Chinese temple in Malaysia and one of the finest in Southeast Asia. Built on a rocky hill, the temple complex consists of several buildings set in 12 hectares/30 acres of gardens. The seven-tier Ban Po Thar (10,000 Buddhas) Pagoda is 30 meters/100 feet high and dominates the complex. This yellow and red building features several forms of architecture. The octagonal base is typically Chinese; the middle tiers are Thai; and the spiral dome is Burmese.

Goddess of Mercy Temple. The soot of many years of joss-stick burning has blackened the expertly carved pillars of this Chinese temple on Leboh Pitt. Built over 150 years ago, the temple belongs to the street people: the noodle makers, trishaw drivers, and housewives who shop in the markets. Amid burning joss sticks, they burden the goddess with their problems or thank her for answering their prayers.

A mosque. Kapitan Kling Mosque, one of Penang's oldest, is also located on Leboh Pitt, southwest of the Goddess of Mercy Temple. Built in the late 1800s, this building with its slender, domed minaret reflects Islamic architecture under Moghul influence.

An imposing wat. Wat Chayamangkalaram, a Thai temple on Jalan Burmah, houses the third largest reclining Buddha in the world. Within the meditation hall of this monastery and spiritual retreat, worshippers, visitors and saffron-robed monks are dwarfed by the 33-meter/108-foot statue of Buddha.

Sri Maha Mariamman Temple. Carvings of Hindu gods and goddesses decorate the facade of this Hindu temple on Queen Street. Inside, gold, diamonds, and other precious stones adorn the statue of Lord Subramaniam.

A Buddhist clan house. Khoo Kongsi, located on Cannon Square at the end of Leboh Pitt, resembles a miniature Chinese imperial palace surrounded by cobblestone courtyards. This clan house—like others in Malaysia—serves as a center for worship and welfare work for people with the same surname, in this case Khoo. The Khoo clan house is particularly elaborate. Stone lions chiseled from green granite guard the entrance, and the roof beams, pillars, and walls — carved, painted, and polished by experts from China — tell of legendary episodes.

MARKETPLACE MEDLEY

Southeast Asia's markets offer visitors an exotic pot-pourri of sights, sounds, and smells. Shaded stalls feature an eye-catching array of goods for sale—baskets brimming with colorful fruits and vegetables, cages filled with cackling chickens, basins swimming with silvery fish, and tables heaped with bolts of batik. The air is filled with a babble of voices—vendors hawking their wares and buyers haggling for the best price. The delicious aromas of sizzling *satay* and frying noodles tempt the hungry.

Part of the intrigue of market wandering comes from the wealth of local produce you'll discover. The deliciously sweet mangosteen (top right) is just one of many tropical fruits you'll find. Produce-laden containers (bottom left) feature such Southeast Asian favorites as star fruit, spinach, green chile peppers, lemon grass, ginger flowers, garlic, and cucumbers. Red chile peppers (bottom right) add zesty spice to many Southeast Asian food specialties.

FESTIVAL TIME

Malaysia's many ethnic groups and religions celebrate an exciting variety of festivals and special events throughout the year. Each group lives by its own annual calendar and celebrates its own traditions and religious festivals. Chinese, Muslim, and Hindu festivals fall on varying dates, so you'll have to check with the Tourist Development Corporation of Malaysia for their exact dates in the year you plan to visit the country. The following list covers some of the country's major celebrations.

Hari Raya Puasa. Held on the first day of the tenth month in the Mohammedan calendar, this day of prayer, feasting, and visiting marks the end of a month-long Muslim fast.

Thaipusam. Hindu devotees honor the birthday of Lord Subramaniam by carrying *kavadis*, wooden frames decorated with flowers and supported by skewers that pierce the back and chest of the carrier. Main celebrations take place at the Waterfall Temple in Penang and at Batu Caves outside Kuala Lumpur.

Birthday of the Deity of Chor Soo Kong. Annual February celebration at Penang's Snake Temple.

Goddess of Mercy Birthday. In Kuala Lumpur, Penang, and Malacca, Chinese temples dedicated to the goddess are the scene of celebrations, including theatrical shows.

Hari Raya Haji. Muslims throughout Malaysia celebrate their *haji* (pilgrimage to Mecca) with mosque services and home entertaining.

Wesak Day. Held in May, this countrywide event commemorates Lord Buddha's birthday with religious rites and lantern processions at temples in Kuala Lumpur and Penang.

Kadazan Harvest Festival. This Sabah holiday in May celebrates a successful harvest with a traditional ceremony and native dances.

Gawai Day. Several traditional Dayak festivals are combined on June 1 for Sarawak festivities and dancing.

Feast of the Hungry Ghosts. Chinese ancestors traditionally return to earth for one day to visit their descendants. Paper money, fruit, and other offerings are burned in small fires to appease ancestral ghosts.

National Day. August 31 marks the day the Federation of Malaya secured its independence from Great Britain in 1957. It's a public holiday, celebrated in Malaysia's principal cities and towns with parades, music festivals, and outdoor shows.

Festival of the Emperor Gods. One of the biggest Chinese festivals, it reaches dramatic peaks at Penang, where a procession winds up Pava Terubong Hill to the temple to celebrate the heavenly return of the nine celestial kings.

Deepavali. The Hindus celebrate the victory of Lord Krishna over a mythical king. The day begins with prayers at the temples, followed by visits to friends and relatives. At night, Hindu homes are lighted by oil lamps.

Pesta Pulau Pinang. During the month of December, Georgetown holds a water carnival with marathon swimming and dragon boat races.

Shopping around

Though Penang is no longer a free port, the island remains an attractive shopping area, offering a wide variety of goods such as stereo and hi-fi equipment, cameras, watches, perfumes, and cosmetics, along with handcrafted Malay carvings, brassware, and pewter. Locally made batiks are an especially good buy. Penang is also noted for its fine locally crafted jewelry.

You can shop in hotel shopping arcades, in stores along Penang Road, or in the Tun Abdul Razak complex. There are also a number of Chinese shops along Leboh Campbell. On Rope Walk, you'll find junk shops through which you can rummage and find everything from old pots and pans to fine Chinese porcelain.

Be sure to visit the *pasar malam* (night market) at which you can bargain for trinkets or batik sarongs, sample the local foods, and enjoy watching the people. It moves to a new location every two weeks, so check the daily newspaper for the current location.

You'll find duty-free shops along Leboh Penang, Jalan Burmah, and Leboh Campbell. The Tourist Development Corporation's duty-free store is at the Tun Abdul Razak complex. Items available at duty-free shops range from perfumes to calculators.

Several batik factory showrooms on the island offer bargains — lower prices than in town — on both batik material and clothing. You can also watch the batik-making process, from hand stamping to drying. Around-the-island tours usually stop at one of the batik factories.

Island sights

The road around the island unfolds along 74 kilometers/46 miles of rubber and spice estates, coconut plantations, rice fields, kampongs of Malay houses on stilts, and stretches of lovely beaches. Where the road becomes winding and mountainous, you'll enjoy beautiful views of the azure sea and green fields far below. Occasionally, a dirt side road leads to remote villages on the coast or inland. If you head south out of Georgetown, there are several stops that will attract you.

Tuanku Abdul Rahman Aquarium. At milestone 4 on the road south of town, this aquarium displays tropical marine life found in Southeast Asian waters. Winding one-way corridors are lined with glass-fronted tanks housing giant Indian carp from inland rivers and spotted eels from offshore coral reefs. The aquarium's marine museum contains exhibits, models, and charts explaining the life cycle of fish and crustaceans and the development of Malaysia's

fishing gear and fish products. The aquarium is open from 10 A.M. to 6 P.M. daily except Wednesdays.

Snake Temple (Temple of Azure Cloud). Hundreds of poisonous pit vipers dwell in this ornate building at milestone 9, a short distance north of the airport. Presumably lulled into a stupor by clouds of heavy incense, these snakes hang from the ceiling, lounge on the altar shrine, and wrap themselves around table legs, chandeliers, candlesticks, and vases. In an annex room, snake lovers can have their photographs taken with a "nonpoisonous" snake or two curled about their arms or neck.

You reach the gold-leafed, red-lacquered temple by climbing a flight of steps lined with refreshment and souvenir stalls.

Batu Maung. About 3 km/2 miles southeast of Bayan Lepas Airport, you can visit this typical Malay fishing kampong. Here, life revolves around the sea — villagers

---

RETURN OF THE TURTLES

come ashore after midnight — usually between 1 and 2 A.M. — and slowly make their way up the beach to favorite nesting spots well above the high-water mark Here, a turtle will use its flippers to dig a nest in the soft, warm sand. Meanwhile, its back flippers are carefully carving out a perpendicular tunnel to receive the eggs.

The eggs are laid in clutches of 80 to 140. The average number is 120 per clutch. Once the egg laying is finished, the turtle laboriously fills the hole and smoothes over the spot before it makes its way slowly back to sea. A female turtle may return several times during the season to lay more eggs, and then return to the same beach the following year, or wait several years before returning.

Turtle eggs are a delicacy bringing a high price in larger cities. Because of this, eager egg collectors are on the beach scooping up the eggs as soon as they are laid. Government controls have been enacted, though, and a Hatchery Conservation area established. More than 50,000 eggs a year are bought from licensed collectors, then taken to the hatchery where they are incubated under natural conditions. The incubation period runs 50 to 60 days, after which the baby turtles are returned safely to the sea.

Popular turtle-watching spots along the east coast are Rantau Abang and Chendor Beach. You'll find convenient nearby accommodations in both areas (see page 100). Spotters armed with flashlights announce the arrival of the turtles. However, sightings on any particular night can't be guaranteed since there are many landing sites along the coast.

In the dark they first appear as black dots swimming furiously through the white surf. Soon they reach shore and their fast graceful pace slows to an awkward, lumbering crawl. These giant leatherback turtles (some reach 2 meters/8 feet in length and weigh 690 kilograms/1,500 pounds) normally dwell in the sea where their size and bulk pose no hindrance to their maneuverability.

Each year between May and September, female leatherback turtles leave the sea and return to beaches along the eastern coast of Peninsular Malaysia — between Kuala Trengganu and Kuantan — to lay their eggs. They

Stilts lift *Malay village near Kota Kinabalu above water; residents' livelihood comes from sea.*

Brilliant batik *sarongs hang on line in Kota Bharu on Malaysia's handicraft-rich east coast.*

fish with nets from small boats in the early morning, sell part of the catch in town, mend nets on the beach, and repair boats pulled up under swaying palms. The fishing families live in wooden, stilt houses with many window openings; some dwellings have attached verandas shaded by coconut trees and surrounded by flowering plants and bushes.

The great outdoors

The highlight of Penang's outdoor scene is its numerous beaches a relatively short distance north of Georgetown. But Penang also offers nature lovers a chance to stroll jungle paths.

Penang Hill. From atop this 3,589-meter/2,230-foot hill west of town, you get not only a good view, but relief from the heat as well, and a chance to explore jungle forest. Riding up the steep incline to the summit by funicular railway, you can enjoy the unfolding view of jungle and blue sea along the way. At each substation, tree-shaded paths wander through the cool forest past private bungalows. The trip takes about 30 minutes, during which time the temperature drops about 10 degrees.

On top of the hill you can see the city, the busy harbor traffic, wide expanses of jungle-covered slopes, and the cultivated valley. Overnight accommodations are available at the Penang Hill Hotel.

The funicular railway runs between 6:45 A.M. and 8:45 P.M. On Wednesdays and Saturdays it continues operation until 11:45 P.M.

Botanical Gardens. Known as Penang's "waterfall gardens," this beautiful park is set in a naturally forested, bowl-shaped site a short distance southwest of town. Paths meander through plantings of native tropical plants and trees. There are pergolas, fern gardens, and lily ponds to enjoy. You might also meet a monkey or two and they're tame enough to be fed by hand. For more animals, visit the miniature zoo with its bears, deer, kangaroos, and orangutans. The park is a popular spot for picnics and jogging.

Secluded sandy beaches. If you drive north of Georgetown to the northern coast of the island, you'll discover a number of beaches ideal for swimming and sunbathing. Most are within a 30-minute drive from town. Secluded white sand beaches are tucked between rock promontories and shaded by swaying palms and leafy casuarinas. Popular beach areas include Telok Bahang (a good fishing area), Batu Ferringhi (where most of the beach hotels are located), and Tanjong Bungah. At the northwestern tip of the island is Muka Head, a popular swimming spot reached only by a trek along an isolated beach, or by boat from Telok Bahang.

Recreational choices

Many of Penang's recreational opportunities focus on the water. At hotels along the north coast, you can sail, fish, skin-dive, wind-surf, or water-ski.

The greens and fairways of Penang's 18-hole golf course are laid out around the island's race track at Batu Gantong. The course has a standard scratch score of 70. You'll find putting greens at the Rasa Sayang, Casuarina Beach, and Golden Sands hotels.

Penang's major hotels, such as the Casuarina Beach, Eastern & Oriental (E & O), Golden Sands, Lone Pine, and Rasa Sayang, have tennis courts. The Penang Sports Club on Leboh Western has several grass tennis courts.

Equestrians can hire horses to ride on Saturdays at the Penang Polo Club on Leboh Western, on weekdays at the Penang Turf Club at Batu Gantong.

MORE WEST COAST ISLANDS

During the 1800s, pirate strongholds on Malaysia's Pangkor Island and in the Langkawi Islands provided safe havens for seafaring bandits who robbed the trading ships plying the Malacca Strait. Today, the same islands provide a restful resort haven for visitors seeking a peaceful vacation away from the mainstream of other travelers.

For island residents, little has changed from the time when pirates dwelled here. The people still live in fishing .kampongs perched on stilts over the water, and they continue to depend on the sea for their livelihood.

Pangkor

Off the peninsula's west coast, about midway between Penang and Kuala Lumpur, lies Pangkor Island. Here fishing, swimming, snorkeling, scuba diving, and sailing are the main resort activities.

You reach Pangkor Island by way of Ipoh, capital of Perak, a 2½-hour drive north of Kuala Lumpur (40 minutes by air). From Ipoh it's a 90-km/56-mile drive through rural Malaysia to the river town of Lumut, and from Lumut it's a 40-minute ferry trip to Pangkor.

Three hotels—the Seaview, Beach Huts, and Pangkor Bay Village—and a small government rest house currently provide the island's accommodations. Most overseas visitors prefer the 55-room Pangkor Bay Village, located on a large coconut plantation facing the Strait of Malacca. Its chalets and Malay-style bungalows are scattered along a 1-mile beach of golden sand. Green headlands rise at either end of the beach, assuring a calm surf.

Langkawi's many islands

The 99-island Langkawi group lies off the north coast of Peninsular Malaysia within sight of Thailand. The only developed island in the group is itself called Langkawi. It offers jungles rich in wild orchids, colored cliffs, waterfalls, black sand beaches, blue lagoons, birds, butterflies, and brilliant flowers. You can reach the island by ferry from Kuala Perlis, Kuala Kedah, or Penang. There's also a 3-day tour from Penang.

Water sport opportunities on Langkawi are numerous. You can relax and sun-bathe on a deserted beach, go for a swim in a quiet lagoon, try snorkeling or skin diving, go boating, or do a little deep-sea fishing for marlin or barracuda. Back on land, you can hike the jungle paths.

Pekan Kuah, the island's main village, has two small hotels and a government rest house. You'll also find accommodations in the 100-room Malaysian-style Langkawi Country Club. Facilities at this sprawling 40-hectare/100-acre resort on the beach just south of town include a 9-hole golf course, tennis courts, horses to rent, and water sport opportunities.

PENINSULAR MALAYSIA'S EAST COAST

Separated from western Peninsular Malaysia by a rugged mountain chain, the quiet eastern seaboard offers visitors still another view of Malaysian life. Here the pace is slow and the life style traditional. Journeying the coastal road, you pass by sleepy Malay villages, undisturbed tropical jungle, and deserted white sand beaches active only during fishing and turtle season. Brightly painted fishing boats with curved prows dot the palm-lined sandy shore.

The people of the east coast are mainly Malay, and Islam dominates their daily lives. Adult farmers and fishermen find pleasure in games like top spinning and kite flying (see page 89). Local villagers still perform traditional dances and *wayang kulit* (shadow plays).

East coast villagers are known for their handicrafts. Their skills are passed from generation to generation. In fact, some of the country's finest craft products — batik, *kain songket* (cloth of gold), woven-leaf products, silver jewelry, and brassware — come from east coast cottage industries.

The east coast's more popular destinations from south to north include Kuantan in the state of Pahang, Kuala Trengganu in Trengganu, and Kota Bharu in Kelantan. In addition, the east coast has many lovely islands blessed with sandy beaches and clear, warm waters.

Getting there

From Kuala Lumpur you can reach the east coast by air (to Kuantan, Kuala Trengganu, or Kota Bharu), or by rail (to Kota Bharu), but it's road travel that reveals the best of the coast. Leaving Kuala Lumpur in the morning, you can drive over the mountainous road across the Genting Pass and arrive in Kuantan—275 km/171 miles away—in time for lunch. (The trip takes about 4 hours.) Kuala Trengganu is 3 hours north of Kuantan, and Kota Bharu another 2½ hours north of Kuala Trengganu. Buses from Kuala Lumpur make the trip to Kota Bharu in about 12 hours. There are also 5 to 7-day tours from KL to the east coast.

From Singapore and Johore Bahru, you can drive up the east coast via Mersing all the way north to Kota Bharu. It's about a 3½ to 4-hour drive from Singapore to Kuantan.

Small hotels and other modest accommodations are available in each of the three main towns and in nearby beach areas.

First stop, Kuantan

From Kuantan, Pahang's capital, you can explore nearby beaches and rural villages where you'll see some of Malaysia's traditional entertainment as well as handicrafts. Local travel agents can arrange for you to visit a village to see demonstrations of top spinning, *bersilat* (the Malay art of self defense), *rodat* (the traditional fishermen's dance), shadow-puppet making, mengkuang leaf weaving, and rice pounding.

Golfers are welcome at the 9-hole Royal Kuantan Golf Course. Sun lovers will enjoy Kuantan's beaches. Skin diving is best near Kuantan in April and May and again in September and October.

Accommodations in the Kuantan area include the Hyatt Kuantan, Kuantan Merlin, Hotel Kuantan, and Hotel Samudra Kuantan. Up the coast —40 km/25 miles north of town—are the Titik Inn and Club Mediterranée Cherating. Chendor Beach, just north of these hotels, is a breeding ground for giant leatherback turtles. Between May and September you can watch them lumber ashore to lay their eggs (see "Return of the Turtles," page 97). There's also a turtle nursery to visit.

Kuala Trengganu

In Trengganu, the state just north of Pahang, you'll find many more miles of sandy white beaches plus another interesting stopover point—Kuala Trengganu, the state's capital. In this town, surrounded by green rice fields and jungled hills, you can explore a colorful public market, see handicrafts in the making, or take a side trip to view giant leatherback turtles (see "Return of the Turtles," page 97).

A colorful marketplace. At Kuala Trengganu's riverside market, women wrapped in batik sit on the ground amidst beautifully woven baskets piled high with colorful fruits and vegetables—fuzzy rambutans, succulent mangoes, and bright green beans. There are tables ladened with freshly caught fish, and crates of live, cackling chickens. You'll find baskets and mats woven into eye-catching shades of purple, yellow, and red, and stalls featuring brassware and batik.

Cottage industries. At Kuala Trengganu's Handicraft Training Centre in Tamar Rusila, young girls come to learn how to weave kain songket and mengkuang leaf products. After their training, they return to their villages to teach others.

Driving south of town, you'll see roadside stalls selling batik, kain songket, colorful kites, and woven baskets and mats. Cottage industries throughout the area welcome visitors.

A place to stay. On the beach south of Kuala Trengganu you'll find accommodations at the Rantau Abang Visitor Centre and at the Tanjong Jara Beach Hotel. The visitor center has a special platform for turtle watching (see "Return of the Turtles," page 97). Other Kuala Trengganu accommodations include Motel Desa, Pantai Motel, Hotel Meriah, and Hotel Warisan.

Kota Bharu

Only a few miles from the Thai border, Kota Bharu is the northernmost town on the east coast. It's also the capital of the state of Kelantan, known for its excellent crafting of silver products, kain songket, batik, and kites. Kota Bharu is best known as a good shopping area for local arts and crafts. Streets are lined with batik and silver shops, and crafts shops selling everything from Malaysian kites to bamboo products.

Like Kuala Trengganu, Kota Bharu has a lively central market where buyers and sellers barter over fruits, vegetables, chickens, and fish. The lantern-lit food stalls at the night market—not far from the central market—offer passers-by a mouth-watering array of local snacks.

Kota Bharu accommodations include the Kesina, Murni, Suria, and Temenggong hotels, as well as the

Resort Pantai Cinta Berahi (facing the beach of the same name).

East coast islands

All along the eastern seaboard there lies a scattered and broken chain of lovely *pulaus* (islands), many of which are only beginning to become tourist destinations.

Just offshore from Mersing, in the southern state of Johore, are Tioman and Rawa islands. Tioman, whose prominent features are twin peaks on its southern shore, offers good skin diving in its clear offshore waters. Delightful accommodations are provided at the Merlin Samudra Hotel. Pulau Rawa has about a dozen chalets for guests.

In the north off the Trengganu coast are Pulau Perhentian and Pulau Redang, two quiet, friendly islands noted for swimming and skin diving around the coral reefs. Perhentian has a rest house. Both islands are accessible from Kuala Trengganu or Kuala Besut.

SARAWAK, LAND OF HORNBILLS

Across the South China Sea from Peninsular Malaysia lies Borneo, an island characterized by jungle-covered mountains and swampy, river-cut lowlands. On the northern rim of this island are Malaysia's states of Sarawak and Sabah. Sparsely settled, Sarawak and Sabah offer visitors a slow pace, a fascinating cultural heritage, and an unspoiled landscape rich with wildlife. They surround the small, independent state of Brunei (see page 104).

Sarawak—nicknamed "land of the hornbills" because of the large-billed jungle birds that dwell here — has 124,450 square km/48,038 square miles. Sarawak's inhabitants include Malays, Chinese, and tribespeople like the Ibans, Bidayuhs, Melanaus, and Kelabits. Each tribal group has its own customs and traditions.

Sarawak's history has long been romanticized by tales of three white rajahs, members of an aristocratic English family who ruled the area for 105 years. The first was James Brooke, who arrived in 1839.

He was a British adventurer with a knack for exploring and pirate-fighting. By 1841, he had settled some disputes, been granted the title *rajah* (prince or king) by the Sultan of Brunei, and become ruler of an uncharted land famed for its headhunters. The family reign continued with his nephew, Rajah Charles Brooke, and Charles' son, Charles Vyner.

Sir Charles Vyner Brooke, the last white rajah, enacted a new constitution in 1941 as a move toward self-government. After the Japanese occupation, Sarawak became a British colony in 1946. Less than 20 years later—in 1963—it joined the Federation of Malaysia.

Getting there

Kuching, Sarawak's state capital, is the main port of entry for the state. Malaysian Airline System (MAS) has regular flights between Kuching and Kuala Lumpur, Singapore, Brunei, and Kota Kinabalu (Sabah). The Straits Steamship Company, sailing to and from Singapore, calls at ports in Sarawak, Brunei, and Sabah. There's also a 3-day tour out of Kuala Lumpur to Sarawak.

Getting around

Once in Sarawak, your best transportation is by air. MAS serves Sibu, Bintulu, and Miri. Most roads outside the towns are unpaved. Land transportation is generally by four-wheel-drive vehicle. You can explore Kuching by taxi, bus, or on foot.

Organized area tours out of Kuching include city sights, a day's visit to a Bidayuh (Land Dayak) longhouse, longer trips to Iban (Sea Dayak) longhouses, and day excursions to Santubong resort, Bako National Park, and the Niah Caves.

Where to stay. Most of Kuching's half dozen hotels have air conditioning and dining rooms; some have nightclubs. Accommodations include the Aurora, Aurora Beach, Borneo, and Longhouse hotels, and the Kuching Holiday Inn. Miri and Sibu also have hotels.

Shopping around. Sarawak craftspeople are noted for their fine beadwork, carvings, and vases. The Sarawak Arts Council Shop—next to the Sarawak Museum—has a display of native crafts, including carvings, masks, weavings, baskets, mats, and ceremonial items made by the various tribal groups.

For more information. The Sarawak Tourist Association Information Office is located on the grounds of the Sarawak Museum on Jalan Tun Haji Openg in Kuching.

Kuching, Sarawak's capital

Located at the southern end of Sarawak, Kuching is spread out along the north and south banks of the Sarawak River, 35 km/22 miles inland from the South China Sea. The main part of town is located on the south bank of the river. Here, you'll find the government offices, State Mosque, churches, temples, wharves, and dockyards.

Kuching's north bank, with its dignified residences set amidst rolling green lawns, presents a sharp contrast to the noisy crowded streets of the south bank. Here is where the white rajahs lived. The former white rajah's palace—now home of the governor—was built in 1870 by the second white rajah. Curved walkways lead to the English-style manor house surrounded by lawns.

Downriver from the palace, Fort Margherita guarded the city from attack. It has been converted to a Police Museum displaying lethal weapons and objects from the white rajahs' times.

Sarawak Museum. In a Normandy-style town house on Jalan Tun Haji Openg, this museum presents a historic and ethnological picture of Sarawak. Artifacts include indigenous tools, fine weavings, carvings, and burial paraphernalia (such as the intricately carved burial pole on the museum lawn). There's an exhibit on Stone Age excavations from the Niah Caves and a re-creation of several rooms of a longhouse (complete with genuine skulls hanging from the rafters).

A nearby excursion. Santubong seaside resort sits at the mouth of the Sarawak River, an hour's express boat trip from Kuching. This quiet fishing village with its chalets and rest houses was an important trading center during the Middle Ages.

Visiting a longhouse

Communal living is a way of life in Sarawak's longhouses. They were originally built so that whole villages could live together, assuring safety from attacks by other tribes and wild animals. Made of ironwood with palm roofs and split-bamboo floors, these houses on stilts can be home for just a few families or for over a hundred families, depending on how "long" the longhouse is.

Within the longhouse, each family has its own quarters with living, sleeping, and cooking space. A door from these quarters opens onto a long communal hall or veranda. Here, the people congregate to relax and gossip, or do chores like mat weaving, basket making, and fishnet mending.

Within a half day's road trip from Kuching, you can visit a longhouse of the Bidayuhs. En route you'll see plantations of pepper plants. Pepper is an economic mainstay of Sarawak.

On a several-day trip from Kuching, you can visit a more isolated Iban longhouse. Ibans live along the interior rivers. (The last part of your journey to one of these houses may be by motorized longboat.) You can arrange to spend the night in a longhouse and enjoy traditional tribal dances, including the *ngajat*, a dance originally performed after a successful head-hunting expedition.

Sarawak's national parks

Sarawak is blessed with several national parks, accessible on a day's trip out of Kuching.

Niah National Park. Discoveries made in the Niah Caves show that man lived in Borneo at least 40,000 years ago. The Sarawak Museum has been excavating these limestone caves since 1957, unearthing all kinds of Stone Age treasures.

Reaching the caves from Kuching requires a 40-minute flight to Miri, a 2½-hour drive to Batu Niah, and a 15-minute longboat ride to Pangkalan Lubang. Here you disembark and negotiate a 4-km/2½-mile trail of planks (slippery when wet) to the caves. (You'll need a guide to explore the caves.) There are accommodations at Batu Niah and Miri.

Bako National Park. You can travel to this park on a short boat trip from Kuching. Situated on the peninsula at the mouth of the Sarawak River, this park features a coastline of sandy bays and steep cliffs. Paths lead through the nearby jungle. Park flora and fauna include ferns, insectivorous plants, sambur, monkeys, and pigs. Park accommodations at Telok Assam include a rest house and two hostels. There's also a camping area.

SABAH, LAND BELOW THE WIND

Early seafarers nicknamed Sabah "land below the wind" because of its location south of the typhoon belt. Within Sabah's 73,711 square km/28,452 square miles you'll find dense tropical rain forests—home to many exotic birds—and nearly 1,450 km/900 miles of beach. Offshore tropical islands offer still more sandy expanses for sun lovers and warm, clear waters for snorkelers and divers.

As in Sarawak, Sabah's inhabitants have a rich cultural heritage. Tribal people include Kadazans, Bajaus, Muruts, Lanuns, Sukuks, and Binadaus.

Getting your bearings

Kota Kinabalu, Sabah's capital, is the state's main port of entry for tourists. Malaysian Airline System (MAS) flies between Kota Kinabalu and Penang, Kuala Lumpur, Singapore, Jakarta, and Hong Kong. Cathay Pacific has flights to and from Hong Kong via Brunei.

Getting around. Internally, Sabah's major towns are linked by MAS. The Sabah State Railways has regular service between Tanjung Aru (near Kota Kinabalu) and Tenom by way of Papar and Beaufort. Other land transportation is mainly by four-wheel-drive vehicles.

Local tours include Kota Kinabalu's city sights, Kota Belud, and Kinabalu National Park.

Accommodations. In Kota Kinabalu, hotels include Ang's, the Capital, the Hyatt Kinabalu International, the Borneo, the Shangri-la, and the Hotel Jesselton and Annex. You'll also find accommodations on the resort isle of Labaun, 124 km/77 miles from Kota Kinabalu, as well as in the Mount Kinabalu area, and in Sabah's other major towns.

Shopping. Locally made woven products such as hats, baskets, and mats are good buys in Sabah. Each tribes' designs are different. You can also buy beadwork, pottery, handwoven cloth, and blowpipes. Semporna, on Sabah's east coast, is known for its cultured pearls.

For more information. You'll find the Sabah Tourist Office at 1 Beach Street in Kota Kinabalu.

Kota Kinabalu, Sabah's capital city

Formerly known as Jesselton, Kota Kinabalu is a compact sea-front town built along a narrow strip of hill-backed land facing Gaya Bay. A string of coral islands dots its natural harbor. During World War II the town was almost completely destroyed, but it has been rebuilt as a well-planned capital. The downtown area has plain, multistory, concrete buildings lining streets planted with trees and shrubs. Many fine homes sit on the woodsy hillsides behind the town. Along the shore, Malay villages are built on stilts over the water or tidal flats.

City sights. Kota Kinabalu can be explored on foot, but there's also taxi service. The central market is the town's busiest area. Launches dock here at the sea wall to unload produce, and suburban buses stop here to unload passengers. Good market buys are woven baskets and mats, brass gongs, native hats, and tropical fruit.

Other sights include the contemporary State Mosque, with its ultramodern minaret capped by a conical-shaped gold dome, and the State Museum, featuring an overview of Sabah's culture and wildlife.

Beach excursions. The beach area at Tanjong Aru, 6 km/4 miles south of Kota Kinabalu, is ideal for swimming and other water sports. There are changing rooms at nearby Prince Philip Park.

(Continued on page 104)

Iban tribesmen, *sporting tattoos and rare feathers, perform warrior dance at Murat village longhouse, about five hours by car and longboat from Kuching, Sarawak.*

Sunday market *in Sabah village finds turbaned woman surveying stacks of rich-colored woven lids, used for covering produce at market.*

BRUNEI — AN OIL-RICH SULTANATE

Only a handful of tourists a year visit the tiny, oil-rich sultanate of Brunei, an independent British protectorate on the northern coast of Borneo. However, business-traveler traffic is heavy.

Oil was discovered here in 1929. Today, this country of 200,000 people produces 250,000 barrels of oil a day, making it economically self sufficient. (There isn't even an income tax.)

Brunei's riverside capital of Bandar Seri Begawan (formerly Brunei Town) is only a 2-hour flight from Kuala Lumpur, or a pleasant stopover between Kota Kinabalu and Kuching. There are also flights between Brunei and Hong Kong, Singapore, and Manila.

Sandwiched between the states of Sabah and Sarawak, Brunei today is a mere remnant of the large and powerful state that once controlled all of Borneo and the southern Philippines. Related to its neighbors by history, culture, and religion, Brunei has had a long tradition of independence. Its present ruler descends from a family of sultans who have ruled the country for 28 generations.

Life in Brunei centers around the Sultan Omar Ali Saifuddin Mosque. Built at a cost of U.S. $5 million, the gold-domed mosque dominates the city skyline. It is surrounded by a tranquil moat.

The over-the-water village of Kampong Ayer sprawls across the Brunei River not far from the mainland town of Bandar Seri Begawan. Considered the largest stilt village in the world (30,000 people), it is really a series of villages. You travel to and around them by boat.

Accommodations include the Ang's Brunei and Puspa hotels.

...Continued from page 102

Several tropical islands lie a short boat trip offshore. The waters surrounding these islands abound with coral and colorful fish.

Trip to a country market

One of the main countryside excursions from Kota Kinabalu is a trip to the Sunday *tamu* (open-air market) at Kota Belud, a 2-hour drive to the north. Early every Sunday morning, rural people from padis, plantations, and forests come to town dressed in their traditional finery for a day of fun and gossip.

Open-front stalls and impromptu arrangements of produce and handicrafts are laid out in a field. The place is alive with activity from 7 A.M. to about noon. People of different tribes barter with each other for all manner of goods and produce — saltfish, betel nuts, batik sarongs, live chickens, and exotic fruit. At one end of the market water buffaloes are auctioned off, and in another area there are cock fights (bloodless).

Tamus are held weekly (usually on Sunday) in towns throughout Sabah. However, Kota Belud's is the biggest. In addition, every town has a special *tamu* once a year. Kota Belud's features buffalo races, native dancing, and demonstrations of riding skills and dexterity by colorful Bajau cowboys. Called the "cowboys of the east," they are well known for their excellent horsemanship. En route to Kota Belud, you'll pass Mengkabong, a Malay fishing village built on stilts over the water. Wooden catwalks connect the wood and thatch houses.

Kinabalu National Park

Southeast Asia's highest peak, 4,101-meter/13,455-foot Mount Kinabalu, dominates Kinabalu National Park, a 712-square-km/275-square-mile wilderness area ranging from mossy rain forest to subalpine scrub. The Kadazans hold this mountain sacred, believing it is home for the spirits of the departed.

Visitors to Sabah can view this intriguing peak from afar while visiting Kota Belud, an hour and a half from the park. If you prefer, you can journey into the park for an overnight stay or a several-day trek up and down the mountain.

From Kota Kinabalu it's a 93-km/58-mile bumpy ride by four-wheel-drive vehicle to the park, or a 25-minute flight to the town of Ranau, followed by a 15-minute trip to park headquarters. The base camp at 1,372 meters/

4,500 feet has a hostel, restaurant, and visitors' cottages and cabins.

The physically fit who want to climb the mountain can begin their trip the next morning by taking a short ride to the 1,829-meter/6,000-foot level where the climb starts. Terraced stairs cover the first 610 meters/2,000 feet of the climb. You'll find aluminum shelter huts spread out about every 2½ hours' walk, the last one at 3,810 meters/12,500 feet, an hour from the summit. Since the peak usually clouds over by 9 A.M., it's best to stay overnight and make the final ascent early the next morning. When it's clear at the top, you can see parts of Indonesia, Borneo, and the southern islands of the Philippines. April and May are the best climbing months.

You'll need a guide for the climb. Make arrangements ahead through the Park Warden, Box 626, Kota Kinabalu.

Still other sights

Sandakan, once the capital of North Borneo, lies on Sabah's east coast, 386 km/240 miles from Kota Kinabalu. The town has an orchid house featuring a collection of rare orchids. The area's biggest attraction for visitors, though, is Sepilok Sanctuary, the world's largest orangutan park. About 24 km/15 miles west of Sandakan, it is home to orangutans (an endangered species) that have been rescued from captivity. They're brought here to be rehabilitated so they can once more live in the wild.

KNOW BEFORE YOU GO

The following practical information will help you plan your trip to Malaysia.

Entry/exit procedures. You need a passport; for a visit of three months or more, you need a visa.

Yellow fever vaccinations are required only if you are arriving from an infected area. However, the U.S. Public Health Service recommends that you have typhoid, tetanus, and gamma globulin shots anyway. If your plans include travel beyond urban areas, check with your doctor for antimalarial treatment.

You pay an airport tax of M $7 when leaving Malaysia for destinations other than Brunei, Sabah, Sarawak, and Singapore. To Brunei and Singapore, it's M $4, and for all other domestic flights it's M $2.

Customs. You may bring in, duty-free, 1 liter of liquor and 200 cigarettes or about 250 grams (8 ounces) of tobacco. If you enter with too many cameras, watches, or other expensive items, you may be required to post an import duty deposit, refundable on departure with the items within 3 months.

Currency. The Malaysian dollar (ringgit) is the unit of currency, and the rate of exchange is U.S. $1 to M $2.25. You are allowed to import M $10,000 and export M $5,000. Money can be converted at any bank or licensed money-changer. Hotels charge a small fee to change money.

Traveler's checks and credit cards are accepted at hotels, restaurants, and stores in the larger cities.

Health conditions. Hospital and medical services are good, and there are many English-speaking doctors. In most large hotels, the water is safe for drinking; in the country, use boiled water.

Tipping. Throughout the country, tipping is not encouraged. Major hotels and restaurants in the cities add a 10 percent service charge to your bill.

Weather and what to wear. Malaysia is warm, but it's not as hot as its position near the equator suggests. Days are sunny and very humid; nights are fairly cool.

Average temperatures in the lowlands range from 22°C/72°F to 32°C/90°F. It's cooler in the hill country, with temperatures between 10°C/50°F and 21°C/70°F. Although the country is not in the monsoon belt, it does have wet months, and short downpours occur throughout the year. Peninsular Malaysia is drenched in rain from October through January. In Sabah and Sarawak, rains are heavy November through February.

You will be most comfortable in lightweight informal sports clothes. Coats and ties or long-sleeve batik shirts are required for men at some deluxe hotels and restaurants. Be sure to bring along a sweater for the cooler highlands areas, and don't forget to pack your umbrella, sunglasses, suntan lotion, and insect repellent.

Time. There is a 15½-hour difference in time between the U.S. west coast and Kuala Lumpur. When it's 8:30 P.M. Friday in San Francisco, it's noon on Saturday in Kuala Lumpur.

For more information. Your best source on travel in Malaysia is the Tourist Development Corporation of Malaysia, MPI, Wisma Building, P.O. Box 328, Kuala Lumpur. Their U.S. office is the Malaysian Tourist Information Center at 600 Montgomery Street, 36th Floor, San Francisco, CA 94111. Malaysian consulates are located in San Francisco, Los Angeles, and Honolulu; the embassy is in Washington, D.C. In Kuala Lumpur, the U.S. Embassy is located in the A.I.A. Building on Jalan Ampang.

Statue *of Sir Stamford Raffles, Singapore's founder, overlooks landscaped plaza at mouth of river, near spot where he stepped ashore in 1819.*

Bumboat plies *Singapore River, bringing cargo from harbor ships to godowns (warehouses) lining river banks. Skyscrapers, in background, contrast sharply with century-old shophouses.*

SINGAPORE

Asia in a modern nutshell — a thriving country
dotted with skyscrapers; accented with parklands; and
blessed with a special blend of Asian people, cultures,
traditions, arts, festivals, and cuisine

aves of progress have rolled across Singapore, leaving in their wake a dazzling modern city with towering office buildings and new hotels set in a garden paradise. Dozens of skyscrapers not far from the harbor's edge appear heavy enough to flip the island over into the sea.

Yet beneath this mass of modern construction, the heart of old Singapore beats on. Century-old several-story Chinese shophouses with red-tile roofs stand within the shadows of eye-catching buildings of glimmering glass. From upstairs shophouse windows, family laundry hangs — as it has for over a century — from long bamboo poles. (You'll even see these bamboo clothes driers jutting from modern high-rise apartment windows.) Victorian-style government buildings lining the Padang green, with its cricket club and weekend cricket matches, still speak of Singapore's colonial past.

Singapore is rich in greenery, so the effects of modernity are further softened by tree-lined boulevards and grassy public squares. Even in Jurong—Singapore's largest industrial estate with hundreds of factories—the emphasis is on greenery: the estate has a series of parklands, including the enormous Jurong Park with its 81-hectare/200-acre lake.

ISLAND FACTS

Singaporeans enjoy a high standard of living. In fact, the island reigns as a showplace for Asian progress. Situated West of Borneo and east of Sumatra, Singapore is dwarfed by its neighbors. Yet its deep-water harbor and its location between the Middle East and the Orient gives it significant stature in world trade. Ships of every description—supertankers, tramp steamers, container ships — anchor in its vast 14-square-km/36-square-mile harbor. Indeed, some 40,000 ships visit the busy waterfront each year, making it the third ranking shipping port in the world.

Manufacturing has also become an important source of funds for Singapore's economy. Over 60 percent of the country's manufactured goods—ranging from garments to precision equipment—is exported.

Some geographic specifics

Only 137 km/85 miles north of the equator, the tiny island republic of Singapore consists of a main, tropical island (572 square km/221 square miles) and about 54 islets. The wide, diamond-shaped main island extends 42 km/26 miles from east to west and 23 km/14 miles from north to south. It lies at the southern tip of Peninsular Malaysia and is linked to the mainland by a 1,056-meter/3,465-foot-long manmade causeway.

Singapore City at the island's southern end occupies only about a quarter of the island. Beyond the central city are industrial suburbs with factories and high-rise apartment complexes. The island's highest point, 166-meter/545-foot Bukit Timah (hill of tin), rises above a central plateau surrounded by reservoirs and forests.

Plants and animals

Until 150 years ago, Singapore was covered with thick vegetation. Tropical forest blanketed nearly two-thirds of the island, and mangrove swamps edged the coast. But land development has devoured much of this original vegetation, and today the island's only remaining virgin forest is the 66-hectare/163-acre Bukit Timah Nature Reserve.

Singapore greenery. Singapore remains tropically green, though, despite the vast development on the island. Nearly 2;000 species of tropical plants flourish. Roadside flowers, such as yellow black-eyed Susans, bloom around the year and Singapore's city streets are lined with flowering trees—African tulip, red flame, and plumeria. Annual plantings of trees and bushes add to the greenery and compensate for the vegetation destroyed by development.

Local wildlife. The mighty leopards and tigers that once menaced Singapore's jungle workers are now found only in the zoo. However, numerous smaller animals, such as

(Continued on page 110)

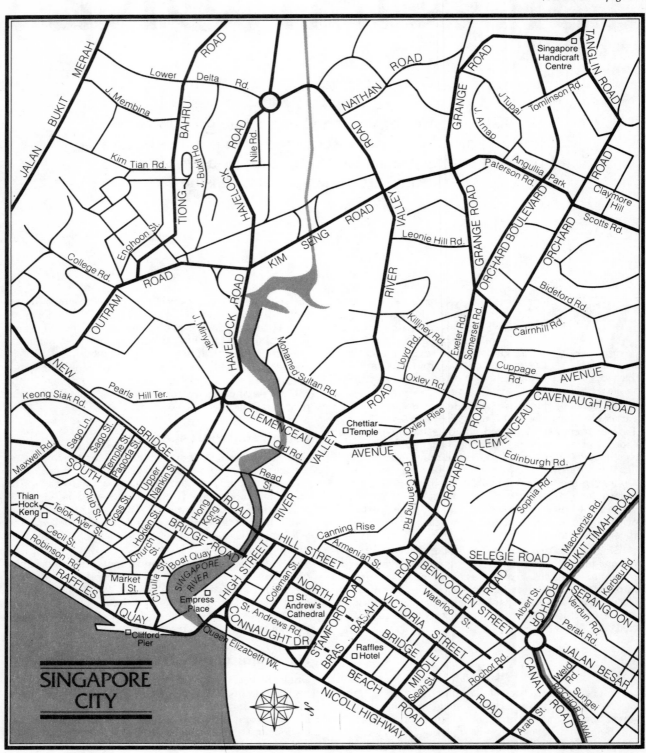

SINGAPORE CITY

THE ESSENTIALS/SINGAPORE

Here are a few basics to help you in planning and taking a trip to Singapore.

Getting there

Singapore is served by air, rail, bus, and sea transportation.

Air. Some 32 international air carriers, including Singapore Airlines, serve the country's international airport at Changi on the northeastern edge of the island, 20 km/12 miles from the center of the city. There's both bus and taxi service to downtown Singapore.

Rail. Malayan Railway provides daily service between Singapore and Kuala Lumpur and Butterworth (Penang) in Malaysia. Three times a week the International Express travels from Singapore to Bangkok, Thailand (with a change of train in Butterworth). Singapore's station is on Keppel Road.

Bus. There's daily bus service between Singapore and such Malaysian towns as Johore Bahru, Malacca, Kuala Lumpur, Penang, Mersing, and Kuantan.

Sea. Singapore is a regular port of call for many passenger and cargo/passenger ships. Ships either dock at the World Trade Centre or anchor in the harbor with launch service to shore.

Accommodations

Visitors to Singapore have a wide variety of hotels to choose from. Most Singapore hotels provide standard international facilities; many also offer swimming pools, health clubs, shopping arcades, and group facilities. All tourist hotels add a 3 percent government tax, and most impose a 10 percent service charge.

Singapore's "hotel row" is Orchard Road—a bustling center of shopping complexes, banks, airline offices, and commercial headquarters. Among the numerous large tourist hotels located along or near Orchard Road are the Century Park Sheraton, Mandarin, Hyatt Regency Singapore, Goodwood Park, Holiday Inn Singapore, Hilton International Singapore, Singapura Forum, York, Ming Court, Ladyhill, Shangri-la, and Marco Polo. Further north are the Royal and Equatorial hotels. The Cockpit and Oberoi Imperial hotels are located between Orchard Road and the business district.

Near the Civic Center, major tourist hotels include the Peninsula and Raffles, a historic landmark noted for its old-fashioned elegance (see page 117). The Apollo, Miramar, and King's hotels are located in a residential area south of the Singapore River. Popular small hotels are the Grand Central, Garden, Orchid Inn, Negara, and Queens.

Getting around

Singapore's complex street pattern, originally planned during the 1800s for pedestrians and bullock carts, has become somewhat confusing, and many streets and alleys have been converted to one-way traffic. For downtown exploration, it's best to rely on public transportation and your feet; rent a car just for trips around the island or to Malaysia.

Taxis are one of the best ways to explore the city and there are over 8,000 metered taxis for hire. Before starting on your trip, make sure the driver understands where you want to go and that he has flagged the meter. (Between 1 and 6 A.M. there is a 50 percent surcharge.) Note that smoking in air-conditioned cabs is illegal and violation of this law carries a stiff penalty. During the morning's peak traffic hours (7:30 to 10:15 A.M.), cars—including taxis—entering the Central Business District are required to have and display a daily area license. The fee of S $2.50 (for taxis) is sometimes payable by the passenger.

The Singapore Bus Service (SBS) provides bus transportation over a network of roads that crisscross the downtown area and circle the island. The buses run from 6 A.M. to 11:30 P.M. You can purchase bus guides showing the bus routes at bookshops and newstands. If possible, avoid riding the bus during peak commute periods (7 to 9 A.M., noon to 2 P.M., and 4:30 to 6 P.M.).

The trishaw (bicycle with sidecar) provides an old-fashioned, leisurely paced transport through the city, especially down narrow lanes and alleys. Try at least a short ride on one since they're fast disappearing from the modern Singapore scene. Establish the price with the driver, though, before you start your trip.

Both self-drive cars and cars with drivers are available for hire. Traffic keeps to the left. If you plan to drive, you'll need an international driver's license.

Tours

There are tours featuring city sights, flora and fauna, arts and crafts, the Jurong area (see page 123), Sentosa (see page 124), and nightspots. You can take city tours by trishaw, and water tours by sampan, motorboat, or Chinese junk.

For more information

The Singapore Tourist Promotion Board at 131 Tudor Court, Tanglin Road (near the Singapore Handicraft Centre) can provide brochures and maps of Singapore. The board is open from 8 A.M. to 5 P.M. daily except Sunday.

...*Continued from page 108*

flying lemurs, civet cats, shrews, flying squirrels, and porcupines, still live on the island.

Among the most commonly seen birds on Singapore island are the yellow-vented bulbul, pied triller, tree sparrow, crow, and dove.

HISTORY IN TRADE

Singapore's history is closely allied to trade. Malay sea gypsies (Orang Laut) and pirates visited the island first, followed by Chinese traders. In the 4th century, Arabs sailed into Singapore harbor en route to the Molucca Islands in eastern Indonesia. Later, Chinese Buddhists and monks arrived.

In the 8th century, a Sri Vijaya prince from Sumatra landed on the island, then known as Temasek (Sea Town). It is said that during his visit the prince spotted a strange-looking animal and was told it was a lion. (This is highly unlikely since there were no lions on the island.) The prince felt that sighting the animal was a good omen, so he renamed the island *Singa Pura* (lion city) and made it part of the Sri Vijaya kingdom. It soon became a flourishing trade center.

Forces from the powerful Javanese kingdom of Majapahit destroyed the town of Singa Pura during their 14th century campaign to eradicate the rival Sri Vijaya kingdom. In the years that followed, Singapore fell into obscurity.

Colonial rule

Singapore's modern era dates from 1819, when Sir Stamford Raffles landed near the mouth of the Singapore River. He had been in search of a good location for a trading station that would protect the southern entrance of the Strait of Malacca and provide a supply base in the India-China trade route. Singapore, with its sheltered deep-water harbor, was ideal.

Raffles and the island's sultan (appointed by Raffles) signed an agreement allowing the British East India Company to establish a trading post at the mouth of the Singapore River. Raffles immediately declared Singapore a free port. When Sir Stamford Raffles landed in Singapore, jungle and swamp covered most of the island. In those first months, a thousand men (mostly Indian convicts) worked at clearing the dense vegetation to make way for a town near the river's mouth.

The town soon grew. Thousands of men from the Middle East and Asia flooded the trading center, and each ethnic group was allotted space. The Arabs and Bugis settled the area between the coast, the Rochor Canal, and the outlying swamps. The Chinese concentrated in the area south of the Singapore River, forming what became Chinatown. Early Indian traders clustered along the river's bank, near what became Chulia, Market, and High streets. Malay fishermen lived on boats or built stilt houses over the water.

From crown colony to independence

Five years after the agreement with the British East India Company was signed, the Sultan of Johore ceded Singapore—together with Penang, Malacca, and nearby islands—to Great Britain in perpetuity. The group was to be known as the Straits Settlement. Singapore became a British Crown Colony in 1867.

Japanese troops took Singapore in 1942 and occupied the island until 1945, when it was returned to British control. Kranji War Memorial, on a hillside overlooking the Johore Strait, honors the Allied Forces who died during World War II. The Memorial Park Land on Beach Road commemorates civilians who died during the Japanese occupation.

In 1959 Singapore became a self-governing state within the British Commonwealth. Four years later, it joined the Federation of Malaysia; but in 1965, Singapore separated from Malaysia and became an independent sovereign state. On December 22, 1965, Singapore became a republic with a president as its head.

Today's government

Singapore's parliamentary system of government is based on full adult suffrage; voting is compulsory for every citizen 21 years of age or older. A speaker, elected by parliament, presides over the 75-member parliament.

Singapore's president, elected for a term of four years, appoints the prime minister. Political power is vested in this prime minister; judicial power is vested in the Supreme Court and several lower courts.

SINGAPORE'S PEOPLE

Like Malaysia, its sister nation to the north, Singapore is a multiracial society rich in a variety of customs, festivals, religions, handicrafts, foods, and life styles. Its population is strongly Chinese. In fact, the Chinese population in Singapore is one of the largest outside China.

Of its 2.3 million people, more than 76 percent are Chinese, mostly Straits Chinese (second and third generation born in Singapore). Malays account for 15 percent and Indians and Pakistanis another 7 percent. The rest of the racial melting pot includes Europeans, Eurasians, Arabs, Indonesians, Thais, Filipinos, and Japanese. They all proudly call themselves Singaporeans.

Changing life styles

Things are changing in Singapore. Old traditions and ways still exist, but they're sometimes hidden behind the sophistication of a modern bustling city.

In times past, whole families lived in two and three-story shophouses in the heart of Singapore. Still other families lived in stilt houses in forest clearings or near the water's edge. Now these low density houses have been replaced by modern, high-rise apartment complexes. These "apartment towns" come complete with shops, markets, schools, restaurants, and food stall (hawker) centers. Although you'll find some of these high-rise apartments in the downtown area, most are located in the suburbs. About 68 percent of Singapore's people reside in these high density blocks in satellite towns.

Dress. Traditional dress is fast disappearing from Singapore's streets. Many of today's residents, prefering western-style dress for everyday wear, reserve more traditional dress for festivals and ceremonial events.

Colorful greetings *frame intent calligrapher in Chinatown. City's Chinese section is one of Southeast Asia's largest.*

Grocer displays *palette of produce along street; locals shop for food amid kaleidoscopic colors and sounds.*

Language. Many residents, particularly the younger generation, speak several languages and dialects. Though the national language is Malay, English is used as the language of commerce and administration. Virtually all the educated people of Singapore speak English. Other official languages are Chinese (Mandarin) and Tamil.

Religion. Most Chinese are Buddhist, Taoist, Confucianist (often a mixture of all three), or Christian. Malays are Muslim, and Indians follow the Hindu or Muslim faith.

THE CITY — A MODERN METROPOLIS

The city of Singapore had its beginning along its river and harbor, and today this area remains a center for much of its commercial activity. Glass and steel high-rises compete for space around the harbor and the river. Still other office towers have found a home along Orchard and Tanglin roads northwest of the harbor. With land at a premium, these modern edifices are edging out structures that recall Singapore's early years. As we've said before, though, tucked between high-rise buildings you'll still find some British-influenced, Victorian-style government buildings as well as several-story Chinese shophouses with their red-tile roofs.

Getting your bearings

Singapore's city area is best explored on foot with occasional taxi rides to more distant points of interest. Before beginning your walk, however, get your bearings and enjoy a panoramic look at the city and its harbor from the observation lounge atop the Mandarin Hotel on Orchard Road. The Singapore Tourist Promotion Board's handy *Weekly Guide Singapore* has a map to help you locate city landmarks; it also contains information on sights to see.

To further orient yourself, take time to view *The Singapore Experience.* This multiscreen, audio-visual presentation gives you Singapore in a 45-minute capsule. You'll learn of its history, its people, its customs, its festivals, and its sights to see. The slide presentation is shown from noon to 6 P.M. daily at the Cultural Theatre, located at the corner of Tanglin and Grange roads (adjacent to the Singapore Handicraft Centre)—a short distance from Orchard Road hotels.

Some downtown sights

It's just a 10-minute taxi ride from the Orchard Road hotel area to downtown. A good place to begin your city tour is at Merlion Park, located on the tip of a promontory on the river's south bank. Here you'll enjoy a fine view of Singa-

A FINE FEATHERED CHOIR

The melodious warbling of talented song birds fills the air on Sunday mornings in Singapore. The feathered-choir concert takes place outdoors along Tiong Bahru and Seng

Poh roads. The participants—thrushes, sharmas, mata putehs, merobok jambols—warble their melodies from elaborate bamboo cages perched atop tall bamboo poles.

Below, their owners squat on sidewalk stools, sip coffee, and listen with rapture to their talented pets. The owners also exchange notes with each other and occasionally haggle over a sale price. Bird doctors, food advisers, food suppliers, cage repairers, brokers, and valuers are also part of the gathering.

On some Sundays, the birds are judged for their musical repertoires. Competition points are given for good looks, quality of performance, and showmanship.

Raising a prize-winning bird is an expensive proposition; some compare the cost to that of keeping a polo pony. Besides the high purchase price, there's an ongoing, costly "grocery" bill for special seeds and insects. The bird's bamboo cage with its intricately carved base is also costly. Wealthy bird owners even hire special servants whose sole duty is to pamper the owner's birds.

To visitors the sights and sounds of a bird concert— usually beginning around 8 A.M.—can add a special touch to the Singapore experience.

pore's famous harbor. Focal point of the park is the 8-meter/26-foot water-spouting Merlion (part fish, part lion) statue — the symbol of Singapore.

A closer look at the harbor. From the park, walk south along the waterfront to Clifford Pier. From here you can take a harbor cruise. On any given day, a variety of ships — from brand-new supertankers to elegant passenger liners and rusting tramp steamers — ride at anchor in the harbor's outer roads.

Your tour — on either a junk or regular boat — includes the harbor and a trip around the southern islands. Some tours stop at Kusu Island for a visit to an ancient Chinese temple, and at Sentosa Island (see page 124). You can choose from daytime, sunset, or evening (dinner) cruises.

Change Alley. The pedestrian bridge from Clifford Pier leads to several shopping alleys, including the well-known Change Alley — one of the narrowest shopping alleys in the world. The lane received its name from the Indian moneychangers who used to congregate here and yell "money change" to passers-by.

These walking, gesticulating bankers are less frequently encountered now. Today, alley strollers will be confronted with hawking salesmen offering a haphazard variety of goods. Stalls and motley shops sell a hodgepodge of gaudy souvenirs, watches, toys, woven baskets, antiques (some genuine, some instant), and even fine luggage and camera equipment.

Raffles Place. Change Alley dead ends at Raffles Place. This busy commercial district of banks, law firms, and shipping companies is undergoing a face lift. Many of its turn-of-the-century Victorian buildings have been torn down to make way for modern office complexes.

On to the north bank. Heading north across Raffles Place, you can cross the Singapore River, near its mouth on the Anderson Bridge or the Cavenagh Bridge. Along the river's northern bank is Empress Place, named in memory of Queen Victoria. Facing Empress Place is Victoria Theatre and Victoria Memorial Hall with its impressive clock tower. A statue of Sir Stamford Raffles — Singapore's founder — stands in front of Victoria Memorial Hall. Not far from here

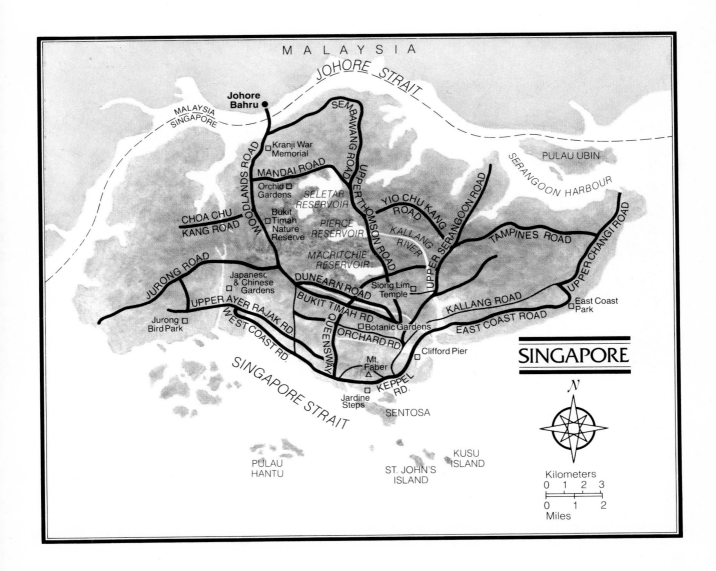

Sari-clad Indians *pass brilliant, sculptured portal of Sri Mariamman, Singapore's oldest Hindu temple.*

On Arab Street, *city's Muslim Malay quarter, trishaw negotiates narrow, shop-lined roadway; bikes provide leisurely paced transport through crowded streets.*

— near the river's mouth — is another statue of Raffles. This one is located near the spot where Raffles first landed in 1819.

The Supreme Court and City Hall, both fronted by Corinthian pillars, face the beautifully maintained lawns of the Padang green a short distance from Empress Place. For more than a century, Singaporeans have played cricket and enjoyed colorful parades on the Padang.

A few churches. At the northwest corner of the Padang stands St. Andrew's Cathedral, seat of the Church of England in Singapore. The Gothic-style cathedral, surrounded by a large lawn shaded by tropical trees, is circled by traffic on four sides. Indian convicts completed work on the cathedral in 1863.

Singapore's oldest Christian church is on Hill Street, a couple of blocks west of St. Andrew's. The Armenian Church, whose proper name is the Armenian Apostolic Church of Saint Gregory the Illuminator, was built in 1835 when there were only three Armenian families living on the island. Services are no longer held in this handsome church, but it's being preserved as a historic landmark.

Along Elizabeth Walk. This promenade, on the harbor side of Connaught Drive, provides a pleasant respite from the traffic and bustle of downtown Singapore. It's hard to realize that this half-mile-long expanse of huge rain trees, flowering shrubs, well-trimmed hedges, and benches was once underwater—part of the harbor it borders—until the land was reclaimed in 1943. (The sandy spit of land just opposite Elizabeth Walk has also been reclaimed and will one day feature housing, parks, and resort hotels.)

Today's Chinatown

The Chinese laborers, merchants, and traders who migrated to Singapore in the 1820s settled in an area south of the Singapore River. These first migrants were from various parts of China and brought with them traditions, dialects, and trades common to their particular provinces. These provincial characteristics were retained because people tended to settle with others from their province. Sometimes whole streets became devoted to a specific trade associated with a particular province.

These first Chinatown residents built two and three-story shophouses in which they lived and worked. The first floor accommodated the family business. The second and third floors were family living quarters, sometimes serving two families.

By the turn of the century, more and more Chinese migrated to Singapore and settled in Chinatown. Space became scarce for new buildings, and existing buildings became overcrowded. The once spacious shophouses were divided and subdivided, and whole families lived crowded together in curtained or partitioned cubicles.

These crowded living conditions continue to exist in Chinatown's ancient shophouses, but like the rest of Singapore, the face of Chinatown is changing. Many of the run-down, overcrowded buildings are being demolished to make room for improved, high-rise housing complexes accommodating more people more comfortably. (Still other Chinatown residents are moving to suburban apartment complexes.) Plans are also being formulated to renovate those shophouses that will be preserved.

Strolling through Chinatown. Today's Chinatown—both old and new—encompasses about 2.6 square km/1 square mile. It's bounded by Anson Road, Tanjong Pagar Road, New Bridge Road, Clemenceau Avenue, and the Singapore River.

Whole blocks of high-rise, concrete flats and business offices now tower over paint-worn, shuttered shophouses, but the exotic array of sights, smells, and sounds that are Chinatown still exist. You'll see streets and alleys still cluttered with awning-covered market stalls heaped with rolls of colorful batik, baskets brimming with red chile peppers, basins of gasping fish, bundles of flowers, cages of cackling chickens, and mounds of colorful fruit and vegetables. At the morning market — stretching between Sago Street, Smith Street, and Trengganu Street—housewives shop for such delicacies as eel and turtle.

The tantalizing aromas of frying noodles and grilling satay also fill the air. Chinatown abounds with tiny, brightly lighted restaurants with tables and chairs that spill out into the street. Sidewalk food stalls are also plentiful, and in the evening whole families gather to dine here.

Cottage industries. Many of the traditional crafts and trades brought from China in the 1800s are still alive in Chinatown. Shops continue to specialize in making lanterns, noodles, carved images, clogs, or paper models. These paper models — of everything from houses and boats to jet planes — are burned by relatives of the deceased at a post-funeral rite to insure that the souls of the deceased are well equipped to cross into the beyond.

During the New Year, people still flock to a letter writer for lucky vermilion scrolls painted with gold characters. During other times of the year these letter writers keep busy writing invoices, business proposals, and letters for illiterate Chinese.

Temples. Singapore is blessed with numerous Chinese temples. In fact, the Yellow Pages (of the city's telephone directory) list over 500 of them. Some of the oldest are located in Chinatown.

Thian Hock Keng (Temple of Heavenly Happiness), on Telok Ayer Street, is Singapore's oldest Chinese Temple. The original joss house (more of a chapel than a temple) was built on this sight in 1821. Today's temple, with its granite pillars, ornamental stonework, and woodcarvings imported from China, was completed in 1840.

Beyond Chinatown, you can visit the Temple of 1,000 Lights on Race Course Road not far from Little India. The temple was named for the electric lights surrounding its 15-meter/50-foot image of Buddha. (For a small fee, you can have the lights turned on.)

Quiet tranquility pervades Siong Lim Sian Si, considered Singapore's most ornate and largest Buddhist temple, located north of the city on Jalan Toa Payoh. Within its halls are carved wooden lanterns, dragons, and phoenixes like those in ancient Peking palaces. Beautifully carved deities can be found everywhere, and all the temple's panels, pillars, and carved altars are painted in rich reds and golds. Footpaths link the temple to spacious Siong Lim Garden (formerly Soochow Garden) where you can walk under flowering shade trees, past small streams and even a carp-filled pond complete with fountain, and across a sculptured marble bridge.

Tours. Besides exploring Chinatown on your own, you can also take an organized tour by trishaw. For reservations, contact Raffles Hotel or Trishaw Tourist Pte. Ltd. on Beach Road.

Little India

The faint twang of sitar music and aromas rich in curry and incense signal your arrival in Little India. Though only 7 percent of Singapore's residents can claim Indian descent, this minority has maintained its culture in art, dance, literature, and food. On Serangoon Road — center of Singapore's Indian colony—you'll find shops selling silken saris, colorful madras bedspreads, gold jewelry, and a host of taste-tantalizing condiments and spices.

Oddly enough, two of the Indian community's most important Hindu temples are not even located in Little India. Chettiar Hindu Temple is located on Tank Road opposite Central Park and Sri Mariamman Temple is in Chinatown on South Bridge Road.

The Chettiar Hindu Temple was built in the 1850s by Nattukkotai Chettiars (moneylenders). It's dedicated to the six-headed Indian god, Lord Subramaniam.

The Sri Mariamman Temple is the city's oldest Hindu place of worship. Its much photographed tower archway features a cluttered but lifelike assortment of brightly painted, stucco sculptures of deities, animals, and human figures. More figures decorate the temple's surrounding wall.

Along Arab Street

You'll find a potpourri of goldsmiths, florists, textile tradespeople, and dealers in semiprecious stones along Arab Street, a thoroughfare linking Beach and Rochor Canal roads. This is Singapore's Malay quarter. Many of the shops are managed by Indians, but their customers are Malay.

The focal point of this Muslim community is the mosque. The lofty, majestic domes and minarets of Sultan Mosque rise above North Bridge Road near Arab Street. Built in the 1920s, it is one of Singapore's oldest Muslim mosques. Surrounding the mosque, tiny shops offer colorful bolts of Indian silks, sari cloth, and batiks.

In and around Central Park

The rolling green lawns of Central Park — marked by flowerbeds, shade trees, and neat walkways — provide a garden setting for the Van Kleef Aquarium and National Theatre. Nearby is the National Museum and Art Gallery. The park is located north of the Singapore River and is bounded on the south by River Valley Road, on the west by Clemenceau Avenue, and on the east by Hill Street.

Van Kleef Aquarium. Set back from River Valley Road among the park's trees, this aquarium contains more than 4,600 specimens of marine life, much of it from local waters. Strolling the long, tank-lined corridors, you'll see giant turtles, eels, carnivorous piranhas, sharks, sea snakes, starfish, king crabs, and octopuses. In smaller tanks, colorful angel, butterfly, and clown fish dart playfully around interesting coral formations or swaying sea anemones. The aquarium is open daily from 9:30 A.M. to 9 P.M.

National Theatre. Built in 1963, a starkly modern building near the Van Kleef Aquarium provides a striking setting for theatrical and musical performances. This theater, with its courtyard entrance enhanced by a fountain, is actually an amphitheater built against a sloping hill.

National Museum and Art Gallery. Located on Stamford Road just east of Central Park, this museum and gallery combination is housed in a white, two-story, domed building whose construction began in 1887.

One of the museum's more popular attractions is the Haw Par Jade Collection, formerly displayed in the House of Jade on Nassim Road. Included in this exhibit are 385 pieces of Chinese carvings. Dating from the Sung and Ch'ing dynasties, the collection is thought to be unrivaled in Southeast Asia.

Other museum exhibits feature Chinese costumes, ancient Thai pottery, Malaysian musical instruments and woodcarvings, weaponry used through the ages, local marine and animal life, butterflies, and ancient coins. One room features early furniture.

The art gallery has paintings and other works of art by local artists.

Both the museum and gallery are open from 9 A.M. to 5:30 P.M. daily.

A SHOPPER'S PARADISE

In Singapore you'll discover an amazing assortment of goods from all over the world for sale at reasonable, if not bargain prices. Many of the imported items — as well as local products — are duty-free.

Bargaining is still an important part of shopping in Singapore. The only place it's not practiced is in department stores where prices are usually fixed. Otherwise, a bit of friendly haggling is expected, and if you don't haggle you won't get the best price. When a price is quoted, make a counteroffer of about half that. You can work up from that to a price that's acceptable to both you and the dealer.

It's also wise to do a little comparison shopping before buying. Initial price quotes can vary between shops. Shops approved by the Singapore Tourist Promotion Board display the organization's official window decal, a gold merlion (half fish, half lion) on a circular red background. The STPB also publishes a helpful *Singapore Shopping Guide*, as well as the *Weekly Guide Singapore*, which contains shopping information.

Where to shop

Half the fun of shopping in Singapore is the variety of shopping locales, from awning-covered, streetside stalls to modern, sprawling, multistoried complexes. Along Orchard Road—not far from many of the major tourist hotels — are shops, elegant boutiques, department stores, hotel shopping arcades, shopping complexes, and Chinese emporiums offering a wide array of goods. Other popular shopping spots include North Bridge Road (electrical appliances, stereo equipment, watches), High Street (gems, pearls, watches, Indian brass, Irish crystal), Arab Street (batiks, basketry, jewelry), Serangoon Road (saris, silks, Indian cottons, Indian jewelry), and Change Alley (souvenirs of debatable quality, cameras).

The maze of alleyways north of the Rochor Canal, from Sungei Road to Kelantan Lane, shelters a hodgepodge of several hundred shops and stalls selling everything from priceless antiques to plastic flowers and fresh fruit. The area is still known as the Thieves' Market, a name that goes back to the days when an article stolen at night could be offered for quick, cheap sale here the next day.

When it started about 50 years ago, the market carried only secondhand goods; now its shops offer a broad range of new goods as well. You can find army survival gear and canned peaches, Japanese cigarette lighters and rusty spanners (wrenches), and clothing and stereo equipment. Business hours are 2 to 6 P.M. daily.

What to buy

Purchases in Singapore can range from Oriental antiques to watches and stereo equipment from Japan. Visitors delight in the treasure trove of crafted items made in Singapore and neighboring Asian countries.

International specialties. If you're interested in fabrics, you'll find batiks from Malaysia, Singapore, and Indonesia. Fabric lovers will be enchanted with Chinese shantung, bold-patterned Thai silk, silver-bordered kelantan from Malaysia, Singaporean khersonese silk, and Indian gold-embroidered pieces ideal for saris.

Carpets from Iran (Persia), China, India, and Singapore are waiting for you in an assortment of colors and patterns. So are figurines and jewelry made from Burmese jade, tribal spears from Borneo, Singaporean pewter, and Malaysian silver filigree jewelry, as well as Indian brassware and Indonesian woodcarvings.

Duty-free items. Many items in Singapore can be purchased duty-free. Prices, therefore, can be from 5 to 40 percent less than the normal list price elsewhere. (Standard list prices are available on demand.) Some of the duty-free purchases you can make include cameras and other photographic equipment, watches and clocks, radios, tape recorders, stereo equipment, calculators, and perfume.

NOSTALGIC RAFFLES HOTEL

In a fast-paced city with its eye to the future, Raffles Hotel stands as a quiet reminder of the simple elegance of its colonial past. In the 1900s, this grand old hotel with its white-washed walls was the center of Singapore's social life. Under its lofty ceilings with their slowly whirling fans, merchants, traders, and sea captains gathered to exchange stories. Well-dressed gentlemen downed pink gins in the bar while ladies in silk sipped tea in the Tiffin Room. It is even said that Somerset Maugham wrote *The Moon and Sixpence* and *Of Human Bondage* while enjoying

the shade of the hotel's courtyard palm trees. In fact, writers such as Maugham, Joseph Conrad, and Rudyard Kipling were frequent guests at the hotel.

The hotel had its beginnings in a small bungalow as a "tiffin house" which served delicious lunches. (*Tiffin* is an Anglo-Indian word for "light lunch.") It gradually developed into a simple hostel. In 1886 the Sarkies brothers, Armenian hôteliers, came to Singapore to seek fame and fortune. They bought the tiffin house/hostel and made it Raffles Hotel. That original bungalow, on the corner of Beach and Bras Basah roads, soon became too small. In 1896, the brothers opened an extension to the building and, by the 1900s, the hotel had become the center of Singapore society.

Today, Raffles stands in an area marked by redevelopment. Raffles Centre—a modern complex of hotels, offices, and shopping centers—is being built adjacent to the hotel. The hotel is being preserved and refurbished.

Although somewhat worn by time, the hotel is still gracious. Its 126 rooms are all spacious semisuites with sitting rooms, bedrooms, dressing rooms, and bathrooms. Its public rooms are equally grand. Dining is still an elegant affair, whether you choose the wood-paneled Elizabethan Grill or the open-air Palm Court with its flickering candles and soft music. In the three-storied Tiffin Room, complete with skylight, you can sip afternoon tea or have breakfast or lunch. The thirsty will enjoy concoctions from the Long Bar where the famous Singapore Gin Sling was created in 1915.

Tailor-made items. Singapore tailors are well known for high standards in men's tailoring. They can even create a custom-made suit in a day. However, for better fit and quality, it's best to give them several days for the job. You'll find good tailor shops in hotel arcades and shopping complexes, and on Coleman Street, Selegie Road, Serangoon Road, North and South Bridge roads, Orchard Road, and Tanglin Road.

What not to buy. The United States restricts the import of products made from animals and plants it has officially listed as endangered or threatened. Even if these items are sold abroad, it does not mean that they will be allowed into the United States. For more information on this, see page 9.

Singapore Handicraft Centre

At the Singapore Handicraft Centre on the corner of Tanglin and Grange roads, you can see Asian arts and crafts being created. You can also purchase them here. The centre is dedicated to the presentation of the arts of Asia and the ancient skills required to produce them.

Between 11 A.M. and 1 P.M. and between 3 and 5 P.M. daily, craftspeople demonstrate how different works of art are created; meanwhile apprentices look on to learn the ancient skills. Demonstrations include batik painting, Persian carpet weaving, rosewood carving, Chinese brush and finger painting, silver crafting, pewter and brass engraving, cane weaving, kite making, mengkuang leaf weaving, and gem cutting.

Many of the items for sale in the centre's 29 shops were made on the premises. You can buy batik, jade carvings, silver filigree jewelry, cane furniture, wooden clogs, paper umbrellas, and semiprecious stones and jewelry.

The centre is open daily from 10 A.M. to 8 P.M. The centre's Beer Garden stays open until midnight.

DINING PLEASURES

Singapore's a diner's delight with a fascinating variety of international cuisines. In addition to Chinese food, you can try Indian, Indonesian, Malay, Korean, Thai, Japanese, and European dishes. There are even a few American fast-food outlets for those who crave "back home" hamburgers or fried chicken.

Places where you can dine are as varied as the types of cuisine. You can try classic European dishes in an elegant, air-conditioned hotel dining room, or take to the outdoors to sample local food favorites at a food stall (hawker) center. (See "Food Stall Dining," page 121.) The Singapore Tourist Promotion Board's *Weekly Guide Singapore* lists many of the best restaurants in various food categories.

Chinese food's numerous styles

With a population that is more than 76 percent Chinese, it's not surprising that Singapore's predominant cuisine is Chinese. There are literally hundreds of excellent Chinese restaurants — ranging from tiny noodle shops to elegant banquet halls.

Ten different regional styles of Chinese cooking are represented in these restaurants. Cantonese dishes feature mildly seasoned meat and vegetables quickly stir-fried in peanut oil. *Dim Sum* — a Cantonese smorgasbord of steamed and fried tidbits composed of meat or vegetables stuffed in flour wrappers or *pao* (light buns) — is a lunchtime favorite with Singaporeans.

Peking's most famous contribution is Peking duck. Szechuan cooking is highly spiced and enlivened with chile peppers and garlic. Slightly less spicy is Hunan cooking with such favorites as minced pigeon in bamboo cup. The Hokkiens have a way with *mee* (noodles) and the Shanghainese make excellent fish dishes and casseroles as well as bird's nest soup and beggar's chicken.

The Teochew people use subtle seasonings and rich sauces. They also make use of the steamboat (similar to a Mongolian hot pot) in their cooking. A Hakka favorite is *yong tau foo* (fried bean curd stuffed with pork and vegetables), and the Hainanese make chicken rice that's well known. The Taiwanese make rice porridge and accompany it with oysters, mussels, or pork stewed in black sauce.

The following are some restaurants to try. You'll also find Chinese cooking at food stall (hawker) centers throughout the city.

- Peking Mayflower, International Building, 360 Orchard Road, for Peking specialties like Peking duck.
- Golden Phoenix, Hotel Equatorial, 429 Bukit Timah Road, for spicy Szechuan specialties.
- Great Shanghai, Mayfair Hotel, Armenian Street, for Shanghainese fried eel.

From the north and south of India

When you think of Indian food, you usually think of hot, spicy curries. But not all Indian dishes — including curries — are hot. North Indian cuisine is mildly flavored with a subtle blending of spices.

The following are some Indian restaurants in the city. Indian food is also featured at food stalls.

- Omar Khayyám, 55 Hill Street, for north Indian specialties.
- Jubilee, 771/773 North Bridge Road, for hot, spicy southern Indian dishes.
- Komala Vilas, 76/78 Serangoon Road, for vegetarian curries.

Malay and Indonesian specialties

The basis of many Malay and Indonesian meals is *nasi* (rice) with side dishes of meat, fish, prawns, and vegetables. *Rijsttafel* (rice table) — a famous Indonesian favorite — consists of numerous dishes, eaten with rice (see page 153). A Malay favorite (also found in Indonesia) is *satay* — beef, lamb, or chicken marinated in crushed spices, then skewered, and grilled over a charcoal fire. A special peanut sauce for dipping accompanies it.

Very few restaurants serve traditional Malay dishes. However, you'll find favorites like satay at food stalls. (Don't miss the Satay Club, a collection of open-air stalls on Elizabeth Walk.) Here is a list of possible choices.

- San Remo, 1st Floor, Orchard Towers, 400 Orchard Road, for Malay dishes.
- Raffles Hotel, Beach Road, for *rijstaffel* lunches on Thursdays.

Smiling schoolgirls on field trip traipse across aviary bridge. Fifty-acre, landscaped Jurong Bird Park caters to familiar and exotic fowl.

...Continued from page 118

- Ramayana, 6th Floor, Plaza Singapura, Orchard Road, for spicy Indonesian cuisine.

Japanese, Korean, and Thai dishes

A number of Singapore restaurants feature such Japanese favorites as *sukiyaki, tempura, sashimi,* and *sushi.* You'll also find restaurants featuring the bold, hot flavors of Korean cooking. Typical Korean dishes include *bulgogi* (specially marinated meat barbecued at your table) and *kimchi* (pickled and highly spiced cabbage). Thai food is very similar to Chinese cooking, but it's spicier and more piquant.

You might want to visit one of the following.

- Yamagen, 19th Floor, Yen San Building, Orchard Road, for Japanese cuisine.

- Korean Restaurant, 4th Floor, Specialists' Centre, Orchard Road, for Korean dishes.
- Siamese Seafood Restaurant, Cockpit Hotel, Oxley Rise, for seafood cooked the Thai way.

Still other dining experiences

Fresh seafood — caught daily — is abundant in Singapore and a number of restaurants specialize in it. You'll also find restaurants featuring continental gourmet favorites.

Seafood galore. You'll find good seafood restaurants all over the island. Most feature informal, al fresco dining and are only open evenings. Menu favorites include chili crab, mussels in soya sauce, and jumbo prawns in black sauce.

FESTIVAL TIME

In Singapore's multiracial and multicultural society, nearly every week brings some holiday or festival. Most of Singapore's festivals fall on different days in succeeding years, though, so check for exact dates in Singapore newspapers, the Singapore Tourist Promotion Board's *Weekly Guide Singapore*, or a current edition of *Singapore Guidebook*. The following are just a few of Singapore's festivals.

Chinese New Year. Red lucky scrolls and banners hanging in shops and outside homes herald this festive season when the Chinese community celebrates the New Year, either at the end of January or beginning of February.

Chingay Procession. This colorful procession held around Chinese New Year features decorated floats, lion dancers, dragon dancers, and stilt walkers.

Thaipusam. This Hindu festival in January honors Lord Subramaniam. A special procession features penitents carrying *kavadis* — decorated frames held in place on the body with steel spikes (see page 122).

Birthday of the Monkey God. Twice a year (usually in February or March and in September), ceremonies are held to honor the Monkey God, T'se Tien Tai Seng Yeh. Activities include processions, Chinese street operas, and puppet shows.

Songkrat. During April, the Thai "water festival" is celebrated in Thai Buddhist temples. To welcome the new year, the image of Buddha is bathed and celebrants and visitors alike are sprinkled with water.

Vesak Day. Held in late May or early June, this Buddhist festival celebrates the birth, death, and enlightenment of Lord Buddha with candlelit processions, feasts, and traditional dramas.

Dragon Boat Festival. This festival in June honors the legendary poet of ancient China, Ch'u Yuan, who drowned himself in protest against corrupt government. Dragon boat races are held on the waterfront.

National Day. On August 9 Singapore celebrates its independence with a giant parade and festivities.

Festival of the Hungry Ghosts. In August, this special festival honors the return to earth for one day of the souls of the Chinese dead. Religious services are held, Chinese opera and puppet shows performed, and Chinese delicacies are offered to the spirits.

Moon Cake Festival. Held in mid-September, this festival commemorates the overthrow of the Mongol warlords by Chinese who hid secret messages in moon cakes. Moon cakes (filled with sweet bean paste and lotus seeds) are exchanged and eaten, and in the evening children light whimsical paper lanterns.

Pilgrimage to Kusu Island. Between September and October, Taoists take offerings to the shrine honoring Tua Peh Kong — god of prosperity — on Kusu Island.

Deepavli (Festival of Lights). In early November, Hindus commemorate the slaying of the tryant King Naragusura by Lord Krishna. Hindu homes are lighted with oil lamps or candles during the festival. At the Sri Mariamman Temple, South Bridge Road, you can see a demonstration of firewalking as men walk across a bed of hot coals.

FOOD STALL DINING

Dining at a food stall center (sometimes called a hawker center) is an excellent and inexpensive way to sample a variety of Singaporean cuisines in an informal atmosphere. Each center features a number of food stalls, and each food stall specializes in certain Malay, Chinese, Indian, or other Southeast Asian dishes. A sign over each stall advertises its specialties.

The best way to choose a meal is to wander from stall to stall to see what's cooking. You can watch chefs deftly prepare a meal using ingredients displayed at the front of the stall. All ingredients used are fresh; food stalls must adhere to strict health regulations. Once you've observed the preparation of various dishes, sit down at a table nearest the food that intrigues you most. Waiters will soon appear for your order.

Until a few years ago, most of Singapore's food stalls were portable affairs. At dusk they would appear on street corners and in car parks. The wheeled carts would be ladened with charcoal cookers, woks, grills, and baskets of fresh produce, meats, and noodles. Now most of the portable food stalls are gone from Singapore's streets, though you'll still find a few in Chinatown at night.

Singapore's modern food stalls are housed in permanent quarters with plumbing. At some food stall centers you'll still dine al fresco along adjacent sidewalks. At still others, you dine inside air-conditioned buildings.

The Rasa Singapura Food Centre (next to the Singapore Handicraft Centre on the corner of Tanglin and Grange roads) features hawkers whose food was recommended by the public and chosen by a tasting committee. This center is open from midmorning to 11 P.M.

You'll find still other food stall (hawker) centers at Boat Quay, Bugis Street, Capital Shopping Centre (North Bridge Road), Old Telok Ayer Market (near Raffles Quay), Cuppage Road, Empress Place, Newton Circus (junction of Newton and Scotts roads), People's Park Complex (New Bridge Road), and Satay Club (on Elizabeth Walk). These food stall centers are open days, evenings, or both.

A continental touch. You'll find western and European cuisine at Singapore hotels and at other local restaurants. Featured dishes can include everything from Italian chicken cacciatore and Russian borscht to Scottish lamb and American steak.

AN ENTERTAINMENT GUIDE

Singapore's entertainment scene runs the gamut from cultural shows to blaring discos.

Cultural offerings

Through Singapore's cultural shows, visitors can learn of the music and dances of Asia. The ancient art of Chinese opera lives on in presentations by wandering theater troupes who perform on makeshift stages in city squares.

Cultural shows. A 45-minute "Instant Asia" show is presented daily at 9:45 A.M. at the Singapore Cultural Theatre, adjacent to the Singapore Handicraft Centre, near the corner of Tanglin and Grange roads. Performances include the Chinese lion dance, the Chinese lotus dance, an excerpt from a Chinese opera, an Indian temple dance, a Malay harvest dance, and a snake charmer complete with snake-filled wicker basket and flute.

Hotels featuring Asian cultural performances include Raffles (nightly), the Hyatt Regency (Tuesday and Friday evenings), and the Mandarin (Wednesday, Thursday, Saturday, and Sunday evenings). The shows at the Hyatt and Mandarin hotels include dinner. At Raffles Hotel, dinner is optional.

Chinese opera. Adorned with brilliant costumes and elaborate makeup, the actors and actresses of Chinese opera recount the popular legends of ancient China through stylized movements. They perform these great stories of old on wooden stages temporarily assembled during festivals on street corners or in city squares. Chinese instruments accompany the story telling.

TIME TO CELEBRATE

Fireworks burst with brilliant patterns of color; crowds pack incense-filled temples; lanterns flicker in windows; and dancers whirl to lively folk tunes—it's festival time in Southeast Asia.

Colorful celebrations, a continuing part of the Southeast Asian scene, herald rice planting and harvesting. In addition to ethnic and religious observances, each country commemorates special holidays.

The festivals on this page are just a few of many visitors can sample. Banner-wielding youths (top right) proclaim Singapore's National Day, an independence celebration. In the Philippines, brightly costumed Bukidron natives (bottom left) perform tribal dances at the Kaamulan Festival. During Thaipusam, Hindu penitents (bottom right) throughout Southeast Asia demonstrate their faith by carrying *kavadis* with back and chest-piercing spikes.

A night on the town

Planning a night out? You can enjoy a theater-restaurant, or a nightclub with dining, dancing, and a floor show. In a different mood, you can spend some quiet, relaxing moments in a cocktail lounge listening to a pianist or guitarist, or boogie the night away at a discotheque. Major Singapore hotels often feature all of these diversions.

Orchestras, musicians, ballet dancers, and drama groups touring Southeast Asia appear in Singapore at the National Theatre on Clemenceau and the Victoria Theatre on Empress Place in downtown Singapore. The STPB's *Weekly Guide Singapore* and the daily *Straits Times* newspaper have information on who is performing and where.

STEPPING OUTDOORS

Singapore has counterbalanced its building boom by remaining an attractive, parklike city. A series of government-enforced programs have transformed sidewalks, traffic circles, and public squares into miniature parklands with flowering trees and shrubs. In addition, the city offers a number of outstanding parks and gardens lush with tropical vegetation. Most of them serve as oases of peace and tranquility in a fast-paced society.

Gardens galore

Outdoor Singapore offers everything from exotic plants and animals to lush jungle and creatures from Chinese mythology. The following are just a few outdoor attractions you'll want to sample.

Botanic Gardens. In the Orchard Road area not far from the Singapore Handicraft Centre, visitors to Singapore's Botanic Gardens can stroll winding, tree-shaded walks and relax on the neatly manicured lawns. From the park's main gate on Cluny Road, the gardens spread over 32 hectares/ 80 acres. Within their spacious confines are some 3,000 different species of native and exotic plants.

Among the most famous plants introduced by the gardens were the 22 rubber trees brought to Singapore in 1877; the rubber industry of Singapore and Malaysia developed from these plants. The gardens also feature an extensive orchid collection. (Singapore is one of the world's leading orchid suppliers.) Plants in bloom can be seen at the Orchid Display Pavilion.

The gardens are open daily from 5 A.M. to 10 P.M.

Mandai Orchid Gardens. Orchids of every shape, color, and size cover 4 hectares/10 acres of hillside in these gardens on Mandai Road north of central Singapore. Here you'll see both ground and climbing orchids. Dedicated orchid fanciers will enjoy visiting the seedling houses where new hybrids are nurtured.

The gardens are open 9 A.M. to 6 P.M. daily. You can reach the park by car or bus. Some island tours also stop here.

Zoological Gardens. A hilly green peninsula jutting into the Seletar Reservoir is the setting for Singapore's Zoological Gardens. The 28 hectares/70 acres of rolling parklands and wooded meadows is home to over 1,000 animals.

Walking the zoo's ring road, you'll see kangaroos, hippos, crocodiles, orangutans, and giraffes.

Located north of the Orchard Road area on Mandai Road, the zoo can be reached by car or local bus. It's open daily from 8:30 A.M. to 6 P.M.

Bukit Timah Nature Reserve. Visitors to this park, which covers Singapore's highest hill, can stroll winding footpaths through primary jungle, lush with tropical vegetation. The 75-hectare/185-acre park on Upper Bukit Timah Road is home to colorful butterflies, forest birds, and small mammals such as squirrels and flying lemurs.

The reserve, which is 12 km/7 miles north of city center, can be reached by car or local bus.

Tiger Balm Gardens. Other Singapore gardens may be filled with tropical vegetation, but not Tiger Balm Gardens on Pasir Panjang Road. Instead, it features brightly painted statues depicting scenes from Chinese mythology.

You enter Tiger Balm Gardens through a red, ornate archway. Once inside, you find yourself surrounded by fat, laughing Buddhas, bright-eyed animals, leering demons, snarling tigers, and carved pagodas. The garish gardens were originally built to advertise Tiger Balm, an ointment that is supposed to cure aches and pains. Throughout the gardens, you'll see statuary vignettes which illustrate the virtues of this product.

Tiger Balm Gardens is open daily from 10 A.M. to 6 P.M. City bus tours make a stop at the gardens; you can also reach them by car, taxi, or local bus.

Jurong parklands

Jurong, on the western part of Singapore island, was at one time nothing more than rolling lands covered with rubber and fruit trees, ponds and swamps, and tiny vegetable farms. Today, Jurong is Singapore's largest industrial estate, with hundreds of factories and high-rise apartments. However, not all of Jurong is concrete and steel. Scattered within the estate, you'll find a number of parklands, largest of which is 364-hectare/900-acre Jurong Park. It includes a bird park and an 81-hectare/200-acre lake with three islands. Two of the islands have gardens, one Chinese and the other Japanese. The third has a golf course.

Organized tours of the Jurong area usually include Jurong Bird Park and the Chinese Garden. All three points of interest can be reached by car or local bus.

Jurong Bird Park. Over 7,000 birds representing 350 different species live in Jurong Bird Park off Jalan Ahmad Ibrahim in Jurong. Like the Zoological Gardens, the key to this 20-hectare/50-acre park is the natural environment for its inhabitants.

Winding, tree-shaded paths take you past flowering shrubs and quiet lakes and across babbling brooks. Tucked amid the greenery and pleasant surroundings are over 90 aviaries featuring everything from tiny owls to giant flightless cassowaries, from colorfully plumed birds of paradise to fierce predators like the eagle.

The park's largest cage is a walk-in aviary with a netted room 22-meters/73-feet high. Within its vast expanse, a variety of birds fly free. A 30-meter/100-foot manmade waterfall provides a dramatic backdrop for the aviary.

(Continued on page 124)

. . . Continued from page 123

Jurong Bird Park is open from 9 A.M. to 6:30 P.M. weekdays and until 7 P.M. on weekends.

Chinese Garden (Yu Hwa Yuan). The landscape design for this 13-hectare/32-acre garden on Jurong Lake's northern-most island (off Yuan Ching Road) is based on typical Chinese garden art. You reach the island by crossing a bridge with 13 arches. Once inside the garden's gateway, you have entered the world of ancient China: palatial courtyards, moongates, many-tiered pagodas, tiny wooden bridges, and pavilions with red-tile, curved roofs. Tranquillity pervades as you stroll past ponds of blooming lotus blossoms.

The garden is open daily from 8 A.M. to 7 P.M.

Japanese Garden (Seiwaen). This 13-hectare/32-acre garden — on an island in Jurong Lake south of the Chinese Garden—is of traditional Japanese design. Footpaths, lined with bamboo and cherry trees, wind through the garden past weathered boulders, massive stone lanterns, a pair of carp-filled ponds linked by streams, a waterfall, and traditional Japanese-style guest houses.

The garden, also off Yuan Ching Road, is open daily from 8 A.M. to 7 P.M.

RECREATIONAL PURSUITS

Singapore's warm tropical climate lends itself to outdoor recreation and the surrounding warm waters are perfect for aquatic activities.

By cable car to Sentosa

To the south of Singapore and visible from the city's sky-scrapers, the resort island of Sentosa rises from the tranquil blue sea. Its 347 hectares/857 acres of unspoiled beauty — rolling hills, golden sand beaches, narrow tree-lined roads, and network of winding walkways — offer an enticing respite from the city's busy pace. And all of this is conveniently located in the southern half of Keppel Harbour, less than a mile from Singapore's waterfront.

You can easily reach this refreshing island by aerial cable car (in bubble-type gondolas) or by ferry. In addition, there is a special 3-hour tour which includes a water excursion from Clifford Pier, a stop at Sentosa with an island tour, and a trip by cable car from Sentosa to the top of Mount Faber, and back to Jardine Steps. There's also a 2-hour harbor tour from Clifford Pier which includes a stop at Sentosa.

The 13-minute aerial trip by cable car travels from the summit of Mount Faber to the cable car station in the Port of Singapore Authority building on the waterfront at Jardine Steps, and then across the harbor to the cable car station on Sentosa Island. Cable cars are boarded at Mount Faber or Jardine Steps; they run from 10 A.M. to 7 P.M. Monday through Saturday, and from 8 A.M. to 7 P.M. on Sunday. You can travel to Jardine Steps by local bus or taxi. Mount Faber is accessible only by taxi.

If you prefer, you can take the 15-minute ferry ride to Sentosa. Boats leave the World Trade Centre ferry terminal at Jardine Steps daily every 15 minutes between 7:30 A.M. and 11 P.M. (11:15 P.M. on weekends).

Recreational activities. Once on Sentosa you'll find numerous recreational possibilities. The palm-lined, manmade lagoon on the south side of the island is ideal for swimming or sunbathing. At the adjoining boating lagoon, you can rent canoes and pedal boats.

Interesting sights. Besides recreational facilities, the island offers several fascinating places to visit. One of these is the Surrender Chamber, a building not far from Sentosa's cable car station.

In the Singapore City Hall on September 12, 1945, the Japanese forces officially surrendered to the Allied forces of Southeast Asia. In the Surrender Chamber you'll see a re-creation of the signing ceremony. Lifelike wax figures reenact the event with the help of a special sound and light show. The Surrender Chamber is open daily from 10:30 A.M. to 6 P.M.

Other Sentosa sights include a fort built in the 1880s to guard the western approaches to Singapore's harbor; a Maritime Museum featuring exhibits about the sea both past and present; and a Coralarium with tanks filled with live coral formations and bright colorful fish. Continuous bus service provides transportation to these points of interest.

Other Singapore playgrounds

Still more sun, sand, and warm swimming waters can be found on offshore islands to the north and south, and along Singapore's east coast.

Islands. Though Sentosa is probably the most famous of Singapore's offshore islands, others are also being developed for recreational use. These islands—including Kusu, St. John's, and Pulau Hantu — make for a perfect day's outing of swimming, sunning, boating, fishing, scuba diving, or snorkeling. They can be reached by regular boat service.

East Coast Park. Singapore's east coast with its stretches of white sand beach has become a recreational parkland for Singaporeans. Within its 350 hectares/865 acres are a beach-trimmed swimming lagoon, an aquatic center with pools and waterslides, a tennis center, a driving range for golfers, jogging and cycling tracks, restaurants, changing rooms, and simple holiday chalets you can rent. You can also rent bicycles and tents.

The park is located about 20 minutes northeast of the Orchard Road area. It can be reached by local bus or car.

Sports to play and watch

Besides swimming and sunbathing, golf and tennis are activities eagerly pursued by Singaporeans.

Golfers will find nearly two dozen courses in Singapore. Nonmembers can play many of the private club courses on weekdays. The best known and most prestigious is the Singapore Island Country Club with its 18-hole course. Sentosa's 18-hole course is lightly wooded with natural water hazards. The course's second hole is on a small, manmade island built on an offshore reef. It's accessible only by a bridge. If you shoot poorly, your ball ends up in the deep blue sea.

One of the finest facilities for tennis is the Singapore

Tennis Centre in East Coast Park. Besides 14 paved tennis courts, the centre has 2 squash courts, as well as lockers, changing rooms, and showers. There are at least a half-dozen other tennis courts open to visitors.

If spectator sports are more to your liking, horse races are held most weekends at the Singapore Turf Club on Bukit Timah Road. Polo matches are held Tuesday, Thursday, Saturday, and Sunday (except November through January) at the Singapore Polo Club on Thomson Road. Other spectator sports include cricket and soccer.

SINGAPORE SIDE TRIPS

Your Southeast Asian experience doesn't need to end when you've completed your exploration of Singapore. Peninsular Malaysia lies less than a quarter of a mile across the Johore Strait. The nearest Indonesian island floats on the distant horizon, and even Thailand and the Philippines are within convenient traveling distance.

Trains, taxis, and buses all make the trip into Peninsular Malaysia on a regular basis. (See "The Essentials" special feature on page 109.) You can also rent a car and drive there yourself. In addition, local tour operators have half-day bus tours featuring Johore Bahru city sights, and full-day bus tours which explore a Johore plantation or take in Malacca. Longer bus tours can include even more of Peninsular Malaysia.

Organized air tours not only can include different Peninsular Malaysia attractions, but also can feature sights in Indonesia, Thailand, or the Philippines. Tours by boat can include ports in Peninsular Malaysia, Sabah, Sarawak, Brunei, Indonesia, Thailand, Manila, or maybe even Hong Kong.

KNOW BEFORE YOU GO

Here are some facts to keep in mind when planning your trip to Singapore.

Entry/exit procedures. Citizens of the United States and other countries recognized by Singapore do not need a visa for visits of 3 months or less. However, a valid passport is necessary.

Yellow fever inoculations are required only for visitors entering from an infected country. The U.S. Public Health Service, however, recommends typhoid, tetanus, and gamma globulin shots. There is also a malaria risk beyond urban areas.

There's an airport departure tax of S $4 for flights to Malaysia and S $12 for flights to other destinations.

Customs. Besides your personal items, you may bring in 1 liter (1 bottle) of liquor, and 200 cigarettes, 50 cigars, or 250 grams (8 ounces) of tobacco.

Currency. The unit of currency is the Singapore dollar; the rate of exchange is U.S. $1 to S $2.08. Singapore has no restrictions on the amount of foreign currency you can bring into the country.

Traveler's checks and credit cards are accepted at hotels, restaurants, and large stores.

Health conditions. Hospital and medical facilities are excellent and many English-speaking doctors are available. Tap water is safe for drinking.

Tipping. Tipping is not a way of life in Singapore. Many hotels and restaurants add a 10 percent service charge.

Time. Singapore is 15½ hours ahead of the U.S. west coast. When it's noon Sunday in Singapore it's 8:30 P.M. Saturday in San Francisco.

Weather and what to wear. Though Singapore is close to the equator, its hot, humid climate is tempered by sea breezes. Temperatures in the daytime average 29°C/85°F; at night, about 24°C/75°F.

The island has no well-defined wet or dry season. Afternoon showers are likely to occur throughout the year, but they last only briefly and can be refreshing. Most of Singapore's heavy rains come during the northeast monsoon, from October through February, with December being the wettest month. The best months to visit Singapore are June through September.

You'll be comfortable in lightweight summer clothes the year around. Don't forget to pack your bathing suit, suntan lotion, sunglasses, umbrella, and a sweater for air-conditioned places.

Important don'ts. Travelers to Singapore should be aware of certain local laws. Pedestrians who jaywalk can be fined S $50. Litterbugs will be fined S $500, and people who smoke in public places can be fined S $500.

For more information. Your best source on Singapore travel is the Singapore Tourist Promotion Board. In Singapore it is located at 131 Tudor Court, Tanglin Road. Its U.S. offices are at 251 Post Street, San Francisco, CA 94108 and 342 Madison Avenue, Suite 1008, New York 10017. Singapore has an embassy in Washington, D.C. In Singapore, the U.S. Embassy is located at 30 Hill Street.

INDONESIA

A country steeped in history and tradition — 13,000
tropical isles rich in tiered rice fields, ancient ruins
of bygone civilizations, exotic wildlife, colorful festivals,
time-honored handicrafts and performing arts, and
unique tribal architecture

 fabled collection of more than 13,000 tropical islands strung out along the equator,
Indonesia is the world's largest archipelago. The countryside is lush and fertile, its face carved by rivers descending
from towering volcanic mountain peaks.

A land of contrasts, Indonesia has modern cities and
quiet, rural districts where gentle people exist on rice terraces still farmed as they were thousands of years ago.
Ancient temples, monumental in size, contrast with tiny
field temples built to appease the rice gods.

The hospitable Indonesians continue to observe
time-honored rituals, including colorful festivals set
against dramatic backgrounds. This intriguing country is
also known for its traditional crafts, costumed dance performances, and puppet plays.

A NECKLACE OF ISLANDS

Indonesia's necklacelike archipelago stretches across 4,828
km/3,000 miles of ocean to encompass 13,677 islands with a
total land area of 1,904,345 square km/735,000 square miles.
Sumatra—on the archipelago's westernmost tip—lies just
west of Peninsular Malaysia. At the island chain's eastern
end, Irian Jaya shares an island just north of Australia with
Papua New Guinea.

Only 6,000 of the country's islands have ever been
named, and of these, only about 900 are permanently
settled. Indonesia's principal islands are Java, Sumatra,
Kalimantan (Indonesian Borneo), and Sulawesi (Celebes).
East of Java is a group of smaller islands, the major ones
being Bali, Lombok, Sumbawa, Sumba, Flores, and Timor.
Strung out along eastern Indonesia are also the Maluku

Islands, the Kai Islands, the Aru Islands, Irian Jaya (on
New Guinea), and smaller island groups.

Indonesia's islands offer visual contrasts: snow-
capped mountains and muddy mangrove-filled estuaries;
dry savanna plains covered in scrub brush and dense tropical rain forests; broad sandy beaches and steep rocky
headlands.

Rich and varied plant life

More than a fifth of the land is covered with dense
hardwood rain forests. Where the rain forests have been
cleared, fields of rice thrive in addition to rubber, palm oil,
coffee, and tea plantations.

Indonesia features more than 35,000 different species
of flowering plants — fragrant frangipani, brilliant scarlet
and orange trailing bougainvillea, and the rare Kalimantan
black orchid, one of the more than 5,000 species of orchid
growing in Indonesia.

Indonesia's animal life

Marsupials common to Australia — such as the tree kan-
garoo and wallaby—can be found on Irian Jaya. Inhabiting
the western islands are the one-horned rhinoceros of Java,
the wild "banteng" ox of Java and Kalimantan, and the
long-nosed tapir and orangutan of Sumatra and Kalimantan. Still other animals include tigers, panthers, elephants,
scaly anteaters, apes, monkeys, wild boars, and a number
of species of deer.

On Komodo Island, 3-meter/10-foot long carnivorous
lizards roam free. These giant monitor lizards, or Komodo
dragons, are believed to be the only living genus left of the
prehistoric *Varanus komodoensis*. Other reptiles — besides
the Komodo dragon — include crocodiles and pythons.

(Continued on page 131)

Silhouetted pinnacles *of Prambanan, 9th-century Hindu temple complex near Yogyakarta, suffused in mist, evoke mystical mood.*

Monkey and lion *performers sit side by side during break in* barong *dance in Bali. Dramatic religious dances reflect contest between good and evil.*

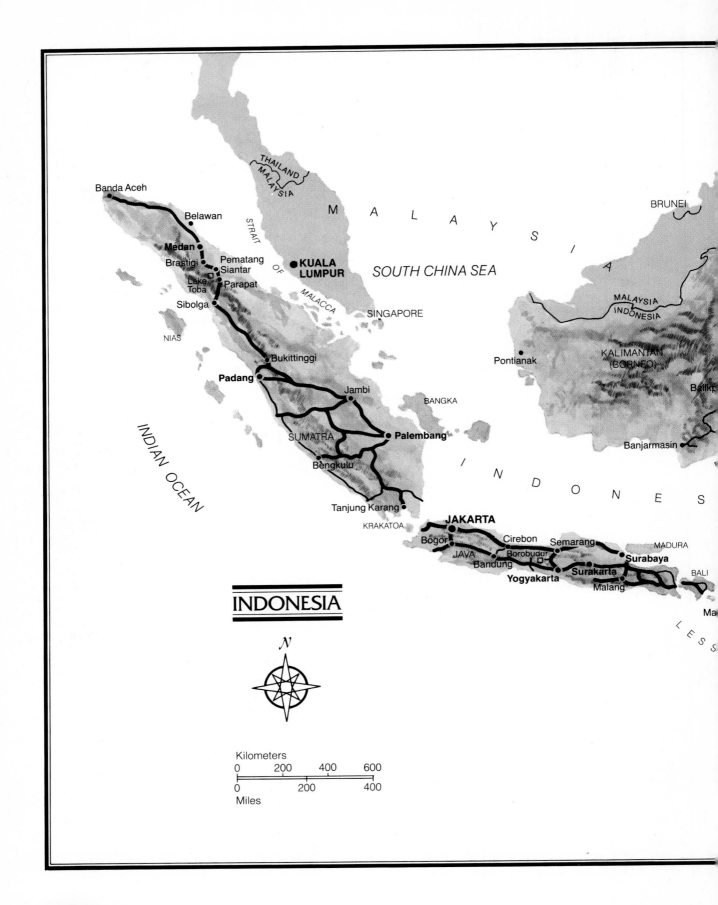

INDONESIA

N

Kilometers
0   200   400   600

0   200   400
Miles

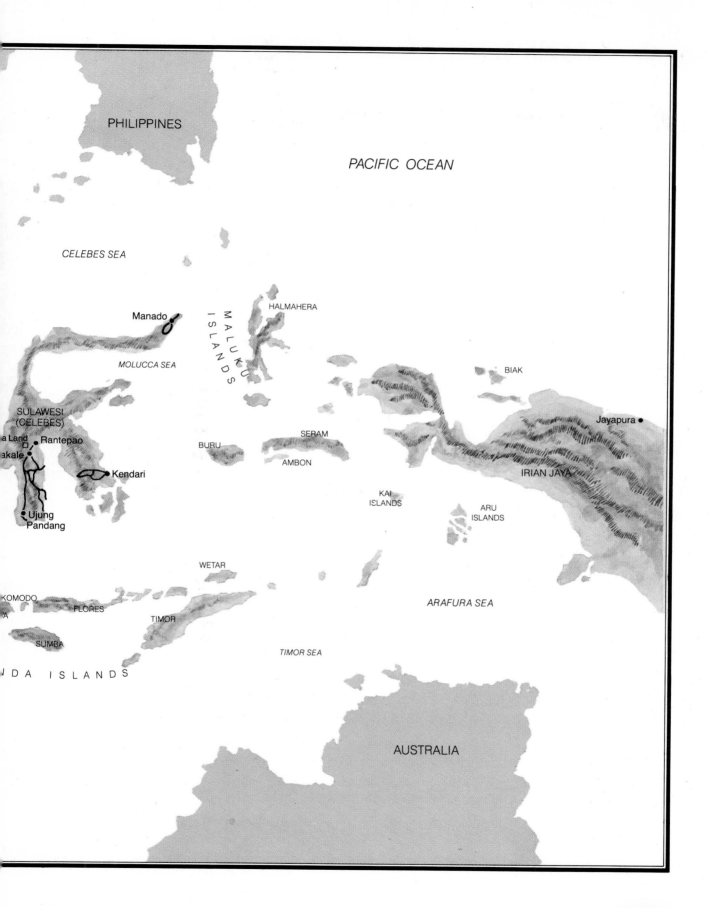

PHILIPPINES

PACIFIC OCEAN

CELEBES SEA

Manado

HALMAHERA

M A L U K U   I S L A N D S

BIAK

MOLUCCA SEA

Jayapura

SULAWESI
(CELEBES)

SERAM

BURU

IRIAN JAYA

a Land   Rantepao

AMBON

akale

Kendari

KAI
ISLANDS

ARU
ISLANDS

Ujung
Pandang

WETAR

KOMODO

ARAFURA SEA

FLORES

a

TIMOR

SUMBA

TIMOR SEA

N D A   I S L A N D S

AUSTRALIA

National Monument, *Jakarta's most impressive landmark, rises 350 feet above Merdeka Square in city's center. For panoramic view, ride elevator to top.*

Rows of tile *roofs crowd Pasar Ikan, Jakarta's old port area. Restored spice warehouses date from Dutch days.*

. . . Continued from page 126

AN ANCIENT HISTORY

Indonesia has been inhabited since the dawn of mankind. In 1891, scientists discovered the fossil remains of *Pithecanthropus erectus* — Java man. Data indicates that this early inhabitant lived on Java around 500,000 years ago.

About 30,000 years ago, waves of dark-skinned pygmy people—Negritos—swept across the archipelago. Next came an Australoid type of people. It is believed that the latter group populated the area 10,000 to 12,000 years ago. Migrants from southern China, termed Proto-Malays, settled in the Indonesian archipelago around 3,000 B.C. They were followed by a second wave of migrants from China — the Deutero-Malays. These newcomers introduced Indonesia to the Bronze Age.

Early empires

As early as the 2nd century, Indian and Chinese traders were doing business in the Indonesian archipelago. They brought with them the Hindu and Buddhist faiths, and by the 7th century, Buddhist and Hindu kingdoms were flourishing throughout Indonesia. Two great temple complexes built on Java—the Buddhist sanctuary of Borobudur and the Hindu complex of Prambanan (see page 145) — remain as architectural monuments of the period.

In the 13th century, the Majapahit Hindu empire of East Java gained control of the entire Indonesian archipelago, a rule maintained for almost a century. The empire's disintegration coincided with the upsurge of Islam, a faith introduced by Persian traders. The first small Muslim state had its beginnings in North Sumatra. From here it spread, undermining the Hindu empire until the Majapahit empire disappeared in the late 15th century. Today, only Bali remains predominantly Hindu.

European domination

The first westerner to visit the Indonesian archipelago was Marco Polo, who landed in Sumatra in 1292. In the 16th century, the Portuguese entered Indonesia in search of spices. They soon took control of the area's spice trade and built fortresses to protect their interests.

At the end of the 16th century, the Dutch ousted the Portuguese and took control of Indonesia. The Dutch ruled the Dutch East Indies (Indonesia) for the next 300 years. Their grip on Indonesia was broken briefly between 1811 and 1816 during the Napoleonic Wars; the English took charge of the government when the Netherlands was occupied by the French.

Fight for independence

The Indonesian movement for independence began in the early 20th century and persisted throughout the World War II occupation of the country by the Japanese forces (1942–1945). On August 17, 1945, two days after the unconditional surrender of Japan, Indonesian nationalists in Jakarta proclaimed the Republic of Indonesia. The Dutch did not recognize the legality of the Indonesia Republic and continued "police actions" until August 1949, when the U.N. effected a cease-fire. A Dutch-Indonesian conference, held at The Hague in 1949, transferred sovereignty from the Netherlands to Indonesia with Sukarno as president.

Ahead of this independent Indonesia lay years plagued by splintered political groups, civil wars, rebellions, and hostile confrontations with Malaysia. On September 30, 1965, the Indonesian Communist Party attempted to turn the country into a communist state. The move was crushed by the Indonesian Armed Forces under General Suharto. Although Sukarno, a communist sympathizer, remained the country's symbolic leader for a brief period following the communist uprising, his era had ended. In 1967 General Suharto was elected president, and in May 1977, Suharto was re-elected to his third 5-year presidential term.

The constitution, written in 1935, established the president as chief executive and supreme commander of the armed forces. Today, the president is elected by the People's Consultative Congress. The president and the Representative Council (parliament) ratify the country's laws.

Indonesia's economy

Agriculture is the basis for much of Indonesia's economy. Four out of every five people work the soil and many of these are small farmers growing rice. Important commercial crops are rubber, tobacco, sugar, copra, palm oil, coffee and tea.

Indonesia is rich in mineral resources, a wealth it has only begun to tap. Even though it's the world's fourth largest producer of tin and prospects for petroleum production are promising, Indonesia's mineral utilization has been limited. Only about 5 percent of the country's total land area has been mapped geologically.

INDONESIA'S PEOPLE

With a population exceeding 139 million, Indonesia is the fifth most populous nation in the world. Its people are a complicated racial mixture representing a number of ethnic groups, each with its own dialect, customs and traditions.

Life style

The heart of Indonesia is still the village. Nearly 80 percent of the country's people live, as their ancestors did, in rural, agricultural communities. Within these villages, life is governed by the family, the community, the dictates of religion, and *adat* (village law based on tradition). Life is communal — families cooperate with one another in growing rice or building a house. Patience and *musyawarah* (the habit of discussing things to arrive at a consensus) serve to make the Indonesians a peaceful people.

Moderation in all things is the Indonesian ideal, whether it be in speech and behavior, eating and drinking, or the possession of worldly things. Extremes in emotion are avoided; a loud voice, hearty laughter, or cries of anguish are considered unbecoming and are regarded with disapproval.

Religious beliefs

Most Indonesians live by the Muslim behavioral code that is prescribed by the Koran, yet only a small percentage are Muslims in the traditional Middle Eastern sense. In East

Java this is particularly true; people are Muslim by affiliation but cling to ancient rituals and customs of animism (attributing a spirit to inanimate objects and natural phenomena).

Though Buddhism waned on Java and Sumatra after the introduction of Islam, there are still Indonesian Buddhists along the coasts of these islands and in Central Java. On Bali, religious practices are dominated by the Balinese-Hindu faith. Bali's brand of Hinduism has been highly modified by ancient Balinese beliefs, including animism and ancestor worship, as well as doctrines adapted from Buddhism and Christianity.

Christian converts are scattered through the country, chiefly among the Torajas and Minahasans on Sulawesi and the Bataks on Sumatra. Frequently, Christian worship, too, is tempered with animist practices.

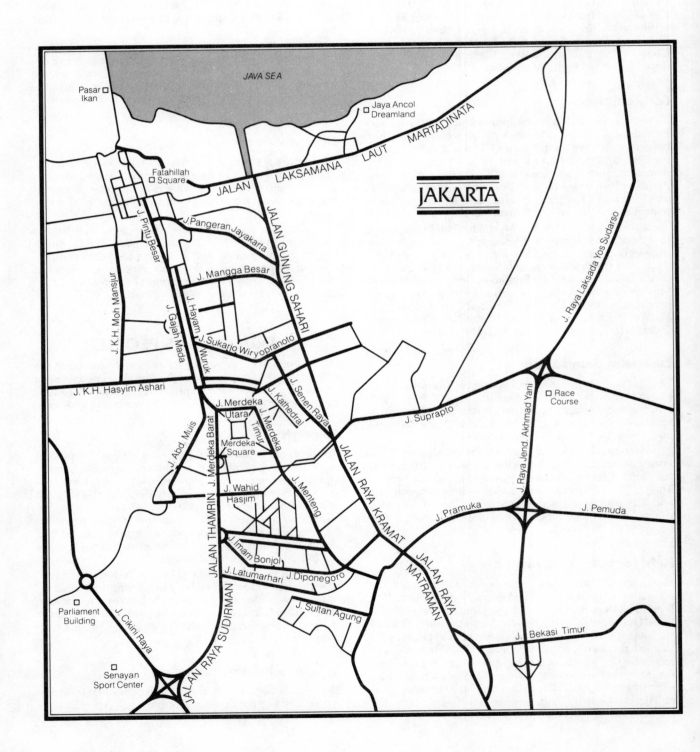

THE ESSENTIALS/JAKARTA

Here are a few basics to help you in planning your stay in Indonesia's capital city of Jakarta.

Getting there

Jakarta is served by air, rail, bus, and sea transportation.

Air. International service to and from Jakarta is by Garuda Indonesian Airways and foreign flag carriers.

Domestic flights by Garuda Indonesian Airways, Merpati Nusantara Airlines, and Bouraq Indonesia Airlines link Jakarta with other Indonesian cities.

Halim International Airport is 16 km/10 miles southeast of Jakarta.

Guests of major hotels can travel from the airport by mini-bus. Taxi service is also available. Kemayoran Airport, near the city center, handles most domestic flights.

Rail. Train routes link Jakarta with other cities on Java. The air-conditioned *Bima Express* and *Mutiara Express* travel daily between Jakarta and Yogyakarta. The non-air-conditioned *Parahiyangan Express* travels several times daily to Bandung.

Bus. Linking Jakarta with other Java cities are air-conditioned night-express buses. It's best to book two seats on these buses since the seats are narrow.

A place to stay

Most of Jakarta's major hotels are downtown. These include the Asoka, Borobudur Inter-Continental, Gadjah Mada International, Holiday Inn Orchid Palace, Hyatt Aryaduta Jakarta, Hotel Indonesia Sheraton, Jakarta Mandarin, Jayakarta Tower, Kartika Plaza, Marcopolo, Natour's Transarea, President, Sabang Metropolitan, Sahid Jaya, Sari Pacific, and Wisata Hotel International. Chinatown hotels include the City and Metropole.

On the road to Halim International Airport are the Jakarta Hilton and the Kartika Chandra. In Jaya Ancol Dreamland, about a ½-hour drive north of city center, are the Pondok Putri cottages and Hotel Horison.

All of the hotels we've mentioned are air-conditioned and have restaurants. Some of the larger hotels also have swimming pools, tennis and squash courts, nightclubs, and shopping arcades.

Getting around Jakarta

The best time to explore Jakarta (and all of Indonesia, for that matter) is during the cooler morning hours. The Indonesian pattern of life is to rise early, get work done during the morning, eat lunch, and rest during the hot afternoon. You'll find museum hours and some shops reflect this life style.

Don't try to drive yourself around Jakarta—traffic jams are commonplace. Taxis are good city transportation, augmented by *helicaks* (motorized *becaks*), *bemos* (motorized three-wheeled trucks), and *becaks* (three-wheeled pedicabs, allowed on Jakarta's downtown streets only at night). City buses are usually crowded.

Tours

Half and full-day tours take in city sights, the Thousand Islands (see page 140), Bogor (page 141), Puncak Pass (page 141), Bandung (page 141), and Samudra Beach (page 141).

Dining adventures

Most of Jakarta's better restaurants are located in the city's hotels, though you'll also find good restaurants, serving a variety of ethnic foods, elsewhere.

• George and Dragon, Jalan Teluk Betung, has a British "pub" atmosphere and serves steak, mushroom and kidney pie, ploughman's cold lunch, lobster bisque, and Irish coffee.

• Oasis, Jalan Raden Saleh, occupies a Dutch Colonial mansion decorated with antique furniture. Rijsttafel (see page 153) leads off the menu. Served also are French and Italian dishes.

• Vic's Viking, Jalan Thamrin (near Kartika Plaza Hotel), features both European and Oriental dishes served buffet-style.

• Mataram Restaurant, Hotel Borobudur Inter-Continental, features authentic Indonesian decor and food, especially rijsttafel.

The entertainment scene

In Jakarta, you can enjoy traditional Indonesian music and dance or modern rock concerts or attend a ballet.

Indonesian cultural shows. Near Halim International Airport, the Indonesia in Miniature complex features performers from various parts of this far-flung nation in regular programs of music and dance. There are also weekly performances of Indonesian music and dance at the Jakarta Hilton's Balinese Theater and at the Hotel Indonesia Sheraton.

At the Taman Ismail Mursuki Cultural Center on Jalan Cikini Raya, you can see traditional Indonesian entertainment like *wayang golek* (plays enacted with wooden puppets) as well as rock concerts and ballets. The center prints a monthly activity guide, which is available at hotels.

Other entertainment. Many of the larger hotels have nightclubs or discotheques.

For more information

Jakarta's visitor information center is located next to the Sarinah Department Store on Jalan Thamrin.

TRIP PLANNING AIDS

A number of international airlines, including Garuda Indonesian Airways, fly direct or connecting flights to Indonesia from the United States, Europe, India, the Orient, the South Pacific, and other parts of Southeast Asia. There are international airports at Jakarta on Java, Denpasar on Bali, and Medan and Padang on Sumatra.

During their Southeast Asia/Orient cruises, both cruise ships and cargo/passenger liners occasionally call at Indonesian ports. There is overnight ferry service between Penang, Malaysia, and Belawan (Medan's port) on Sumatra.

A variety of accommodations

You'll find a number of international standard hotels in Indonesia. In recent years, large international hotel chains have built quite a few on Java and Bali. Amenities at these hotels can include air conditioning, swimming pools, restaurants, shopping arcades, and nightclubs.

If you're on a limited budget, try Indonesia's inexpensive "national standard" hotels. Outside Jakarta or Denpasar, though, some of these do not meet western standards, either in facilities or cleanliness.

Other possibilities for the budget-conscious are youth hostels and YMCA accommodations.

Hotels charge an 11 percent room tax, and many also add a service charge of 10 percent to the bill.

Local transportation tips

Because distances are great between Indonesian points of interest, the most efficient way to travel in Indonesia is by air. But efficiency isn't everything, and if you rely solely on air transportation, you'll miss seeing Indonesia's beautiful countryside. Ground transportation options include rail, bus, and chauffeur-driven car.

Indonesia's scheduled domestic air service reaches to the far corners of the country. Garuda Indonesian Airways has the most extensive schedule. Other local air carriers include Merpati Nusantara Airlines and Bouraq Indonesia Airlines. When traveling by air, it's advisable to make reservations well ahead and always reconfirm them. For domestic service, the airlines request that you arrive at the airport 2 hours before departure; gates are closed to all except transfer passengers 1 hour before the scheduled flight time.

Taking a train. Java's extensive rail network connects the island's major cities. There are three separate rail networks on Sumatra. Use air-conditioned coaches, if possible.

Traveling by bus. Express buses link larger towns in Indonesia. During the rainy season, though, some express routes may be cancelled because of flooding.

Local buses serve the countryside around towns as well as the towns themselves. Preferred by the local people, these buses can be very crowded.

Journeying by boat. Daily ferry service links Ketapang on Java with Gilimanuk on Bali. Ferry services also operate between several other island groups.

Car plus chauffeur. Chauffeur-driven cars are available for hire for day-long tours of city sights or longer trips. (On longer trips you may be expected to pay for the driver's accommodations and meals.) It's not advisable to rent a car without a chauffeur.

Taxis and pedicabs. The best way to get around major tourist centers is by taxi. All taxis are metered. For short journeys around town, the *becak* (a three-wheeled pedicab) is a convenient, cheap alternative to the taxi. These brightly painted, people-powered vehicles can also be hired by the hour as well as for just a short trip. In either case, be sure to arrange the fare before climbing on board. The motorized version of the becak is the *helicak*. Also available are the larger, three-wheeled trucks called *bemos*.

Tours. Each major tourist center has tours of local city sights. On Java and Bali you'll find coach tours that feature sights throughout the islands.

Your choice of cuisines

Indonesian food offers great diversity in ingredients, styles of preparation, and manners of serving. Aromatic eastern spices, famed for centuries, are used lavishly to give bold, rich flavors to Indonesian dishes. The Indonesian staple, rice, is accompanied by various side dishes of meat, eggs, fish, and vegetables that are prepared many ways.

Indonesia has a number of popular local dishes, with varations from region to region. For example, Central Javanese food tends to be spicy and sweet, but not hot. East Javanese food is somewhat saltier and a little hotter. Dishes cooked the Sumatran way are very spicy and full of chile peppers. You'll find spicy Sumatran food served at Padang restaurants in Jakarta and other major towns throughout Indonesia.

Local specialties you might want to try are *nasi goreng* (fried rice with eggs, meat, tomatoes, cucumbers, and chile peppers), *gado gado* (vegetable salad with a peanut sauce), and *soto* (soup made with coconut milk flavored by spices). *Sambal* is the spicy hot sauce made from ground red chile peppers. The hottest form of this sauce comes from the Padang region. *Sate* — pieces of marinated beef, chicken, prawns, or fish barbecued on a skewer and served with a spicy peanut sauce — is still another local favorite.

The entertainment scene

Indonesia's traditional music, dance, and drama are an important part of Indonesian life and dominate the entertainment scene. Held on a scheduled basis at hotels and in formal theaters, performances can be seen in villages and temples during local festivals and special events.

Traditional Indonesian performing arts date back to ancient times and have their roots in religion and folklore. Many of the performances are based on two ancient Hindu epics — the Ramayana and the Mahabharata. The *gamelan* orchestras that accompany these performances can include bronze gongs, chimes, cymbals, long drums, and bamboo xylophones.

Wayang. Traditional Indonesian drama includes *wayang kulit* (shadow plays with puppets made of leather), *wayang golek* (plays enacted with wooden puppets), and *wayang*

Native *in traditional dress passes entrance to Kraton Yogya, palace compound displaying sultans' effects and antique gamelan pieces.*

To create batik, *artist applies design in liquid wax to fabric length. After dyeing, fabric is washed in hot water to dissolve wax, leaving previously covered area uncolored; process is repeated for each color added.*

orang (dance dramas with human actors). A gamelan orchestra usually accompanies these wayang performances.

Other entertainment. Western-style entertainment and floor shows are limited to the large hotels and a few nightclubs in Jakarta, Bandung, and Surabaya.

Handicraft treasures

For centuries, Indonesians have blended themes from Arabia, India, China, and the West with their native styles and techniques to create art works of exceptional beauty. They excel in painting, sculpture, textiles, woodcarving, metalwork, and woven-leaf products.

Indonesia's most famous craft product is handpainted or printed *batik* (see special feature below). Other locally made fabrics include silk and a beautiful cloth woven with silver and gold threads.

Silver is fashioned into intricately designed jewelry as well as bowls, flatware, and tea sets. Particularly gifted are the silver artisans of Yogyakarta. You'll also find beautifully crafted gold jewelry in Indonesia.

The Indonesian's skill in woodcarving can be seen in masks, statuary, and furniture. Still another Indonesian skill is stonecarving. You might also consider purchasing leather wayang kulit puppets, woven bamboo baskets, and Balinese watercolors or oil paintings.

BATIK, INDONESIA'S NATIONAL CLOTH

Wherever you go in Indonesia, you'll see batik. Local men and women wear batik sarongs as everyday attire. Batik bedspreads, drapes and wall hangings decorate hotel rooms. When shopping, you'll see a variety of goods made from it — bathing suits, shirts, skirts, scarves, table placemats, and tote bags.

The word "batik" does not actually refer to the cloth itself. It refers to the wax and dye process used to achieve the design on the fabric. "Batik" means wax printing in Javanese.

The original technique of hand decorating fabric through a wax and dye process was developed by Persians and Egyptians and brought to Indonesia by the early traders. The Javanese amplified and improved the technique.

To make fine, hand-decorated batik, the cloth — usually cotton — first has its original starch removed; it is restarched, then softened by beating with wooden mallets. Artists create the design on paper, then trace it onto the cloth. Liquid wax is applied with a *canting* (a small, spouted copper container) to those areas that are not to be colored during the first dyeing process. After the dyed fabric has dried, the wax is then scraped from the areas of the fabric that are to receive the second color. The area that has already been dyed is covered with a protective wax coating, and a second dyeing takes place. The number of times this wax and dye process occurs depends on the number of colors to be included in the final design. In the final stage, all the wax is removed by immersing the cloth in boiling water.

Hand drawing with wax is a time consuming and costly batik art. An intricately patterned batik could take 2 to 3 months to make.

Some batik makers use an engraved copper block called a *cap* to produce their batiks. The cap, a 20-cm/8-inch square block containing the design, is dipped in melted wax and applied to the fabric repeatedly until the desired areas of fabric are covered in wax. Then the dyeing process takes place. A batik made in this manner can be produced in a week and therefore costs less.

In the early 1960s, some manufacturers began to machine print batik patterns on fabric. These are not really batiks since no wax is involved. Hand drawn or stamped batiks have their designs printed on both sides, but machine printed fabrics don't.

Java is the center for Indonesia's batik-making business. Each area of the island has its own colors and designs. The three major batik-making areas are Yogyakarta, Surakarta, and Pekalongan in Central Java.

Batik making is also popular in Malaysia and Singapore.

THE STORY OF RAMAYANA

The Ramayana—a classic epic of good versus evil—was written by an Indian poet and sage, Valniki, over 2,000 years ago. The popularity of this morality play spread throughout Southeast Asia, and the story was passed from generation to generation.

During your Southeast Asian travels, you'll continually witness the influence of the Ramayana epic on the art and drama of the area. You'll see parts of the epic told in Indonesian *wayang kulit* (shadow plays) and *wayang orang* (dance drama) and Thai *khon* (masked drama). The dances of Bali recount scenes from the Ramayana, and two Indonesian dance festivals—one at Prambanan and the other at Pandaan—feature it. You'll see segments of the Ramayana told in the paintings of Bali; Southeast Asian woodcarvings often portray Ramayana characters. Throughout Southeast Asia, temples are decorated with sculptures and bas-reliefs based on the Ramayana epic.

Although the tale varies somewhat from region to region, the basic Ramayana epic tells the story of Prince Rama, who was born to rid the world of a demon named Ravana. Driven from his father's court at Ayutthaya, Rama, an incarnation of the god Vishnu, escapes to the forest followed by his wife, Sita, and his brother, Laksmana. Ravana abducts Sita and unsuccessfully attempts to court her. Meanwhile, Rama assembles an army that includes the monkeys led by the monkey king, Sugriva, and the monkey general, Hanuman. Rama and his supporters slay Ravana and rescue Sita. Rama, Sita, and

Laksmana return triumphantly to Ayutthaya, and Rama becomes King.

Indonesians know the Ramayana epic by heart and delight in seeing the various Ramayana characters come to life on stage. Visitors too—even those with only a slight knowledge of the plot—can enjoy a performance that dramatizes segments from the Ramayana. By listening to the response of the audience, you'll soon be able to separate the good guys from the bad.

Things not to buy. The United States restricts the import of products made from animals and plants that it has officially listed as endangered or threatened. The fact that these items are sold abroad does not mean that they will be allowed into the United States. For more information on this, see page 9.

Bargaining. Prices are fixed in shopping complexes and department stores. At small shops or local markets, though, it's customary to bargain.

Store hours. Shops are usually open from 9 A.M. to 8 P.M. Monday through Saturday. However, a few shops are open for a half day on Sunday. You will find some shops closed daily between 1 and 5 P.M. for siesta time.

JAKARTA, A BUSY ISLAND CAPITAL

Jakarta, a hustling, noisy metropolis of 5½ million people, is the political and economic capital of Indonesia and a major entry/exit point for visitors.

Located on the northwest coast of Java, this sprawling city of 622 square km/240 square miles has a history dating back at least 450 years. In its early days, it was the site of a Hindu kingdom, then a Portuguese fort; later it became a Muslim city named Djayakarta. The Dutch took command in 1619, razed the old city, and built a new town, Batavia. During World War II, the Japanese occupied the city. In 1945 Batavia was renamed Jakarta, capital of the new Republic of Indonesia.

The architectural influences of Jakarta's Dutch-ruled period are still prevalent in Jakarta today. The reds of tiled, gabled roofs brighten the older sections of the city. Dutch-designed canals, reminiscent of those in Holland, flank some of the city's wide thoroughfares. Intermingled with these ancient reminders of the city's colonial days are soaring skyscrapers.

The city's heart — Merdeka Square

Spread across a broad plain with much of its real estate reclaimed marshland, Jakarta is monotonously flat.

The heart of the downtown area is Merdeka Square. To

Sightseers *to late 8th-century Borobudur near Yogyakarta add only spot of color to latticed stupas, dome-shaped shrines containing Buddha images.*

the north of this square is the older part of the city, including a restored area called Old Batavia (see below). Running south from Merdeka Square is broad Jalan Thamrin, bordered with multistory office buildings, hotels, and apartments.

National Monument. Jakarta's most impressive landmark is located in the center of Merdeka Square. The National Monument—a 107-meter/350-foot white tower—is topped by a torch covered with 70 pounds of gold leaf. The torch commemorates Indonesia's nationhood and is called the "Flame of Freedom." Inside the base of the tower is a museum featuring dioramas that depict the country's history from prehistoric times to independence. An elevator ascends to the top of the monument for a panoramic view.

National Museum. Recognized as one of the finest of its kind in Southeast Asia, the National Museum is located on Jalan Merdeka Barat, bordering the west side of Merdeka Square. Strolling its halls, you'll see excellent collections of the arts and crafts of various Indonesian peoples, and scale models of their traditional buildings. Here, too, is a fine collection of Hindu-Javanese friezes, reliefs, and statues that date from the 5th through the 14th centuries, and ancient Chinese porcelain excavated from Indonesian soil.

The museum is open Tuesday through Sunday. Hours are 8:30 to 11 A.M. on Fridays, 8:30 to 1:30 on Saturdays, and 8:30 to 2:30 other days.

Other area buildings. The 100-year-old Merdeka Palace, official residence of Indonesia's president, lies on the north side of Merdeka Square. Just northeast of the palace is Istiqlal Mosque. Faced with Javanese marble, this imposing mosque with its minarets and white dome took 17 years to build.

Old Batavia

In an effort to preserve some of the sights and atmosphere of early Dutch Jakarta, a 3-block-wide, 2-mile-long section of the city north of Merdeka Square is being restored. Known as Old Batavia, the development includes three areas: Fatahillah Square, site of the Stadhuis (city hall) built in 1710; Pasar Ikan, the old port and today's fishermen's wharf; and Glodok, the historically important Chinese quarter.

Fatahillah Square. This restored square was once the center of administration for the Dutch East India Company. From here, the company governed the far-flung colony and controlled the spice trade. Closed to auto traffic, the old square has been recobbled and decorated with plants and shrubs. Many of the square's 18th century, gabled Dutch buildings are being restored for use as shops.

Once a flourishing city hall, the Stadhuis, facing Fatahillah Square, now houses the Jakarta Historical Museum. You'll see old etchings, maps, paintings, porcelains, beautifully carved furniture, and other relics of the days of the Dutch East India Company. The museum is open Tuesday through Sunday. Hours are 8:30 to 11 A.M. Fridays, 8:30 to 1:30 Saturdays, and 8:30 to 2:30 other days.

Pasar Ikan. This old harbor area was once alive with the activities of Indonesia's spice trade. Ships laden with the goods of the world came to call here. They took away with them the rich spices of Indonesia.

Today's cargo liners dock at Tanjung Priok, a much larger harbor area northeast of town. However, small interisland sailing ships and fishing fleet boats still dock at Pasar Ikan.

Not far away, two of the thick-walled warehouses, built in the 1600s to store the spice shipments, have been restored: one as the Spice Trade Museum and the other as a maritime museum displaying past and present sailing craft.

Glodok. This Chinese quarter centers around the Jalan Pintu Besar area and features old tile-roofed houses that line canals, marked by drawbridges reminiscent of 17th century Netherlands. Glodok comes to life each evening when hundreds of small shops and stalls are set up along its narrow streets. The local inhabitants jam the streets, moving from stall to stall, haggling with the sellers for a better bargain. Stalls and shops carry all types of food, clothing, household goods, and gifts. Handcarts and pedicabs add to the congestion.

Other museums

Some of Jakarta's diverse museums help chronicle the country's crafts.

Museum Wayang. This puppet museum on Jalan Pintu Besar west of Fatahillah Square features leather puppets and wooden puppets as well as the gamelan instruments that accompany these puppets when they perform. The museum is open Friday, Saturday, and Sunday from 9 AM. to noon. On Sunday at 10 A.M. there are puppet performances.

Textile Museum. Indonesia's fabrics — from Javanese batiks and Sumatran weavings to tie-dyes from Timor—fill a 19th century colonial house on Jalan Jatipetamburan. Some fabrics in the collection date back more than 100 years. The museum is open daily from 9 A.M. to 2 P.M. On Fridays it closes at 11 A.M. and on Saturdays at 1 P.M.

Indonesia in miniature

Taman Mini Indonesia Indah or Beautiful Indonesia in Miniature introduces visitors to the cultural mosaic of Indonesia's richly diverse ethnic groups. Located near Halim International Airport, this 100-hectare/247-acre complex features traditional buildings, costumes, and handicrafts of 27 different Indonesian provinces.

Each cluster of life-size model buildings is like a tiny village: stilted Dayak longhouses from Kalimantan, Sumatran houses with roofs curved like buffalo horns, and richly decorated Balinese temples. Within each cluster, people dress in the traditional costumes of that region, demonstrate local handicrafts, and perform local entertainment.

In the center of the complex is a giant lake in which small, vegetation-covered islands have been placed to duplicate the islands of the Indonesian archipelago. For the best view of this pint-size Indonesia, take the aerial cable car that travels across the lake in its journey from one end of the complex to the other.

(Continued on page 140)

. . . Continued from page 139

You can get around the large complex by mini-train, mini-bus, pedicab, or horse-drawn cart. Indonesia in Miniature is open from 9 A.M. to 4 P.M. daily. Museum Indonesia is open from 10 A.M. to 4 P.M. daily except Monday. Many of the cultural shows are held on Saturday and Sunday evenings.

Shopping around

Jakarta is a shopper's delight. Streetside stalls, tiny neighborhood shops, and modern department stores offer a multitude of locally made handicraft items such as stonecarvings, batiks, and Balinese paintings as well as Oriental antiques.

Some shopping places. The Sarinah Department Store, on Jalan Thamrin near the Hotel Indonesia Sheraton, is Indonesia's largest emporium. Fifteen air-conditioned floors are stocked with every imaginable type of merchandise. One whole floor is devoted to Indonesian crafts.

The city's major shopping areas include Blok M in the Kebayoran Baru area, Pancoran in Chinatown, and Pasar Baru on Jalan Pos. This narrow street, lined with a number of fabric shops, fills with the tantalizing aromas from food stalls in late afternoon. There are also many interesting new shops in the restored Old Batavia district.

Special handicraft centers. The Jakarta Hilton's Indonesian Bazaar houses 5 hectares/12 acres of shops selling Indonesian handicrafts and Oriental antiques. Here, you'll find Balinese paintings, stone and woodcarvings, silverwork, batiks, and leatherwork. The bazaar also has a theater featuring regular weekly performances of Indonesian music and dance. The Bazaar's shops are open daily from 10 A.M. to 6 P.M.

The Batik Federation, south of the downtown area near the Senayan Sport Center, has one of the country's best displays of batik. You can also purchase fabric here. If you are a serious collector of batik, investigate the numerous small batik factories and batik boutiques throughout Jakarta. Check with Jakarta's Tourist Information Center on Jalan Thamrin for locations.

Antiques. A fascinating flea market on Jalan Surabaya in Menteng — about 10 minutes from the major hotels — is certainly worth a visit. Lining one side of the street for about 3 blocks, the market's stalls display everything from old furniture to Ming china, from new shoes to old coins and brasswork. Though some of the "antiques" were obviously manufactured yesterday, you can often find excellent authentic pieces. Be prepared to bargain with a vengeance. The stalls along Jalan Surabaya are open daily from 9 A.M. to 5 P.M. Sunday is a popular local shopping day at this flea market.

Outdoor pleasures

Visitors wishing to enjoy Jakarta's tropical outdoors will find abundant opportunities to do so.

Jaya Ancol Dreamland. One of the most ambitious amusement centers in Southeast Asia is Jaya Ancol Dreamland (Taman Impian Jaya Ancol) on the north edge of the city not far from Kemayoran Airport.

Situated along a beautiful waterfront, the complex area was nothing more than a mosquito-infested marshland until the 1960s. Now it is a 139-hectare/343-acre amusement and sport center featuring an oceanarium with fish tanks and dolphin and sea lion performances; a swimming pool complex with five different pools, including one with waterslides; a marina area with water sport equipment as well as tennis courts and horseback riding facilities; an 18-hole public golf course; a 40-lane bowling alley; a lagoon equipped with boats to paddle or sail, and edged by a sand beach for sunning; a drive-in movie theater; and a race car circuit. Guests can stay at a multistory hotel or at beach cottages; eat at the complex's many restaurants; wile away the hours at its nightclubs or jai alai stadium; or relax at its open-air theater for cultural performances or art market featuring Indonesian craftspeople and craft shops.

Other recreational possibilities. The Senayan Sport Center, south of the city center, has tennis and badminton courts, a swimming pool, a shooting range, an ice skating rink, and the 18-hole public Kebayoran Golf Course. The sports spectator will find horse racing at Pulo Mas on Jalan Raya Jend. Akhmad Yani, greyhound racing at the Senayan Sport Center, and jai alai at the stadium at Jaya Ancol Dreamland. Other popular spectator sports include badminton and soccer.

Thousand Islands

The turquoise blue waters of the Bay of Jakarta are dotted with over 600 small coral islands, a few of which have been developed for tourists. Blessed with golden sun, white sand beaches, and colorful coral reefs alive with tropical fish, the Thousand Islands are ideal for time devoted to sunbathing, swimming, or skin diving.

Pulau Putri, the most developed island, has a 102-room resort with fan-cooled bungalows equipped with kitchens and outdoor barbecue pits. When you tire of cooking for yourself, enjoy the resort's restaurant and bar. Pulau Putri sports possibilities include water-skiing, sailing, fishing, snorkeling, and skin diving.

Located only about 64 km/40 miles northwest of Jakarta, the Thousands Islands make a perfect day trip from Jakarta. It's only a 20-minute flight to Panjang Isle — Pulau Putri's airstrip — then another 35-minute boat trip to Pulau Putri. The Thousand Islands can also be reached by boat from the mainland — a 3-hour trip. There are organized cruises and diving trips to the Thousand Islands as well.

WEST JAVA, A SPLENDID TAPESTRY

Home of the friendly Sundanese, West Java is a rich tapestry of rice fields and terraces, tea plantations, dense jungles, towering mountains (many of them still-smouldering volcanoes), and beautiful beaches.

From Jakarta, on the province's north coast, good roads and railway systems provide access to a number of interesting West Java destinations. There's also regular air service to major cities and attractions. In fact, the province's transportation network makes West Java one of the easiest parts of Indonesia to explore.

A short trip to Bogor

An easy and rewarding day excursion from Jakarta is the 56-km/35-mile trip south to Bogor. Tucked into mountain foothills, this city is famous for its Botanical Gardens and Presidential Summer Palace. Averaging a daily temperature of 25°C/77°F, it's also a cool retreat from the sizzling climate of Jakarta.

A new four-lane toll road connects Jakarta with Bogor. Travel time is only 30 to 45 minutes. There are both full and half-day tours from Jakarta to Bogor. Another transportation possibility is electric train service from Jakarta.

Famous Botanical Gardens. Begun in 1817, the Botanical Gardens cover 111 hectares/275 acres and feature an impressive collection of more than 15,000 tropical plants and trees. Bougainvilleas, conifers, rubber and showy flamboyant trees, oleanders, philodendrons, bamboo, and 400 different types of palm trees prevail. Rafflesia, with its bloom of 1 meter/3 feet in diameter — the world's largest flower — grows here. The garden's Orchid House has one of the world's largest collections, featuring more than 3,000 registered hybrids.

Presidential Summer Palace. Adjoining the Bogor Botanical Gardens is the Presidential Summer Palace, summer home and retreat for President Suharto. Surrounded by banyan-shaded, rolling green lawns where deer freely roam, this pillared, white colonial mansion was built in the early 1800s. It became the official residence for the Dutch governor general in 1870. President Sukarno made it his summer palace, and President Suharto continues to use it for the same purpose. You'll need special permission to enter the palace grounds; your hotel or a local travel agent can help with this. You can see the palace—at a distance—from the Botanical Gardens.

Onward to Puncak Pass. Heading southeast of Bogor, you enter the Puncak mountain region. After leaving Bogor you climb steadily, twisting through hills covered with tea plants and steep mountainsides terraced in rice fields. Near the top of the spectacular 1,500-meter/4,921-foot pass, the scenery changes to magnificent forests of pines and other conifers.

The Puncak Pass area is a popular holiday resort region for Jakarta residents. The district has a number of small hotels, several with swimming pools, gardens, and golf courses.

Some tour operators include both Bogor and Puncak Pass in a full-day tour from Jakarta.

Bandung, West Java's capital

The road through Puncak Pass winds on to Bandung, the capital of the province of West Java. The third largest city on Java, Bandung is one of the island's educational and cultural centers. Situated atop a plateau 762 meters/2,500 feet in elevation and ringed by imposing mountains, Bandung's mild, springlike climate produces a rainbow of temperate-zone flowers. In fact, the city is locally known as Kota Kembang or City of Flowers.

About 161 km/100 miles southeast of Jakarta, Bandung may be reached in about 4 hours by road (through Bogor), 3 hours by train, or 30 minutes by air.

Music, dance, and drama. The colorful folk dances and melodic music of the Sundanese have been particularly well preserved in Bandung. You can hear concerts featuring the *angklung* — a unique, local musical instrument — daily at the Saung Angklung, a model of a Sundanese folk house.

Crater trips. Bandung is located in an area of active volcanoes. Mount Tangkuban Prahu is about a 45-minute drive north of the city. Park near the edge of the crater and walk to the volcano's rim to peer into its vast gray-brown mass of bubbling mud, steam, and stinking sulphur.

About 15 km/9 miles south of Bandung is Mount Papandayan, still another bubbling volcano, rank with sulphur. You have to hike a distance to reach the crater.

Both craters should be visited in the early morning before clouds move in.

Accommodations. Bandung accommodations include Hotel Istana, Savoy Homann Hotel, Grand Hotel Priangan, and Panghegar Hotel.

West Java beaches

You'll find beautiful beaches along Java's southern and western coasts. The waters off the southern coast tend to be rougher than those off the western coast.

Samudra excursion. Samudra Beach, on the southern coast of Java 160 km/99 miles from Jakarta, is a pleasant overnight excursion from the capital city. The drive to Samudra Beach from Jakarta—through forests, rice fields, and villages—is superb. En route you can stop to explore Bogor. Or you can by-pass the drive and fly from Jakarta to Samudra Beach.

Lodging is at the Samudra Beach Hotel, at the edge of a palm-fringed beach. Swimming here can be dangerous since the beach drops off sharply just offshore, and there's a strong undertow. It's advisable to restrict your swimming to the hotel pool.

The nearby fishing village, with its armada of black-hulled, outrigger fishing boats, is a pleasant excursion from the hotel. The early morning fish market is a bustling affair with fish of all shapes and sizes being offered for sale.

Beaches and a volcano. You'll find warm, calm seas and sandy beaches characterize Java's west coast from Merak to south of Labuhan.

Carita Beach, 159 km/99 miles from Jakarta, is a starting point for excursions to Krakatoa volcano and the Ujung Kulon Nature Park (see page 144).

Krakatoa made its presence known to the world on August 27, 1883. On this date the volcano—located in the Sunda Strait between Java and Sumatra — erupted with such force that it literally blew itself apart. The explosion was heard as far away as Bangkok and Australia. Dust from the explosion circled the globe for 2½ days, and devastating tidal waves destroyed 165 villages. Nearly 40,000 people were killed.

Since then, the volcano has been slowly rebuilding itself on the ocean's floor. Today, Anak Krakatoa (child of Krakatoa) is a gently sloping 152-meter/500-foot smoking cone. You can hike to the summit of the volcano if you like.

(Continued on page 142)

. . . Continued from page 141

You can reach Anak Krakatoa on a 6-hour round-trip boat ride from the Carita Krakatoa Beach Hotel. The hotel has rustic, bungalow-style accommodations. There are also accommodations at the Anyer Beach Hotel to the north.

CENTRAL JAVA, RICH IN TRADITION

For more than a thousand years, Central Java has been the cultural center of the Javanese people. Here, clustered in and around Yogyakarta and Surakarta (Solo), you'll see some of Indonesia's greatest treasures — the world's largest Buddhist sanctuary, Borobudur; the massive Hindu temple complex of Prambanan; and ancient palaces and royal tombs.

Many of the crafts of Indonesia have their roots in Central Java. Here, you'll find craftspeople highly skilled in the art of batik making. Still others are excellent silversmiths or leather workers. Traditional theater arts also thrive in Central Java. Stylized Javanese court dances are still taught and performed here. Wayang kulit is a popular form of local entertainment along with gamelan music.

Like West Java, Central Java's landscape includes smoking volcanoes, awesome craters, neatly manicured rice fields, rugged coastal cliffs, rolling surf, and sandy beaches.

Captivating Yogyakarta

Many visitors to Indonesia consider Yogyakarta one of the country's most fascinating cities. Located in the southern part of Central Java midway between Jakarta and Bali, Yogyakarta is a showcase of Javanese arts, crafts, culture, and history. Its nearby neighbors are the imposing edifices of Borobudur and Prambanan.

Located 499 km/310 miles southeast of Jakarta, this city of 400,000 can be reached by air, rail, bus, or car. Once you've arrived, taxis, ponycarts, and becaks can get you around. Local tours can include city sights, arts and crafts centers, Borobudur, Prambanan, or Solo.

The city's largest and most popular hotel is the Hotel Ambarrukmo Sheraton. Other local accommodations include the Airlangga Guest House, Mutiara Hotel, Natour's Hotel Garuda, Puri Artha Cottages, and Wisma L.P.P. II.

The sultan's palace. The heart of Yogyakarta is its royal palace, Kraton Yogya. Built in the mid 1700s, it is still the home of Yogyakarta's sultan. Yogyakarta's royal court enjoys the status of being the highest-ranking court in Indonesia, a court responsible directly to the central government in Jakarta, not to the provincial head of Central Java.

Though the palace is still the home of the sultan, visitors are allowed to tour parts of it between 8:30 A.M. and noon daily. Uniformed guides lead visitors through the complex.

Surrounded by thick walls, the palace is an outstanding example of classical Javanese court-architecture. Of particular interest are the *pendopos* or open-sided pavilions with their gleaming marble floors, carefully carved teak pillars and panels, and gilded rafters. Included in special palace displays are royal carriages, a sultan's sedan chair, beautiful batiks, and ancient musical instruments.

Sono Budoyo Museum. Also near the palace, housed in the Sono Budoyo Museum, is one of the country's finest collections of Javanese, Madurese, and Balinese arts and crafts. Exhibits include an 18-carat gold Buddha statue, antique gamelans, wayang golek wooden puppets, old Javanese weapons, batiks, and Bronze Age household relics. The museum is open Tuesday, Wednesday, and Thursday from 8 A.M. to 1 P.M. It closes at noon on Friday, Saturday, and Sunday.

Royal tombs. About 16 km/10 miles south of the city, at Imogiri, are the tombs of the Mataram kings, where royal families have been buried since 1645. To reach the tombs, you must climb 345 steps up a shaded stairway. If you wish to enter the courtyards (possible on Mondays, Thursdays, and Fridays), you are asked to wear formal Javanese court dress (available at the site).

You can reach Imogiri by bus, taxi, or car.

A center for artists. Craftspeople in the Yogyakarta area are well known for their skills in batik making, silver crafting, and leather working.

At the Batik Research Center on Jalan Kusumanegara, you can see a permanent exhibit of batik that will introduce you to the history and the production of the fabric. The center is open daily from 9 A.M. to 2 P.M.

At Yogyakarta's several dozen batik factories — many on Tirtodipuan south of the sultan's palace — you can observe the batik process first-hand. Fabric is for sale in the factory showrooms.

Kota Gede, 5 km/3 miles east of Yogyakarta, is the center for Java's silver crafting industry. Visitors are welcome to wander through many of the factory showrooms and watch the craftspeople hammer, file, polish, heat, and solder pieces of silver into works of art. All work is done by hand. Delicate silver filigree jewelry, molded from thin silver alloy wire, and intricately decorated coffee sets, plates, ash trays, and flatware are available for purchase.

Yogyakarta is also known for its leather products. Skilled locals craft hand-tooled suitcases, shoulder bags, shoes, boots, belts and wayang kulit puppets.

Drama. An intrinsic part of the Javanese way of life is the wayang kulit, a shadow play using leather puppets. Based on episodes from the Ramayana and Mahabharata epics, the plays feature a single puppeteer, the *ki dalang*, who negotiates all the puppets and narrates the story from behind a lamp-illuminated screen. All the audience sees are the shadows cast by the intricately carved leather puppets. A gamelan orchestra accompanies the movements of the puppets while the tale is told.

Traditionally such a play goes on all night (from 9 P.M. to 5 A.M.), children falling asleep on their mothers' laps. (Some adults also doze.) This lengthy version of wayang kulit can be seen on the second Saturday of the month from 8 P.M. to 5 A.M. at Sasono Hinggel, Alun 2 Kidul, in Yogyakarta. A 2-hour evening performance is held weekly at the Ambarrukmo Sheraton Hotel.

Dance. Other highlights of Yogyakarta cultural entertainment are performances of classical Javanese dance and Ramayana ballet. There are weekly performances of Javanese dance and the Ramayana ballet at the Ambarrukmo Sheraton Hotel.

(Continued on page 145)

They're off! *Jockey crouches on sled between flanks of yoked bulls as they race for finish line; annual event attracts hundreds of visitors to Madura Island.*

Draped against cold, *guide stands by pony on Mount Bromo's rugged slopes. To arrive at East Java's active volcano by sunrise, Surabaya tour parties brave several hours of night riding.*

INDONESIA'S NATURE RESERVES

Indonesia is blessed with a rich and varied landscape. There are vast areas of unexplored rain forest, miles of pristine beaches, and countless lava-spewing volcanoes with bubbling calderas. The country is also blessed with a multitude of unusual mammals, reptiles, and birds—many found nowhere else in the world. Unfortunately, many species face extinction because of overhunting. In order to protect Indonesia's endangered wildlife, the Indonesian government has set aside 2 million hectares/5 million acres as wildlife reserves.

Visitors willing to rough it a little can explore some of these reserves. Since the parks usually lie off the beaten path, even getting there can be an adventure, and once there, accommodations are rustic.

The best way to visit Indonesia's nature reserves is on a specialized tour, because the tour operators will take care of transportation, accommodations, and any permits you might need to enter the reserves. Several Jakarta tour companies offer nature reserve trips.

Ujung Kulon Nature Park. This nature reserve, on the southernmost promontory of West Java, was established to protect Java's one-horned white rhinoceros from extinction. Other Ujung Kulon inhabitants include bantengs (cowlike animals), wild pigs, barking deer, flying foxes, green sea turtles, crocodiles, and several rare species of hornbill. Since there are no roads into the reserve, you must fly into Ujung Kulon by helicopter from Jakarta, or take a boat out of Labuan on Java's west coast.

You'll find simple accommodations at rest houses on Haudeuleum and Peutjang islands just off the coast. The best time to visit Ujung Kulon is April through October.

Baluran Game Reserve. This most accessible of Indonesia's reserves is located on the northeastern tip of East Java, just off the main Surabaya-Banyuwangi Road. It's a 5-hour bus ride from Surabaya to the reserve.

Here the country is dry—a land of open forests and scrublands bordered along the Madura Strait by beautiful beaches. Bantengs, barking deer, black monkeys, peacocks, and wild pigs all call this reserve home.

The best time of year to visit is during Baluran's dry season—from August to November—when animals must move into the open for grazing.

You'll find clean, forest authority bungalows at Bekol, 13 km/8 miles from the park entrance.

Gunung Leuser Nature Reserve. Within this North Sumatran nature reserve is the Bohorok Orangutan Rehabilitation Center. Here, tamed orangutans are trained to return to the wild. The best time to view them is during their late afternoon feeding. Three other endangered species—the Sumatran rhinoceros, elephant, and tiger—have also found a protective home in Gunung Leuser Nature Reserve.

The reserve can be reached from Medan by road. You'll find a rest house near Kotacane.

Kutai Game Reserve. This reserve, on the east coast of Kalimantan, is the major home of Indonesia's orangutans. Also found here are proboscis monkeys, civet cats, gibbons, and wild pigs. Most of the reserve is impenetrable jungle sliced by swift-flowing streams.

To get to the park, you have to fly to Balikpapan on Kalimantan and then take either a four-wheel-drive vehicle or taxi boat into the park. The trip by road takes 8 hours.

Komodo Reserve. The famed Komodo lizard, sole survivor of carnivorous dinosaurs who lived 130 million years ago, dwells in this reserve on Komodo Island in the Sape Straits east of Bali. Komodo lizards can be as long as 4 meters/12 feet.

The island's only other inhabitants are a few fishermen and wild deer, cattle, and pigs.

To see a Komodo lizard, you must have patience. It sometimes takes several days to track one down. Once lured out of its cave by an animal carcass, a lizard can devour its own weight in food in 17 minutes. After the lizard has eaten, it can go without food for three months.

Accommodations in the island's fishing village are primitive. It's best to go to Komodo Island on a boat tour that provides accommodations on board. The time to visit Komodo Island is March through September.

. . . Continued from page 142

An open-air theater in front of the Prambanan (see below) is used for staging the colorful Ramayana Ballet Festival, held on four successive nights during periods of the full moon from June through October. A floodlit stone temple provides a dramatic backdrop for the performances, which can include two gamelan orchestras, sixty singers, and hundreds of costumed dancers. For more information on the Ramayana epic see page 137.

Borobudur, a Buddhist sanctuary

Lying 42 km/26 miles northwest of Yogyakarta is Borobudur, the largest Buddhist sanctuary in the world. Built in the 8th century, Borobudur is several hundred years older than Cambodia's Buddhist temple of Angkor Wat.

Consisting of approximately 2 millon cubic feet of stone, the massive monument is over 38 meters/125 feet high. Thousands of craftsmen, engineers, laborers, sculptors, and stone masons worked for decades to complete it. Yet, not long after it was built, it was abandoned, because the center of the Buddhist culture shifted. Over the next 1,000 years, the monument was buried under layers of lava from a nearby volcano. Rediscovered by Sir Stamford Raffles in the 1800s, the sanctuary had been excavated by the beginning of this century.

The shape of things. Encircling a hill, the sanctuary has ten terraces—seven square lower terraces topped by three round upper terraces—rising in tiers to form a pyramidlike monument. Bas-reliefs on the walls of the lower square terraces depict episodes in the life of Buddha, showing the stages through which man must pass before he attains the Buddhist heaven, *nirvana*.

The upper circular terraces contain 72 latticed stone *stupas* (dome-shaped shrines), each with a seated Buddha hidden inside. On the uppermost terrace is the main stupa, symbol of the highest sphere in the Buddhist universe.

The climb up the steep stone stairs is a tiring one, but the view from the top is worth it. Removed from the babel of civilization below, you can gaze in peace across the rice fields and palm groves. The best time to stand atop Borobudur is at dawn when the stupas are silhouetted in the warm orange light of early day.

Current restoration. Since the foundation of Borobudur has grown weak, the monument is beginning to collapse under its own weight. In addition, poor drainage is causing the bas-reliefs to erode. Because of this deterioration, Borobudur is being dismantled stone by stone as part of a massive United Nations-sponsored renovation. Each stone is numbered, dried, and treated. The foundation is being reinforced and the drainage system improved. This work is taking place section by section; thus visitors can still see parts of the monument.

Getting there. From Yogyakarta, it's about an hour's drive to Borobudur. You can hire a car and driver, take a local bus, or join a tour.

Prambanan, the Hindu complex

The Hindu temple complex of Prambanan is located 16 km/10 miles east of Yogyakarta on the road to Surakarta (Solo). The complex—easily reached from Yogyakarta by taxi, bus, or tour—was originally built in the 9th century by Central Java's first Hindu king. Rice fields around the Prambanan complex are strewn with the remnants of other temples, built in the same period. Like Prambanan, these temples were abandoned when the Hindu-Javanese kings moved from Central to East Java.

A 49-meter/160-foot-high temple dedicated to Shiva, God of Destruction, dominates the Prambanan complex's central courtyard, one of several. The other two temples in this courtyard are dedicated to Vishnu and Brahma. In another courtyard lie the ruins of 224 minor shrines or temples. Prambanan's bas-reliefs include dynamic dancing figures, celestial musicians, trees-of-heaven, rams, deer, cats, and monkeys. Scenes from the Ramayana are also depicted.

SPEAKING THE LANGUAGE

Of the 200 languages spoken in Indonesia, only one is the national language—Bahasa Indonesia. Adapted in 1928 from the traditional Malay, it has evolved into a national language. Within the country, the people of each region also have their own language: Sundanese in West Java, Javanese in Central Java, Madurese in East Java, and Balinese in Bali.

The Indonesian language uses the same alphabet as English, and the letters are pronounced the same way, with these few exceptions: *c* is pronounced *ch* as in *chip*, *sy* has the *sh* sound of *shop*, and *kh* has the *k* sound of *kite*.

In recent years, some Indonesian words have undergone a change in spelling. Words that were formerly spelled with a *dj* are now spelled with the *j* only; thus *Djakarta* has become *Jakarta*. The letter *j* in old spellings has been changed to *y*, so *Surabaja* is now spelled *Surabaya*. The *tj* combination of consonants has been changed to *c*, so that *betjak* is now spelled *becak* and pronounced *bechak*.

To ease communication problems, all hotels, transportation facilities, and tour offices have multilingual employees. You will find, though, that once you get off the beaten path, very few people speak English.

The following are a few words to help you get started in speaking Bahasa Indonesia.

Good morning—*"Selamat pagi"*
Good afternoon—*"Selamat sore"*
Good evening—*"Selamat malam"*
Goodbye—*"Selamat tinggal"*
How are you?—*"Apa kabar?"*
Yes—*"Ja"* (pronounced *"Ya"*)
No—*"Tidak"*
Thank you—*"Terima Kasih"*
What's the price?—*"Berapa harganya?"*
Where is the restaurant?—*"Dimana restoran?"*
Where is the toilet?—*"Dimana kamar kecil?"*

Costumed dancer's *graceful movements and clanging of gamelan orchestra lend enchantment to dramatically lighted* **legong** *performance outside Balinese temple.*

With offerings held securely *atop their heads, colorfully dressed mourners advance toward site of cremation ceremonies. It's an occasion not for solemnity but for joy; visitors are welcome.*

Side trip to Surakarta

Surakarta (also known as Solo) is still another superb repository of Javanese art and culture. Located 65 km/40 miles east of Yogyakarta, Solo was the capital of the Mataram Kingdom from 1745 to 1755. Many people consider it the least westernized city on Java.

It's about an hour's drive to Solo from Yogyakarta. Local Yogyakarta tours feature Solo, or you can travel there by car or bus. Overnight accommodations include the Mangkunegaran Palace, Cakra, Kusuma Sahid, and Sahid Sala hotels.

A royal palace and museum. The 17th century walled Kraton Kasunanan with its shady courtyard is larger than the sultan's palace of Yogyakarta. Most of the superb decorations in the palace — gilded columns, marble statues, crystal chandeliers — were chosen by Sultan Pukubuwono X, who reigned in the early part of this century. Today, the palace is the home of the current ruler of Solo.

Adjacent to the palace, the Royal Museum contains exhibits of Solo's social, cultural, and political history. Of particular interest are the figureheads from royal barges that once journeyed the Solo River between Surakarta and the coast. Other museum displays include old Hindu-Javanese bronzes and antique Chinese porcelain. The museum and palace are open from 9 A.M. to noon daily.

Kraton Mangkunegaran. This palace is smaller than the Kraton Kasunanan, but equally lavish in architecture and furniture. The ceiling of the giant *pendopo* (pavilion) is painted with signs of the zodiac. There are Italian marble floors and European chandeliers. Open to the public, the inner royal residence features cabinets displaying antique jewelry, dance costumes, and masks from Java and Madura.

Colorful marketplaces. Solo has several markets with a fascinating array of goods. For batik, go to Pasar Klewer at the eastern end of Jalan Secoyudan near the Kraton Kasunanan. This entire two-floor market is devoted to the selling of batik. Hundreds of stalls offer thousands of varieties of batik and a few other local fabrics.

At the toy market on Jalan Slamet Riyadi near the Sriwedari Amusement Park, you can buy imaginative (if fragile) toys made while you wait. Pasar Triwindu, off Jalan Diponegoro, is Solo's flea market, selling odds and ends of all kinds: old uniform buttons, stoneware bottles, and brass and copper household goods.

MOUNTAINOUS EAST JAVA

Lying between Jakarta and Bali is East Java, a countryside of smoking volcanoes and temple-studded rice and sugar cane fields. Pleasant mountain resorts, classical Javanese dance, and the added attraction of bull races on nearby Madura Island (just off East Java's north coast) make the visit a special one.

You'll find the East Javanese intensely traditional. Women wear bright sarongs, usually topped with lacy, long-sleeved overblouses; most of the men also wear sarongs. Ceremonial dance is a favorite form of entertainment.

Industrial Surabaya

With a population exceeding 2.6 million, Surabaya is one of the country's principal industrial cities. Located on the Kali Mas River at the western end of Madura Strait, Surabaya is second only to Jakarta in size and economic importance. Its harbor, Tanjung Perak, is a main port of call for ocean-going ships. Nearby Ujung is Indonesia's famous naval base.

Surabaya is a mix of old and modern structures, Dutch colonial buildings and minaret-topped mosques, and boldly executed military memorials (commemorating Indonesia's heroes in the 1945 war of independence) and Hindu statues.

City sights. The highlight of a Surabaya sightseeing tour is the city zoo. Largest in Southeast Asia, the zoo is home for sloe-eyed sambars, droll orangutans, black apes, and the fierce-looking Komodo dragons. Aviary inhabitants include cockatoos, pheasants, cassowaries, and hornbills. A nocturnal house and dolphinarium round out the collection.

Other city sights to visit are Chinatown, the Arab quarter, the harbor, the governor's mansion, and the city museum. The latter includes exhibits of prehistoric tools, ornately carved antique furniture, and East Javanese daggers, puppets, and masks.

Ramayana Festival. About an hour's drive south of Surabaya, at Pandaan near the mountain resort of Tretes, is the Candrawilwatika Amphitheatre, the setting for a series of Ramayana ballet performances held between May and October. Presented on two successive nights each month during the period of the full moon, the dances feature a version of the Ramayana based on East Java temple carvings. There are tours from Surabaya to the Ramayana Festival performances.

Getting to Surabaya. By air, Surabaya is an hour from Jakarta, a half-hour from Bali. You can also reach the city by rail and road.

Local transportation. Surabaya city transportation includes taxis, becaks, and buses. Local tours feature city sights, Mount Bromo, the Madura bull races, or ancient temple ruins.

A place to stay. Air-conditioned comfort and dining facilities are available at such Surabaya hotels as the Grand Park, Hyatt Bumi Surabaya, Majapahit, Mirama, Ramayana, Simpang, and Jane's House. The latter is furnished in restored Javanese and Chinese antiques.

Across the strait to Madura

Separated from Surabaya by a narrow strait is the island of Madura, best known for its bull races held regularly on the first Sunday of every month (except January). To reach the island, take a 25-minute ferry ride from Surabaya. The races are held at Bangkalan Stadium, a 16-km/10-mile bus ride north of Madura's ferry terminal.

Each year in September, at the close of the harvest season, Pamekasan, the island's capital, hosts a championship bull race. Two bulls from each district on the island — winners of a series of local elimination races — are brought to Pamekasan. The morning of the race, the carefully groomed and elaborately decorated bulls are paraded through town to the race course. Musicians and huge crowds add to the festivity.

For the race, the bulls are yoked in pairs, with a tapering wooden sled harnessed between them. The end of the sled trails on the ground. The jockey, balancing himself on a narrow shelf of the sled between the two bulls' rumps, lines up his team beside the other pairs of bulls on the field. The signal is given, and the race is on. A fast bull team can do the 111-meter/121-yard-long course in 9 to 10 seconds.

East Java temples

The rice fields of East Java are strewn with the ruins of temples. Within driving distance of Surabaya, many of these temples are regularly included on countryside tours.

Majapahit ruins. One hour southwest of Surabaya by way of Mojokerto lie the 13th century archeological treasures of the Majapahit Empire, an advanced and powerful Hindu civilization. The empire's capital, in the vicinity of Trowulan, was a magnificent walled city with lavish pavilions, temples, palaces, pools, and plazas. Today you'll see only the remains of walls, temples, and *gapuras* (gateways).

Panataran complex. You'll find East Java's largest temple complex just 10 km/6 miles north of Blitar. Begun in the late 1100s, construction of this complex took 250 years and spanned two eras: the Singosari and the Majapahit kingdoms. Much of the major work was done during the Majapahit reign.

The complex consists of three walled courtyards with temples, dance/play platforms, and shrines. Temple wall bas-reliefs depict coiled serpents, winged lions, strange griffins, and animal tales.

Besides this large temple complex, there are a number of smaller temples in the Blitar area.

Rugged trip up Mount Bromo

From Surabaya you can arrange for a tour to 2,187-meter/7,176-foot Mount Bromo, an active volcano about 129 km/80 miles southeast of the city. The steaming crater, which last erupted in 1842, is part of the massive Tengger Mountains, a chain of volcanic peaks extending across this part of East Java.

The best time to view the mountain is at sunrise, when the rugged landscape is at its most dramatic. In order to accomplish this, you must leave Surabaya about 11 P.M., drive by way of Probolinggo, and arrive about 2 A.M. at the small mountain village of Ngadisari, where you transfer to ponies. Wind whistles through the tall pine trees, and stars in these clear southern skies seem incredibly close as the sure-footed pack animals carry you up the slopes of Bromo's neighbor, Mount Batok, and down into the desolate Sea of Sands.

After 2 hours on ponyback, you dismount and climb 250 steep stairs to Bromo's crater rim in time to see the sunrise. From the rim you gaze down into the crater at the cone, veiled by smoke and encrusted with striking lava formations. Nearby Mount Batok looms above you, and steaming sulphur beds seethe below you.

You can be back in Surabaya by midday. The trip can also be made during daylight hours, but you miss much of the mountain's mystique. There are also sunrise tours to Mount Bromo from Malang. Night or day, it's cold on the mountain, so be prepared with a heavy sweater, jacket, hat, and gloves.

MAGICAL, CHARMING BALI

For centuries, from the days of the early traders to the present, Bali has been known as the enchanted island. Much of its charm lies with the people — the graceful, beautiful Balinese who live in mystical harmony with their natural surroundings.

Another part of the enchantment is the lush, green, 5,426-square-km/2,095-square-mile island itself. An east-west chain of volcanic mountains—some of them still active—dominates the northern part of the island. To the south of these towering peaks are the island's rice fields, carefully sculptured terraces that extend from the valley floors to the tops of the steep hillsides. An intricate irrigation system composed of dams, canals, pipes, and bamboo spouts controls water flow so that each terrace gets just the amount of water it needs.

Separated from the eastern tip of Java by a narrow, 3-km/2-mile channel, Bali is easily reached by air from Jakarta (about an hour's flight) and from other Indonesian cities. Garuda Indonesian Airways and other international airlines fly to Bali from cities in Southeast Asia, the Orient, and Australia. The international airport is 19 km/12 miles south of Denpasar, the island's capital city (see page 149).

Overland bus tours out of Jakarta feature Java sights plus a trip to Bali. There's daily ferry service between Ketapang, Java, and Gilimanuk, Bali.

A traditional life style

The Balinese life style is a rural one. The lands are cultivated communally by families that cluster together in villages. Each extended family — often consisting of several generations — lives within a walled compound that comprises thatch-roofed houses.

Village living. Farmers rise early to take care of chores, such as tending the rice fields, before the day grows hot. They return to the shade of the compound at midday, completing their chores in the late afternoon. Evening is a time for entertainment like wayang performances.

Religion dominates. Bali-Hinduism, practiced by about 90 percent of the people, dominates the life of the Balinese. Since they believe that their island is a gift from the gods, the Balinese continually thank the gods for this gift through dance, music, and art.

To honor the gods, temple festivals that feature music, dance, and offerings are held. These celebrations take place at least once a year at each of the island's temples. Since there are 10,000 temples in Bali, you'll find a religious festival somewhere on the island nearly every day. It's not uncommon to come across a long procession of women, dressed in their best finery, walking gracefully along the road, offerings of multicolored rice cakes, fruit, and flowers atop their heads.

Besides temples, there are numerous shrines honoring the gods. Family compounds have them, and portable ones are carried to the rice field to assure a good harvest. You'll even see them atop Denpasar's traffic lights and at busy country crossroads. Daily, offerings of rice and flowers are brought to these shrines.

A Balinese cremation—an elaborate event with colorful decorations, music, and dance—is a joyful time. With the cremation, the soul of the dead person travels to heaven to be reincarnated, returning, hopefully, to the beautiful island of Bali.

Visitors are welcome at temple festivals and cremations, as well as other local celebrations.

Island orientation

Denpasar, Bali's capital city of 75,000, is located on the southern tip of the island. Here also are the international airport and several beach resort areas.

Denpasar. Traffic-congested Denpasar is Bali's largest city. Include in your tour of city sights the Denpasar Museum, which has a collection of Balinese arts and crafts dating from early times to the 20th century, and the Abian Kapas Art Center, also featuring Balinese art.

Denpasar accommodations include the Bali and Denpasar hotels.

Nearby beach resorts. The beautiful beach areas of Sanur, 5 km/3 miles southeast of Denpasar, and Kuta, 7 km/4 miles southwest of Denpasar, offer opportunities for swimming, sunbathing, fishing, and boating. Most of the major hotels have tennis courts, and there's a 9-hole golf course opposite the Bali Beach Inter-Continental in Sanur.

First-class accommodations abound in the Sanur and Kuta beach areas. Amenities include restaurants and swimming pools. Sanur accommodations include Alit's Beach Bungalows, Hotel Bali Beach Inter-Continental, Bali Hyatt, Bali Sanur Bungalows, Beach Hotel and Bungalows Diwangkara, Gazebo Cottage Beach Hotel, La Taverna Bali Hotel, Santrian Beach Cottages, Hotel Sanur Beach and Seaside Bungalows, Hotel Segara Village, Sindhu Beach Hotel, and Tandjung Sari Hotel. The Hotel Bali Oberoi, Kartika Plaza, Legian Beach Hotel, and Pertamina Cottages are in the Kuta area.

Another beach resort area is being developed on a section of land south of Sanur and Kuta. When finished, Nusa Dua, a 425-hectare/1050-acre parcel of land on the Bukit Peninsula south of the airport, will feature hotels, shops, theaters, sports facilities, and a garden.

Getting around the island. For island touring—most of Bali's sights are some distance north of Denpasar and the beach areas—you can hire a car or a car with driver. Motor scooters and bicycles are also available for hire. Local island transportation includes buses and bemos. There are organized tours featuring Denpasar city sights, arts and crafts villages, and religious temples.

Music fills the air

The Balinese people love music and dance. No Balinese ceremony or festival is complete without some form of dance performance.

Many hotels offer dance entertainment during special hotel dinners. Local tours also include various dance performances held in nearby villages. Still another good way to see Balinese dance is to attend a festival or celebration. Check with your hotel or a local travel agent for the current festival schedule.

Three dance performances you might see during your stay on Bali are the *legong, kecak,* and *barong* dances.

Legong. This dance ballet is the most beautiful of Bali's classical dances. Lovely Balinese maidens, clad in colorful, silk sarongs and flower headdresses, perform graceful, flowing motions in perfect unison. The dance tells the story of an arrogant king in pursuit of an unwilling princess.

Kecak or Monkey Dance. In this dance, performed at night, a chorus of 200 men sit cross-legged in a circle in the middle of a shadow-filled arena. Chanting, chattering, hissing, moaning, and bellowing in perfect unison, they stretch their arms and sway from side to side as if one body. In the center of this eerie group, dancers act out a sequence from the Ramayana. The dance tells how King Rama and the monkey army of Hanuman, represented by the all-male chorus, helped to rescue Rama's wife, Sita.

Barong. In this dance, a good, mythical, dragonlike beast—the *barong*—fights *rangda*, the queen of the witches and evil. At the end of the dance, rangda uses her powers to turn humans against themselves: the entranced dancers try to stab themselves with *krisses* (daggers). Surprisingly enough, because the dancers are in a trance there is no injury.

Arts and crafts villages

In the 13th century, when the early Javanese Hindus moved to Bali to escape Islam, they took with them their Javanese classics and poetry, arts and crafts, music, dance, sculpture, and theater. On Bali, these immigrants continued to cultivate their arts with little influence from outside sources. As a result, you'll find a wonderfully distinctive style in Balinese arts and crafts that is unique to this island.

A wide selection of Balinese arts and crafts are found in hotel gift shops. In addition, there are more and more compounds where you can see a variety of crafts produced and sold in one place. However, to really see Balinese art forms and have the time to browse, it's best to visit the villages that specialize in a particular craft or crafts. You can do this on your own or on a tour.

Batubulan. In this village, northeast of Denpasar, you'll find expert stonecarvers. They are kept busy sculpturing works for Bali's many temples and shrines. Many of the shops will ship for you.

There's a performance of the barong dance here daily at 10 A.M.

Celuk. Fine gold and silver jewelry (rings, bracelets, brooches, and pendants) is produced in this town, north of Tegaltamu. Besides the shops along the main street, be sure to explore the back-lane shops. Here, you can view craftsmen at work as well as make purchases.

Mas. Still farther north, on the road to Ubud, is this village of expert woodcarvers. From teak, coconut, ebony, and hibiscus wood, these craftspeople create works that portray the Balinese myths, legends, and way of life.

At the Tilem Gallery, you can see woodcarvers at work. There are also carvings for sale.

Ubud. This village, north of Mas, is considered the center for Balinese fine arts. Set amid green hills, pastoral Ubud is home to several hundred artists (painters and carvers), superb dance groups, and gamelan orchestras.

Ubud is well known for its paintings—both traditional and modern. Balinese paintings have a unique style and bold colors. The Puri Lukisan (Palace of Fine Arts) houses a permanent collection of paintings and sculptures that shows the development of Balinese art chronologically.

Bedulu. On the road to Tampaksiring, 24 km/15 miles north of Denpasar, lies Bedulu. The people here weave colorful baskets in a variety of shapes and sizes.

Just west of Bedulu is Goa Gajah, the Elephant Cave. This cave is believed to have been a Buddhist monastery in the 11th century.

Religious sights

With more than 10,000 temples available for viewing, tourists have ample opportunity to visit at least a few. Many are included in local tours, or you can explore them on your own. The temples are at their colorful best during the temple festival, when even the statues of the deities are decked out in hibiscus flowers and sarongs.

When entering a temple, you must wear a sash around your waist. These are usually available from your tour guide or you can rent one at the more visited temples. Even better, buy one. Then you'll be prepared if you happen upon a temple festival procession and want to join the celebration.

Mengwi. Built in 1634 by the Mengwi, Pura Taman Ayu is one of Bali's loveliest temple complexes and one of the largest. Because it is situated on high ground surrounded by a water-filled moat, it appears to float in the middle of a lake.

Mengwi is northwest of Denpasar on the main south-to-north highway.

Sangeh. Hundreds of monkeys live in this sacred forest, 20 km/12 miles north of Denpasar. *Pala* trees — not native to Bali — thrive in this forest. The Balinese have declared the area is sacred, and the monkeys who dwell here share in this sacredness. Unafraid of strangers, they'll flock around you for peanuts. (These can be purchased at the site.) Be careful, they have been known to bite the hand that feeds them.

Tanahlot. This seaside temple on Bali's southwest coast sits on a high, rocky outcrop just offshore. At low tide, it's possible to wade out to it. The temple is particularly spectacular at sunset, when the tiered structure stands silhouetted against a flaming orange sky.

Bangli. Pura Kehen, Bali's second largest temple complex, is located near Bangli northeast of Denpasar. Bangli was the capital of the Gelgel Dynasty during the early part of its 14th century reign. Inscriptions in the temple date back to 1050.

Pura Kehen features three courtyards on ascending levels of a terraced hillside. Ornamental carvings decorate the balustrades of the stairways connecting the courtyards.

Besakih. The oldest and most sacred temple complex on Bali is located 60 km/37 miles northeast of Denpasar at Besakih, on the slopes of Mount Agung. This "mother temple," probably built in the 2nd century (before Hinduism was established on Bali), is the largest temple complex on Bali and is considered to be the royal ancestral sanctuary.

NORTH SUMATRA

Sumatra, located northwest of Java, is the second largest island in Indonesia and the fifth largest in the world. In contrast to Java and Bali, it is sparsely populated—only 20 million people live on the large island. Tourist facilities are limited on Sumatra. But the traveler who is willing to forego some of the amenities is awarded a look at charming, noncommercial Indonesia.

Geographically, the island is set at an angle, running 1,770 km/1,110 miles from northwest to southeast, with the equator slicing through its middle. Paralleling its western coast is a rugged range of mountains. East of the range lies a wide coastal plain, traversed by broad rivers that flow through the coastal mangrove swamps to join the Strait of Malacca and the Java Sea.

The island's main gateway is Medan, the capital of North Sumatra and a busy commercial center. Visitors to this province, located across the Strait of Malacca from Peninsular Malaysia, can enjoy the cool mountain resort of Lake Toba as well as visit Batak tribal villages.

Medan, a tropical trading center

Located inland from the northeast coast of North Sumatra, Medan is a cosmopolitan trading, processing, and manufacturing center. More than 60 percent of Indonesia's exports are shipped from its port of Belawan, on the coast 26 km/16 miles north of the city. Nearby plantations produce rubber, palm oil, and fine Deli tobacco.

About transportation. Medan is one of Indonesia's three international gateways. International airlines — including Garuda Indonesian Airways—serve Polonia International Airport with direct flights from Singapore, Penang, Kuala Lumpur, and Tokyo. There's also ferry service between Belawan and Penang, Malaysia.

Garuda Indonesian Airways and Merpati Nusantara Airlines link Medan with other Indonesian cities. There's train service between Belawan, Medan, and Banda Aceh.

Transportation in Medan includes unmetered taxis, becaks, and buses. There are half-day tours of Medan and several-day tours to the Lake Toba area.

A place to stay. Medan's comfortable hotels include the Danau Toba International, Dharma Deli, Dirga Surya, New Belawan International, Garuda Plaza, and Polonia. Most are air-conditioned and have restaurants.

Swayback roofs *of Toraja homes attract visitors to Sulawesi's lush countryside. District's friendly villagers act as guides and festival escorts.*

Local sights. Sightseeing opportunities in Medan are limited. The town best serves as a jumping-off point for trips to the Lake Toba area.

During your stay in Medan, you might want to visit the Maimoon Palace of the Sultan of Deli on Jalan Pemuda. Built in 1888, the palace is embellished with cupolas and gingerbread trim. The nearby Mesjid Raya — Great Mosque — with its beautiful minaret and reflecting pool was built in 1906.

En route to Lake Toba

Lake Toba, a crater lake about 177 km/110 miles south of Medan, is Sumatra's only developed tourist area. Lying at 914 meters/3,000 feet above sea level, it offers vacationers a springlike climate the year around.

FESTIVAL TIME

Practically every event in an Indonesian's life calls for a colorful ceremony. Each of the country's numerous ethnic groups has its own festivities connected with birth, marriage, and death, and celebrations are an integral part of the country's different religions.

The following list covers a few of the more intriguing events. Check Indonesia's current calendar for exact dates.

Galungan. An important Balinese celebration symbolizing the victory of good over evil, this twice yearly event is celebrated with decorations, temple offerings, and gamelan music.

Waicak. The annual full moon festival, held at Borobudur Temple near Yogyakarta in early May, commemorates the birth and death of Buddha. Climax of the event comes at 4 A.M. when the worshippers, each carrying a lighted candle, walk up the stairs of the temple and circle clockwise toward the main stupa.

Idul Fitri. The end of Muslim fasting months is celebrated with mass prayers in mosques and public squares.

Idula Adha. Cattle and goats are slaughtered as offerings and given to the poor on the eve of Haji (annual Muslim pilgrimage to Mecca).

Grebeg Maulud. Muslims celebrate Mohammed's birthday. In Yogyakarta, a procession travels from the Sultan's Palace to the mosque. Surabaya festivities include carnivals and a traditional mask festival.

Ram fighting. Annually on the first Sunday after August 17th, the grand finale of the year's ram fighting trials takes place in Bandung. Highlight of the event is the performance of the *gendang pencak* (traditional fighting dance).

The highland area around Lake Toba is Batak country. Here, you'll see the architecture and lifestyle of a people living much as their ancestors did.

Two main roads lead to Lake Toba: one passes through the mountain resort of Brastagi, and the other — called the "plantation road" — passes through mile after mile of rubber, palm oil, and cocoa tree plantations. The Brastagi route, though longer, is more scenic and less traveled. It takes about 6 hours to reach Lake Toba on this road; the "plantation road" takes only 3 hours. You can combine the two for an enjoyable loop trip; if possible, allow 2 to 3 days and stay over at Lake Toba.

Tours that extend over several days usually include a stay at the lake. You can also hire a car and driver for the trip.

A mountain resort. Brastagi, 68 km/42 miles south of Medan, is the main highland resort en route to Lake Toba. It was developed during colonial times by rubber plantation owners desiring a place to escape from the lowlands heat. With its temperate climate and volcanic soil, the area has been a major growing region for vegetables, fruits, and flowers (roses, carnations, gladioluses, and orchids).

The Batak people. The Batak tribespeople are descendants of neolithic mountain dwellers from northern Thailand and Burma. About 1,500 years ago, invading Mongols forced these mountain people to move to the shores of Southeast Asia. Unhappy away from the mountains, these ancient Bataks migrated to Sumatra and made their way into the highlands. The first groups settled on Samosir Island in Lake Toba. From here, tribes spread throughout the area. Today, there are several subgroups, known collectively as Bataks. Though each subgroup speaks its own particular dialect, it shares a common cultural framework with the other Batak tribes. The largest group is the Toba Bataks. Other notable groups are the Karo, Simalungun, Dairi (Pakpak), Angkola, and Mandailing.

The Batak village is typically clusters of multifamily dwellings. In early times, each village was well fortified with thick walls topped by a bamboo fence because of continual battling between villages. As you travel through Batak country, you'll see remnants of these early fortifications as well as examples of traditional houses. High above the ground, these houses rest on piles. They have heavy plank walls and soaring, sway-backed roofs, peaked sharply on both ends. Built without any nails, some of these structures are over 100 years old.

Batak villages. On your Toba excursion, you can visit several Batak villages.

Lingga, 15 km/9 miles south of Brastagi, has several traditional stilted Karonese houses that are being preserved by the government. Karonese folk dancing is occasionally performed here.

At Pematang Siantar, 128 km/80 miles southeast of Medan, a palace of a Simalungun Batak king has been preserved to serve as a museum. Inside this beautiful structure with its graceful sway-backed roof, you'll see antique armaments and artwork, as well as ancient iron tools.

In Pematang Purba, 140 km/87 miles southeast of Medan, a traditional royal Simalungun village is preserved as an open-air museum. The village contains interesting houses, a courtroom, and an execution yard.

RIJSTAFFEL, A PLENTIFUL FEAST

You'll find variations of this wonderful feast served in all parts of the world, especially Holland. However, to have it at its very best, try it in Indonesia—its country of origin.

In Dutch, *rijstaffel* means "rice table." In reality it's a "mini" (or, in some cases, "maxi") banquet highlighting rice with a wide variety of meat, chicken, fish, and vegetable side dishes, accompanied by such condiments as

sambal, Indonesia's notoriously hot sauce made from chile peppers. Rice has always been the main part of the Indonesian meal. To rice are added side dishes. The Dutch colonial settlers—rich in money, servants, and leisure time—took this local pattern of eating and turned it into a sumptuous, 2 to 3-hour banquet. All the best dishes of the area were prepared. One by one they were paraded before the guests by white-coated waiters. Care was taken that each dish would vary in flavor or texture from the previous one.

Today's rijstaffel is not quite as elaborate as those of the Dutch colonists. Though some restaurants still serve the different dishes at your table, many now prepare rijstaffel dishes only for Saturday or Sunday buffet lunches. The number of side dishes may vary from 12 to 50, but rice is always the most important item.

Possible rijstaffel selections include *opor ayam* (chicken in coconut milk), *sayur choisin ayam* (Chinese cabbage with chicken), *babi rica* (spiced pork), *ikan pepes* (fish fillet in banana leaves), *sate campur* (mixed meats on skewers with peanut sauce), *gado gado* (vegetable salad), and *soto ayam* (gingered chicken soup).

Not every rijstaffel is the same. Each region will feature its own side dish specialties. To sample Indonesia's gastronomic variety, try a rijstaffel. Check with your hotel for information on local possibilities.

Beautiful Lake Toba

This shimmering stretch of water is so large it's more like an inland sea than a lake. The 80-km/50-mile long lake is twice the size of Switzerland's Lake Geneva. It's surrounded by high mountains and jungle-covered plateaus; Samosir Island fills more than half the lake basin.

Parapat. You'll find Lake Toba tourist accommodations in the small town of Parapat, 179 km/111 miles southeast of Medan. Set back in a bay, the town affords a sweeping view of the lake and the mountains. Popular hotels include the Hotel Danau Toba, Hotel Parapat, and Wisma Pertamina International.

Enjoy the resort's many activities: swimming, water-skiing, boating, hiking, mountain climbing, and fishing. These strenuous activities can be combined with a trip to a nearby village market or an excursion to Samosir Island. Hotels occasionally hold performances highlighting Simalungun and Toba Batak folk music and dancing.

Trip to Samosir Island. On this 1,036-square km/400-square mile island are several Toba Batak villages. From Parapat, you can reach the island by speedboat in 20 to 30 minutes. Tour launches provide scheduled tours.

However, if you want to travel as the natives do, take the much slower local ferry.

On a trip to the island, your first stop will be Tomok. The village's royal cemetery has stone sarcophagi of early Batak kings. At the village market, you can buy everything from handwoven cloth and woodcarvings to old coins and Batak calendars carved into bamboo. Bargaining will get you the best price.

Farther west on the island's coast is Ambarita. This town can be reached by boat from Tomok. Traditional wooden houses with sway-backed roofs and elaborately decorated walls border a central square. The stone chairs and tables in the square mark what was once an outdoor courtroom where kings and chiefs presided.

Nias, a mysterious island

The people of Nias lived in a Stone Age culture well into the 20th century. On this island, lying off the upper coast of North Sumatra, you'll see ancient pyramids, stone terraces believed to have been the center of sacrificial ceremonies, and ritual dances and festivals. The Nias tribespeople were well known as fierce warriors and headhunters. Today, most islanders are Christians and prefer hymn singing to

Every detail *of carving adds prestige to owner's home. Life-size carvings of sacred buffalo also embellish boat-shaped houses.*

At first glance, *effigies on Toraja's hanging tombs appear to be apartment dwellers, surveying the scene below. Celebrants at elaborate, month-long funeral festivals welcome guests.*

warring. However, you can still see demonstrations of their fierce war dances.

You can reach Nias by boat from Sibolga or Padang, or by plane from Medan. Cruise ships also call here.

Visit fascinating Teluk Dalam, a hillside town reached by steep stone stairs. The village is a stunning surprise: a large cluster of houses raised off the ground by pilings, and all topped with steeply pitched roofs. Groups visiting the village are entertained by men attired in full battle regalia—headdresses, face masks, shields, and spears. Women participating in the ceremonies wear beautifully embroidered dresses and gold headdresses. Carrying on a tradition performed by Nias warriors for centuries, the younger men exhibit their jumping skill; barefooted, they leap over a 2-meter/7-foot-high stone wall set up in the main village square.

WEST SUMATRA

Located on the midwestern part of Sumatra, the province of West Sumatra is the home of the Minangkabau tribe. The area of some 38,860 square km/15,000 square miles is predominantly mountainous and features high-walled canyons, sparkling waterfalls, blue lakes, and tiny hamlets tucked into lush, green valleys.

Gateway cities

West Sumatra's principal cities, Padang and Bukittinggi, are not tourist attractions in themselves but are access points for Minangkabau villages.

Padang. This city, the area's main seaport, can be reached on regularly scheduled flights from Jakarta, Medan, and Singapore. Though lacking in major tourist attractions, the town does offer visitors little shops, narrow lanes, broad avenues, and old wooden houses.

Back country loop trip. An excellent way to see the Minangkabau country is to hire a car and drive a loop from Padang to Bukittinggi to Lake Singkarak and back again. The journey from the lake back to Padang is on an up-and-down twister of a road, but intriguing villages and magnificent mountain scenery make the journey a rewarding experience.

Tours out of Padang travel to Bukittinggi and Minangkabau country.

Bukittinggi. This thriving commercial center, 92 km/57 miles north of Padang, is the capital of West Sumatra. Located on the Agam Plateau on the lower slopes of the Bukit Barisan mountain range, Bukittinggi is a pleasant hill resort with a cool, sunny climate.

One of the city's attractions is its Rumah Adat Baandjuang Museum. Housed in a 100-year-old traditional, sway-back roofed, Minangkabau-style building are traditional wedding dresses, unusual musical instruments, hunting weapons, antique jewelry, and ancient cooking vessels and utensils.

Accommodations. In Padang choose between the Mariani and Muara hotels. In Bukittinggi, you can stay at the Dymens Hotel.

Touring Minangkabau country

It is believed that the Minangkabau kingdom came into being between the 12th and 14th centuries. The Minangkabaus have a matrilineal society—the grandmother is the grand matriarch. In this society, the women dominate the family. When it comes to proposals of marriage, women do the asking. A daughter who marries stays with her family. The new husband has a choice: he can stay with his family, visiting his wife as a guest, or he can establish himself permanently with his wife's family.

Local architecture. The houses of the Minangkabau people have roofs shaped like buffalo horns. The ridge poles of the roofs are strongly curved to form scooped, sway-backed roofs with high spirelike tips — the buffalo horns. The horns are the sharpened ends of the long ridge poles used to support the roof of the house.

The house, thatched with thick layers of black fiber from palm trees, sits well above the ground on beautifully carved wooden pillars.

Some villages. At Padangpanjang, 17 km/11 miles south of Bukittinggi, the "buffalo-horn" spikes of the village's many traditional houses pierce the sky. The music conservatory here specializes in the teaching of traditional Minangkabau music and dance.

A mosque marks the center of ancient Pariangan, a village on the slopes of Mount Merapi. Surrounding the temple are picturesque houses with rice barns; there's also a traditional council house.

SPIDER-SHAPED SULAWESI

The island of Sulawesi, formerly known as Celebes, straddles the equator just east of Kalimantan. It's a mountainous land of misty plateaus, fertile valleys, meandering rivers, shimmering lakes, tumbling waterfalls, pleasant hot springs, and palm-lined beaches.

The 264,249-square-km/102,000-square-mile island is divided into four provinces — North, Central, Southeast, and South. For visitors, the most important are South Sulawesi and North Sulawesi.

Sulawesi is just beginning to develop as a tourist destination, so accommodations and land transportation are limited. Daily air service connects Ujung Pandang, South Sulawesi's capital, with Jakarta, Denpasar, and Surabaya. Manado, North Sulawesi's capital, can be reached by air from Ujung Pandang. Accommodations in Ujung Pandang include the Grand, Pasanggrahan Beach, Victoria, and Raodah International hotels. Manado hotels include the Kawanua City, Wenang, Minahasa, and Ricardo.

South Sulawesi, Toraja Land

The province of South Sulawesi offers visitors hot springs, exotic butterflies, and romantic beaches. It is home for the famous Bugis seafarers and the Torajas, a tribal group with unique houses and burial customs.

Ujung Pandang. Located on the island's southwest coast, Ujung Pandang (formerly called Makassar) is Sulawesi's chief seaport. Its harbor is crowded with *prahus*, Buginese double and triple-masted sailing ships handhewn from teak. In past years the Buginese — capable of sailing the seas without benefit of sextant or compass — have been slave runners, pirates, and warriors as well as traders. Today, their schooners carry merchandise between Jakarta and other Indonesian islands.

You can accomplish town sightseeing in a *becak* or a *tigaroda*, two bicycle-operated pedicabs. Also, there are sightseeing tours of the city and local tours to offshore islands for swimming and diving. Ujung Pandang is also the starting point for the full-day bus or jeep trip into Tanah Toraja (Toraja Land).

Into Toraja Land. About 306 km/190 miles north of Ujung Pandang lies the scenic countryside of the Torajas, an ancient race of Proto-Malays. According to legend, the ancestors of these people used the boats that brought them to Sulawesi from Indochina as roofs for their new homes. Today, the traditional Toraja house faces north — the direction from which the original Torajas first appeared — and has a roof shaped like a double-prowed boat.

You can reach the Toraja area by jeep or mini-bus tour out of Ujung Pandang. The trip takes 8 to 10 hours one way. Accommodations are available at Rantepao, the cultural center of the tribespeople, and nearby Makale, political center of the Torajas. Hotels include the Misiliana and the Toraja Cottage in Rantepao and Barana Wisma in Makale.

Tanah Toraja sights. Here in Tanah Toraja (Toraja Land) are unique houses and burial caves. Take a short trip from Rantepao and Makale to see both attractions.

In the villages, houses capped with boatlike roofs seem to float above the surrounding rice fields like ships at anchor in a harbor. Built atop thick pole pilings, the houses feature outer walls elaborately decorated with geometric designs painted in ochers, whites, and blacks. The curved roofs are made of layers of bamboo poles.

Many of the Toraja dead are buried in "hanging graves," located not far from the villages. These burial caves are tombs that have been cut into the sides of steep cliffs and sealed at their entrance with decorative, wooden doors. Standing in rows in recessed balconies on the cliff face are wooden statues of the deceased. The clothed figures, their white painted eyes perpetually open, gaze eerily across the rice fields. The clothing of each statue is regularly replaced by family members.

Before the dead are buried in the "hanging graves," they are honored with a Toraja Feast of the Dead, an elaborate, month-long celebration. Relatives and friends gather and bring gifts to the deceased; the most valued gift is a water buffalo. The funeral ritual takes place in a temporary village that is burned following the ceremony. The funeral day is a gala time climaxed by cockfights and dancing. The deceased is then buried.

North Sulawesi, Minahasa country

On the northern arm of Sulawesi, you'll find colorful ports, plantations of cloves and nutmeg, rice fields, hot springs, beautiful lakes, and a half-dozen active volcanoes. It's also the home of the Minahasa tribespeople.

Jutting northwards, the tip of North Sulawesi is only 644 km/400 miles from the Philippines.

Manado. This coastal city, on the province's northwest tip, is North Sulawesi's capital. For over 300 years, it has been a thriving trade center for cloves and copra. Within the city, parks and statues are juxtaposed with souvenir shops and markets. Offshore, divers and snorkelers find spectacular reefs, sponges, anemones, clams, brightly colored tropical fish, and the remains of shipwrecks.

Minahasa country. North Sulawesi is the home of the Minahasa, a Proto-Malay race whose ancestors migrated to the area in megalithic times. A short distance from Manado, you can see several ancient Minahasan burial sites. These early tombs have high, roof-shaped covers because it was the custom in those early times to inter the dead in a sitting position.

THE MYSTICAL OUTER ISLANDS

Indonesia has thousands of other islands including many that might be of interest to an adventurous traveler. On these islands, you'll find age-old cultures as yet uninfluenced by technological changes. Accommodations and transportation are limited, but the experience of visiting these primeval islands and seeing the primitive life styles of their people can be rewarding.

Islands the adventurous traveler might want to explore include Kalimantan, Irian Jaya, and Malukus.

Kalimantan, forested nature world

Three quarters of the island of Borneo (third largest island in the world) is called Kalimantan and belongs to Indonesia. The northeastern section of the island embraces the Malaysian states of Sabah and Sarawak and the independent Sultanate of Brunei.

Predominantly mountainous, Kalimantan is covered with dense equatorial forests. Flowering plants, including many varieties of orchids and rhododendrons, thrive here. Within its jungles live crocodiles, orangutans, proboscis monkeys, gibbons, panthers, and rhinoceroses.

The original people of the island were Dayaks, a wild inland people once notorious as headhunters; many Dayak tribes still remain. They live on the edge of rivers in communal houses on stilts. For more information on these "longhouses," see page 102.

Three of Kalimantan's major coastal cities have long been trading centers and timber-shipping ports: Banjarmasin, capital of the province of South Kalimantan; Balikpapan, in East Kalimantan; and Pontianak, capital of West Kalimantan. Each can be reached by air from Jakarta. You'll find accommodations in all three cities.

Island transportation is limited almost entirely to river boats. One Jakarta tour operator offers a 7-day Kalimantan excursion that transports you upriver by houseboat to visit villages, enjoy local entertainment, and lodge overnight in village longhouses.

Primitive Irian Jaya

Irian Jaya, the easternmost territory of Indonesia, occupies the western half of the island of New Guinea. It shares the island—the second largest in the world—with Papua New Guinea.

From its sweltering, swampy lowlands to its snow-capped mountains, Irian Jaya is primitive and un-developed. Inhabitants include Papuans, Negritos, Melanesians, and some Indonesians.

Irian Jaya's tribal villages are perhaps its biggest attraction. Many of them are built on low, swampy ground, with wooden walkways between the houses and between adjoining villages. These tribespeople live much as their ancestors did centuries ago.

Air service is available between Jakarta and several towns in Irian Jaya, including Jayapura, the capital (formerly called Sukarnapura). Accommodations are meager.

A special permit, obtainable through local Indonesian travel agents, is needed to visit Irian Jaya.

Maluku, the spice islands

The fabled spice islands of Maluku (formerly called the Moluccas) lie between Irian Jaya and Sulawesi. They are famed for their abundance of nutmeg, mace, cinnamon, cloves, and pepper. In centuries past, merchants and explorers risked their lives in search of these spice-laden islands.

Ambon is the provincial capital and main port of the island group. You can reach it by air from Jakarta and Ujung Pandang. Besides simple accommodations, the town offers historic buildings and offshore coral reefs.

KNOW BEFORE YOU GO

To help in planning your trip, here are some important details you will want to know:

Entry/exit procedures. To visit Indonesia you must have a valid passport and a visa issued by an Indonesian embassy or consulate. A tourist visa is valid for 30 days from day of entry; with an additional payment, the visa may be extended 2 weeks. Indonesian consulates are located in San Francisco, Honolulu, and New York. The embassy is in Washington, D.C.

If arriving from an infected area, you will need an international health certificate showing inoculation against yellow fever. In addition, the U.S. Public Health Service recommends that you have typhoid, tetanus, and gamma globulin shots. Because there is a malarial risk, check with your doctor regarding antimalarial treatment.

Air passengers departing Indonesia pay an airport departure tax of 1,000 Rp. When flying between Indonesian cities, you pay an airport departure tax of 800 Rp.

Customs. Indonesia allows you to bring in two liters of liquor, 200 cigarettes, 50 cigars or 100 grams (3½ ounces) of tobacco, and a reasonable amount of cameras and film. It's wise to declare valuables such as cameras and jewelry upon your arrival, so you'll have no trouble when you leave the country.

Currency. The official rate of exchange for the Indonesian rupiah (Rp.) is approximately 666 Rp. per U.S. dollar. The rupiah cannot be purchased outside the country nor carried out on departure. Money can be converted at the Bank of Indonesia or at any other authorized bank or moneychanger. You'll find that credit cards are seldom honored in the country's outlying areas.

Health conditions. Hospitals and medical services are good in the major cities but quite limited when you get into the countryside. Drink only boiled or bottled water.

Tipping. Though not compulsory, tipping is appreciated. It's not necessary if a service charge has already been added to the bill.

Time. The time difference between the U.S. west coast and Indonesia is 15 hours. When it is noon Monday in Jakarta, it's 9 P.M. Sunday in San Francisco.

Weather and what to wear. Indonesia straddles the equator, and its hot, tropical climate is influenced by monsoon winds. The best time to visit is from April through September.

The average year-round temperature at sea level is 26°C/79°F. The highlands are cooler, with temperatures dropping about 1° for each 91-meter/300-foot rise in elevation. Humidity remains high throughout the year, especially in the lowland areas.

Dress is casual. For men, sports shirts and light-weight trousers are good. Women will be most comfortable in loose fitting cotton dresses or skirts and tops. Bring a sweater for air-conditioned buildings and cooler mountain areas. You'll also need suntan lotion, mosquito repellent, a bathing suit, and an umbrella.

For more information. Your best sources of information on travel in Indonesia are the Directorate General of Tourism, 81 Jalan Kramat Raya, Jakarta; Jakarta Metropolitan City Tourism Development Board, 8-9 Merdeka Selatan, Jakarta, Indonesia; and the Indonesian Tourist Promotion Board, 323 Geary Street, San Francisco, CA 94102.

INDEX

Elaborate carving *and bright paint transform Thai rowboat into work of art.*

Photographers

Dave Bartruff: 39 top and bottom, 42 bottom, 127 top.
Bob/Virginia Brunner: 154 bottom. **Directorate General of Tourism, Indonesia:** 130 top, 143 top and bottom, 151.
Phyllis Elving: 98 top, 130 bottom, 135 top, 138, 154 top.
Lynn Ferrin: 66 bottom. **Jack Fields:** 15. **Shirley Fockler:** 10 top right, 31, 47 bottom, 63 top, 71 right, 135 bottom. **Jim Gebbie:** 71 left, 82 top, 90, 98 bottom, 103 left. **Thomas Holdiman:** 87 bottom. **Cliff Hollenbeck:** 10 bottom right, 55 top, 58. **Jane Keator:** 119. **Martin Litton:** 146 top. **Lynne Morrall:** 106 top. **Philippine Ministry of Tourism:** 23 top, 42 top, 122 bottom left. **Karen Rantzman:** 127 bottom. **Frederick M. Rea:** 26 left. **Dick Rowan:** 18, 23 bottom, 26 right, 34 top and bottom. **David Ryan:** 47 top, 50 top, 55 bottom, 66 top, 79 bottom, 111 right, back cover left. **Napan Sevikul:** 63 bottom, 159. **Carol Simowitz:** 95 bottom right, 146 bottom.
Singapore Tourist Promotion Board: 2, 10 bottom left, 111 left, 122 top right and bottom right, back cover right. **Joan Storey:** 50 bottom, 114 left and right. **Tourist Development Corporation, Malaysia:** 74 top and bottom, 79 top, 82 bottom, 87 top, 103 right. **Nikolay Zurek:** 95 top right and bottom left, 106 bottom.